My Father's World

My Father's World

Celebrating the Life of Reuben G. Bullard

EDITED BY
JOHN D. WINELAND, MARK ZIESE,
AND JAMES ESTEP

WIPF & STOCK · Eugene, Oregon

MY FATHER'S WORLD
Celebrating the Life of Reuben G. Bullard

Wipf & Stock
An Imprint of Wipf and Stock Publishers
199 W. 8th Ave., Suite 3
Eugene, OR 97401
www.wipfandstock.com

ISBN 13: 978-1-49825-423-6

Manufactured in the U.S.A.

This is my Father's world,
and to my listening ears
all nature sings, and round me rings
the music of the spheres.

This is my Father's world:
I rest me in the thought
of rocks and trees, of skies and seas;
his hand the wonders wrought.

—Maltbie D. Babcock

The world is Mine, and all that is in it.

—Psalm 50:12

Dr. Reuben G. Bullard

Contents

Foreword William G. Dever ix
Preface John D. Wineland xv
List of Contributors xix

1 Studying the Word and World of God:
   The Life of Reuben G. Bullard 1
   James R. Estep, Mark Ziese, and John D. Wineland

2 Bibliography and Activities: Reuben G. Bullard, PhD 22
   James Riley Estep Jr. and John D. Wineland

3 Letters of Remembrance and Obituaries 31
   Complied by Mark Ziese and John D. Wineland

4 The Labor of Animal Husbandry in the Biblical World 49
   Mark Ziese

5 Archaeological Insights into the Crucifixion of Jesus 72
   James Riley Estep Jr.

6 *Crurifragium*: An Intersection of History, Archaeology,
   and Theology in the Gospel of John 86
   Brian Johnson

7 Population, Architecture, and Economy in Lower Galilean Villages
   and Towns in the First Century AD: A Brief Survey 101
   David A. Fiensy

8 Roof Tiles and How They Relate to the Interpretation
   of the Synoptic Gospels 120
   Robert W. Smith

9 Digital Publication of Pottery 143
   John Mark Wade

10 Antiquarian Power in Ancient Mesopotamia 158
        Sara Fudge

11 Aspects of Warfare in the Bible: Insights from Egypt 170
        Kevin Morrow

12 Dark Ages and Little Ice Ages: Millennial Scale Climate Change
        and Human History 186
        Nigel Brush

13 Mosaics at Abila 200
        Timothy Snow

Foreword

William G. Dever

I FIRST MET REUBEN Bullard in the Spring of 1966 as the newly-
appointed director of the Hebrew Union College (HUC)-Harvard
Semitic Museum Excavations at Gezer. The Cincinnati branch of HUC
was headed then by Dr. Nelson Glueck, a noted explorer and biblical archaeologist. Dr. Glueck concurred with me that the Gezer project, which
we envisioned as pioneering newer American field methods in Israel,
should be multidisciplinary. And where better to look for a key member
from the natural sciences than in Cincinnati?

Reuben Bullard was already teaching at Cincinnati Christian
University, finishing his doctorate in geology at the University of
Cincinnati. He was deeply immersed in the Bible and the biblical world,
but he had no experience in the Holy Land, and certainly not in archaeology. Reuben came to the attention of Dr. Glueck, and we invited
him to join our nine-person "Core Staff" in 1966 for what was to be a
ten-year project. Gezer became one of the largest and longest running
archaeological projects in Israel at the time.

Gezer was also the first major American dig in Israel, with all eyes
focused on its claim to be doing the "New Archaeology." Reuben Bullard
became the first full-time professional geologist to be a member of the
supervisory staff of an archaeological excavation in the field in Israel.
There had been a few part-time, post-season geological consultants before, especially on prehistoric digs. But absolutely no one in the field of
biblical archaeology at that time had any idea what to do with a geologist
in the dirt, and certainly not us!

But it turned out that the geologist (not us biblical scholars) knew
what the dirt was; how it came to be deposited; where it was; why it

looked that way; and how it existed as a part of a once functional, but extinct cultural system that we were trying to reconstruct. Reuben Bullard gave "dirt archaeology" new meaning.

Yet integrating Reuben into the "Gezer system" was not to prove easy, but neither did it prove uneventful. I recall how my first impression of him was not too promising. My own father had been a Christian Church preacher, and indeed while he ministered to Christian Churches in Sebring and Akron, Ohio during my boyhood, I had visited the Cincinnati Bible College (now Cincinnati Christian University) with my dad. And I later graduated from Milligan College in Tennessee, another Christian Church college that was known for its liberal arts program, and then continued my education at the Disciples of Christ Seminary, Butler School of Religion in Indianapolis (now Christian Theological Seminary). But having moved on to a pastorate in a liberal Congregational church in the Boston suburbs while completing my Ph.D. at Harvard, I felt that I had outgrown my fundamentalist roots. All of this made me wary of Reuben Bullard, who I feared was a "Bible-Thumper."

However tough-minded Reuben may have been theologically (and, I hoped, scientifically), he seemed a bit unsuited to fieldwork. He had a fairly serious limp from an accident years before, and especially when weighted down with all that apparatus he wore around his geologist's belt, he appeared rather ponderous. That was until he limped out into the field that first day, and left us all behind in the dust (and he even had a name for the dust)!

Reuben was indestructible, although as I look back on it now he must have been in some pain much of the time. We all soon called him "Reuben, the Rock Man." And whenever anyone turned up in the field some mysterious soil deposit, or an enigmatic stone tool, the call went up: "Where's Reuben, the Rock Man"? And he was everywhere, doggedly making his daily rounds, pronouncing with certitude on anything he could get under that ubiquitous field lens of his. We soon found Reuben an invaluable member of our Core Staff, intimately involved in every field decision we made. How did we ever do without a geologist? Or more precisely, a "Geo-archaeologist," for that was the sub-discipline that Reuben created almost single-handedly in Israel (and later in Jordan).

Geo-archaeology is taken for granted today; but when Reuben appeared on the scene in the 1960s no one envisioned it or saw any need for it. Seldom does one individual contribute so much to changing the focus of a discipline, least of all one as traditional as biblical archaeology was back then. The field has changed dramatically now, of course, and even the name is often different: "Syro-Palestinian" or "Southern Levantine" archaeology, a more independent, highly professional field. But Reuben Bullard, an "amateur archaeologist" whose personal disposition and interests were much more narrowly biblical, turned out, to our surprise, to be in the forefront of the progress toward "secularizing" our discipline. And now we see that the new style of more scientific archaeology has yielded even more precise and positive results for our understanding of the biblical world.

Reuben did live to see the bulk of the impact of the newer approaches that he helped to pioneer, and I must admit that he was not altogether happy with them. I remember that I gave a talk some years ago at a plenary session of the Annual Meeting of the American Schools of Oriental Research, entitled "What Remains of the House That Albright Built?" My answer was "Not much, except the foundations; and these are in ruins." Now William Foxwell Albright had been the dean of American biblical archaeology, and the teacher of all of our teachers. I was told afterward that Reuben sat in the back of the hall, becoming more and more agitated. At the end of my paper he burst out to bystanders: "This is heresy!" Yet that was an uncharacteristic outburst. Overall, Reuben was an exceptionally tolerant and good-humored fellow, keeping his non-scientific opinions to himself (on scientific matters, however, he could be dogmatic). But what would he have made of a couple of my recent state-of-the-art popular books: *What Did the Biblical Writers Know and When Did They Know It? What Archaeology Can Tell Us About the Reality of Ancient Israel* (Eerdmans, 2001); and *Did God Have a Wife? Archaeology and Folk Religion in Ancient Israel* (Eerdmans, 2005)?

Living with the Gezer gang in the close quarters of our dig camp, and socializing with the Core Staff on weekends, could not have been easy for Reuben, given his background. The student volunteers, more than 100 each season, were a motley crew, mostly worldly secularists, many of them Jewish, typical American youngsters far away from parental control, and admittedly a bit rowdy. So was the Core Staff, even those of us who had been clergymen before we had moved on ("not defrocked," we insisted, "only unsuited"). At staff meetings each evening there was an open bar, and some of the language stemming from the day's frustrations in the field was a bit strong.

Growing up as I did in the Christian Church tradition, I remember vividly how uncomfortable some social situations could be, when one feels inevitably like the "outsider." Yet I must state for the record that Reuben never once seemed judgmental to me. He held to his own convictions, of course. But he did so with quiet dignity, never confrontational, always congenial. He was a man of unswerving principle, but of essentially generous spirit.

To be candid, I think that Reuben also tolerated the rest of the Core Staff out of his innate professionalism. This was about the work (the "vocation," he would have said), and that required teamwork. Reuben was always a professional, a team-player, whatever his personal reservations. He was enormously disciplined, clearly focused on our common goals, and never distracted by anything that in the end would prove trivial. That professionalism was a mark of Reuben's character; and I have no doubt that it was also part and parcel of his Christian beliefs. Salvation is by grace for sure; but the Apostle Paul (not to mention the Protestant Reformers) didn't discount "good works."

Reuben was a member of our Core Staff for every season of "Phase I," 1966 through 1971 (when I left HUC for the W. F. Albright Institute of Archaeological Research in East Jerusalem). The essence of the newer stratigraphic methods we were introducing at Gezer was the focus on the "third dimension." The traditional approach had been two dimensional, concentrating only on architectural features and larger building complexes. That goal was important; but such large-scale clearance often resulted in empty buildings, robbed of their context, which alone could have dated them and explained their function. In archaeology, context is what gives the lifeless remains meaning.

It was the venerable Dame Kathleen Kenyon who showed us at Jericho in the 1950s that it was the "debris" (the dirt) that held the clues. And that meant carefully cutting deep trenches to separate debris layers. Then she drew "sections" of the sides of trenches to document the buildup of successive strata. Such meticulous digging yielded more precise dates; and the soil layers revealed clearer phases of construction, use, reconstruction, and abandonment over long periods of time. Thus the characteristic "tells," or multi-layered mounds of the Middle East (and the Biblical world), could be coaxed to yield their secrets. But, as Kenyon insisted, everything depends upon recognizing the nature of the "debris," the rubbish that earlier archaeologists had discarded.

In the Gezer staff's training at Shechem in the early 1960s, under the legendary biblical archaeologist G. Ernest Wright, we had already emulated Kenyon's "debris layer" approach. So at Gezer we knew how to separate red dirt from brown dirt from black dirt, largely on the basis of color and texture. But what was this stuff? And what did it mean for understanding the history and culture of the levels in which it was observed and recorded? That is where Geo-archaeology comes in, and Reuben Bullard's specialized expertise.

Two or three examples of Reuben's unique contributions at Gezer (among hundreds I could relate) may be illuminating for the non-specialist:

(1) In Field VI, on the acropolis, we were excavating deep 12th-11th century BC levels over a large area. They were characterized by alternating layers of hard packed buff soil and dark ashy deposits. Elsewhere, such ashy levels had been taken as "destruction layers" that were supposedly evidence of "Israelite destructions" at the time of the Conquest. But as we carefully separated these levels, and sieved the organic remains in them, Reuben was able to prove under the microscope that they were successive dirt threshing floors, burnt periodically in order to clear them, and thus filled with burnt wheat and barley grains. Furthermore, they could then be related to a nearby granary with painted Philistine pottery in it; so much for "Israelite destructions." The ugly fact killed the elegant theory! We joked that we had found the remains of the Philistine wheat fields that Samson and his foxes with firebrands on their tails had burnt. (Even Reuben was amused.)

(2) In 1968 we excavated the famous Gezer "High Place," dug by R. A. S. Macalister before the First World War, in the infancy of biblical archaeology. He thought this unique monument was a Canaanite place for child sacrifice, reminiscent of the Biblical view of the horrendous Canaanites ("High Places," or *bamot*, are vociferously condemned in the Bible). When we carefully sectioned through the scant debris layers that Macalister had left untouched (our only chance at correct interpretation), we turned over the carefully sieved samples to Reuben.

Whatever "Biblical" motivation that Reuben might have held, Reuben the scientist saw under his microscope the answer to the riddle. The soil around the "High Place" was saturated with tiny fragments of burnt sheep and goat remains. Only the teeth had survived the hot fires; but that was enough to show that the "High Place" was a cultic installation for animal sacrifice, not unlike the biblical customs, although in this case pre-Israelite. Another myth laid to rest.

(3) One of the enduring mysteries of the archaeology of ancient Palestine is the long "Dark Age" between the Early and Middle Bronze Ages, ca. 2400-2000 BC. We had thought that Gezer, like so many large urban sites in Palestine, had been abandoned throughout that entire period. But in examining the soil deposits that we had carefully dug through, Reuben was able to show that these deep layers constituted a "buried secondary humus layer," i.e. topsoil that had accumulated during a long hiatus in occupation, then built over by a new occupational horizon. This natural soil-formation process takes centuries to develop. So there was our "Dark Age," no longer merely a hypothesis.

Reuben Bullard's pioneering efforts to establish the discipline of Geo-archaeology began at Gezer, but they did not stop there. Later he joined the staff as a field consultant in geology at several sites in Jordan, among them the great 3rd millennium BC site of Bab edh-Dhra'. Perhaps more important, he helped to recruit and train several other geologists who continued to make (and still make) signal contributions to Palestinian and Biblical archaeology. Among these converts to archaeology was his own student, Frank Koucky, who worked at the site of Idalion in Cyprus (excavations now directed by my wife Pamela Gaber, who met Reuben at Gezer in 1971).

Reuben Bullard's legacy continues, and it extends far beyond the original circle that the most prescient of us could have foreseen. The fact, however, is that his work was so far ahead of its time that even the most up-to-date handbooks on our branch of archaeology include a chapter on "Geo-archaeology," as seen from Suzanne Richard's edited volume *Near Eastern Archaeology: A Reader* (Eisenbrauns, 2003). It is also true, unfortunately, that Reuben did not write much, even in preliminary field reports.

His 1969 doctoral dissertation, "The Geology of Tell Gezer, Israel, and Its Excavation," was never revised for its intended publication in the Gezer publication series (now up to six volumes). The truth is that Reuben, although highly disciplined, was enthralled by fieldwork, being a real "dirt archaeologist." Nevertheless, his legacy lives on in the work of an entire generation of younger archaeologists excavating today in Israel, Jordan, Cyprus, and even beyond. That is an enduring tribute to a modest, devout man who knew his calling.

Preface

I MET DR. BULLARD in the spring of 1981 during my first year of seminary studies at Cincinnati Christian Seminary, which was the graduate division of Cincinnati Christian University (CCU). Midway through
that semester one afternoon, Dr. Bullard requested that I visit him in his
office high atop Old Main. He asked me to consider becoming his graduate assistant. He had heard, through his son Rick, that I had earned a BS
in biology with a minor in chemistry from Valparaiso University. I soon
realized that it was rare to find anyone with a science background on the
CCU campus, and he worked on convincing me that I could be of great
help to him as his assistant. I hesitated at first, warning him that I was no
geologist, but he assured me that I would learn. Little did I know when
I agreed to work for him that it would change my life in unimaginable
ways.

During the summer of 2004, I was leading students on my second
archaeological and historical study tour to Turkey. While I was on that
trip, I thought often of Dr. Bullard, as it had been twenty-one years earlier, during the summer of 1983, that I went on my first study tour with
him. He liked to call it the "BOAT" tour, but officially it was known as
the *Book of Acts Tour*. We visited scores of sites and museums in three
weeks of hectic travel to Turkey and Greece. His knowledge of the sites
and passion for archaeology impressed and inspired all of us. Now I was
leading my own study tours to Turkey, and hoped that I could be half
as inspiring as he had been two decades earlier. I had been thinking
back on what an impact he had made on my life, remembering how
Dr. Bullard often told his students at the beginning of a course or trip,
"This will change your life." I thought about how really it was Dr. Bullard
himself who had changed my life. Because of him I changed my entire
course of study, which changed the direction of my life, eventually leading me into a career in field archaeology, and as a professor of ancient
history and archaeology.

Sadly, when I arrived home from Turkey that summer a message on my answering machine from Jim Estep informed me of Dr. Bullard's untimely death. I was shocked and saddened by the news. I often thought, while on that trip, about how I wished I could contact him and reminiscence about his study tours and share with him the details of my own. Dr. Bullard, in many ways, was a like a father to me, certainly as an academic mentor, but also in a much more personal way. For instance, he always found creative ways to help me, a very poor graduate student, finance my participation on his study tours, by one time lining up a donor to underwrite part my fees, and another time by offering to give me a discount on a trip for helping him recruit people. I was privileged to spend a great deal of time with him in many different settings. Over the four plus years as his graduate assistant I spent about 10-15 hours a week with him. Besides this I traveled on two of his study tours, and spent a month with him in the field at the Abila excavation in Jordan.

I helped him initially organize his famous Cumberland Falls-Mammoth Cave Earth Science class field trip, which became somewhat legendary on the campus of the CCU. I also helped him organize, as well as participated in two of his study tours to the Mediterranean area. But ultimately, what had the greatest impact on me was serving as his assistant in the field during the 1984 Abila of the Decapolis expedition. We hiked miles and miles over the hills and wadis of the area examining the topography and geology of the region. Even though I was thirty years his junior, I had to work hard to keep up with him, and always by noon I would be loaded down with thirty pounds or more of geological samples he had found! Once we returned from Abila, he encouraged me to join, attend, and present papers at the annual meetings of the Near East Archaeological Society and the American Schools of Oriental Research. Not only would I run into him at those meetings, but we often shared meals, and at times were even roommates.

During the fall of 2007 I had lunch with Jim Estep in Lexington. We decided to try to put together a volume to honor Dr. Bullard. The essays in this volume are all written by former students and colleagues of Dr. Bullard, and the diverse range of topics highlights his broad interests in geology, archaeology, and biblical studies.

I must take this opportunity to acknowledge the work of my fellow editors, James R. Estep and Mark Ziese. I would also like to thank all of the contributors to this volume for their contribution and patience. My special thanks goes also to Connie Wineland for her diligent work as copy editor.

Finally, this book is a celebration of the life of Dr. Reuben G. Bullard, who encouraged, inspired, and influenced so many people, certainly each contributor to this volume. The diversity of the articles is a reflection of the interdisciplinary approach of Biblical studies, archaeology, history, and geology which he championed. Its title was taken from one of Dr. Bullard's favorite hymns, *This is My Father's World*. He would often lead his classes in a lively acapella rendition. He especially enjoyed leading this song at the beginning of his 8:00 a.m. earth science class located all the way up on the third floor of Old Main. He used it not only to wake up his students, but in typical fashion, to inspire them to understand the connection between God and his creation. He especially emphasized this part of the verse: "I rest me in the thought of *rocks* and trees, of skies and seas; his hand the wonders wrought."

List of Contributors

CHAPTER CONTRIBUTORS

Nigel Brush, Associate Professor of Geology, Ashland University, Ashland, Ohio

David A. Fiensy, Professor of New Testament, Kentucky Christian University, Grayson, Kentucky

Sara Fudge, Professor of Hebrew and History, Cincinnati Christian University, Cincinnati, Ohio

Brian Johnson, Professor of New Testament, Lincoln Christian University, Lincoln, Illinois

Kevin Morrow, Good News Productions, International, Joplin, Missouri

Timothy Snow, Ph.D. student, Catholic University of America, Washington, D.C.

Robert Smith, Professor of History and Bible, Mid Atlantic Christian University, Elizabeth City, North Carolina

John Mark Wade, Assistant Librarian, Emmanuel School of Religion, Johnson City, Tennessee

LETTER CONTRIBUTORS

Steven Bowman, Professor of Judaic Studies, University of Cincinnati, Cincinnati, Ohio

Warren D. Huff, Professor of Geology, University of Cincinnati, Cincinnati, Ohio

Gerald L. Mattingly, Professor of Biblical Studies, Johnson Bible College, Knoxville, Tennessee

Dale R. Meade, Missionary to Columbia, South America, Instructor, Columbia Bible College, Bogotá, Columbia

George ("Rip") Rapp, Regents Professor Emeritus of Geoarchaeology, University of Minnesota [deceased]

Joe D. Seger, Director, Cobb Institute of Archaeology, Professor of Religion, Mississippi State University, Mississippi

Keith Schoville, Professor Emeritus, Department of Hebrew and Semitic Studies, University of Wisconsin, Madison, Wisconsin

Jon Weatherly, Vice President for Academic Affairs and Professor of New Testament, Cincinnati Christian University, Cincinnati, Ohio

Edwin Yamauchi, Professor Emeritus, Department of History, Miami University, Oxford, Ohio

FOREWORD

William G. Dever, Professor Emeritus, University of Arizona, Tucson, Arizona

EDITORS AND CONTRIBUTORS

John D. Wineland, Professor of History and Archaeology, Kentucky Christian University, Grayson, Kentucky

Mark Ziese, Professor of Old Testament, Cincinnati Christian University, Cincinnati, Ohio

James Riley Estep, Jr., Professor of Christian Education, Lincoln Christian University, Lincoln, Illinois

Studying the Word and World of God:
The Life of Reuben G. Bullard

By James R. Estep, Mark Ziese, and John D. Wineland[1]

T HE STUDY OF THE word of God and the world of God are rigorous pursuits. They demand the brightest and best, as answers often
come slowly, and perhaps even painfully. To engage the word of God is
to enter into the domain of the theologian. Here, text, language, and interpretation swirl about in primary patterns. Deep reflection is critical.
To engage the world of God, on the other hand, is to venture into a very
different mix: the domain of the scientist. Here, meaning is sought in
patterns of another order entirely; they are scientific, elemental, micro-
scopic, and galactic. Meditation remains critical. Few individuals pursue
both the study of the word of God and the world of God on an academic
level. Even more rare is the person who engages these studies to a degree
of excellence that is recognized by his peers. This is what makes Reuben
G. Bullard of such interest. To understand something of the man, his
development, achievements, and legacy requires a survey of some "four-
score years" of life (Psalm 90:10).

THE EARLY YEARS AND THE DEATH
OF HIS FATHER (1928–1945)

Reuben George Bullard came into this world on March 18, 1928 in
Wheeling, West Virginia. He was born to Reuben G. Bullard of Wheeling,
and Vada Catherine Bixler of Mitchell, Indiana. He had one younger

---

1. The authors would like to acknowledge the great assistance and information received from the Bullard family.

brother, Richard. Though theirs was a small family, they had a grand spiritual heritage. Vada's grandfather was a preacher who, in the 1830s, established several churches in the area of Bedford, Indiana. These churches were a part of a frontier revival movement radiating from Cane Ridge, Kentucky. This spirit of restoration was carried into their new Wheeling home, and formed an integral part of Reuben's childhood.

Besides being a place of faith, the Bullard household was also a place of music. As a young woman, Vada studied at the Cincinnati Conservatory of Music, a finishing school already of some fame by the turn of the twentieth century. She was an accomplished pianist, while her husband played the violin. Early memories of Reuben and Richard include evenings listening to their parents play duets. Music was a staple for all.

At the age of seven, Reuben began to study the piano under his mother's tutelage. It would become his earliest passion. In time, he also learned to play the clarinet, and joined the Triadelphia High School band. Those who wore the red and black uniforms were well known in the upper Ohio valley for precise playing. Even though Reuben did not own the highest quality instrument, through regular practice and attention to detail, he earned the position of first chair of the clarinet section.

Reuben thought himself fortunate to have two uncles teaching in Triadelphia High School. One taught biology, and the other taught world history. So not only did Reuben play in the band, he worked hard to become an honor roll student, becoming top in his class in chemistry and physics. Tragedy struck at age fourteen, however, with the sudden death of his father. As the oldest child, this prompted him to work a series of jobs to help support the family.

During his teenage years, Reuben delivered daily newspapers by bicycle, his route taking him almost two hours to complete. However, not satisfied with his standard factory-model bike, he tinkered with it, making several improvements. He added lights on the front, lights on the back, a control panel on the handlebars, a bracket for a water container, and several other gadgets. These modifications made it easier for him to ride great distances. His work as newsboy lasted a year, after which he then took a job as a messenger for the Western Union Telegraph Company; the "improved" bicycle again served as his mode of transportation. In this role, he delivered news of the war. Some of the messages he carried were reports of death; others concerned soldiers missing in action. These telegrams were carried not only to the better neighborhoods, but also to the poorer neighborhoods, as well as to the "red light district." This work kept him out late, often past midnight. As one might expect, his mother waited up, watching from her bedroom window for the flicker of the lights of his bicycle. It was not that she necessarily feared for his personal safety (these were different times), she just needed to know that he was home.

As his "improved" bicycle suggests, Reuben enjoyed tinkering. He built model airplanes, cutting the pieces from wood, and gluing them together. He once made a rocket, which he shot across his high school football field. He made his own toy soldiers and cowboys by melting lead and pouring it into the tiny molds. Outlasting all these interests, though, was a fascination with photography. It began with his mother's Kodak Brownie camera which he borrowed to shoot scenes in the local park. Soon this interest grew into a passion. He learned darkroom skills, and printed his own black and white photographs. Once, later when he moved to Mitchell, Indiana, he climbed, with camera bags slung over each shoulder, to the top of the water tower at the Lehigh Portland Cement Company. From that vantage point, he took pictures of the plant and the distant landscape. Reuben was not afraid to peddle far or to climb high! This inclination would prove to be true in many more ways.

THE MOVE TO MITCHELL AND GRADUATION
FROM HIGH SCHOOL (1946–1948)

At the end of the Second World War, and after his junior year in high school, Reuben, his younger brother, and his widowed mother returned to south-central Indiana. Compared to the bustling city of Wheeling, the town of Mitchell was a very small place. But strong roots were there. Reuben's Uncle Victor was the chief clerk for the local cement company. Knowing of the boy's knack for chemistry and attention to detail, Victor secured a job for Reuben. He worked nights in the plant, monitoring various stages of the cement production process. He watched the tremendous power of the gears and engines reduce the hard limestone into soft powder. This interest in machines would eventually be transferred into a love of rail travel and steam locomotives, another hobby that occupied him for the rest of his life. Meanwhile, Reuben began his senior year of high school in Mitchell as he continued to work fulltime, often overnight, at the Lehigh plant. This occupation continued for three years after his graduation in 1947.

Reuben was always a self-learner. Once while on a swim outing with his family, he determined that he would dive from the high board. In this he was successful. On another occasion he rewired his grandfather's home, a structure which still stands to this day with no electrical problems. He also continued taking photographs and developing them in the darkroom. He even purchased and taught himself to drive a sleek 1947 Buick convertible. And he always had his music. On the occasion of his high school graduation, he stepped up to the piano, not in a cap and gown, but in a tuxedo! He entertained the graduates and their guests with Richard Addinsell's *Warsaw Concerto* and Chopin's *Military Polonaise*. For a year after graduating from high school, Reuben continued taking private piano lessons at the University of Indiana in Bloomington. He favored the music of Rachmaninoff, Tchaikovsky, Beethoven, and Grieg. But he also loved more modern compositions, especially George Gershwin's *Rhapsody in Blue*.

AN AUTOMOBILE ACCIDENT
AND A CHANGED LIFE (1949)

Beyond the death of his father, another tragedy proved pivotal in Reuben's young life. As he was traveling home one late afternoon, he asked his friend to drive his convertible while he snapped pictures along a scenic Indiana highway. Reuben later drifted off to sleep. As he slept, his friend hit an oil spot in the road and lost control of the vehicle. The Buick overturned in a field. Since this was before the time of seatbelts, both young men were thrown from the car. The driver escaped with a scraped chin, but Reuben was caught under the post of the doorframe. The weight crushed his pelvis, and extensively damaged his right leg and foot. He suffered a great loss of blood before being rushed to the hospital. Fortunately, a former Air Force surgeon and bone specialist was available to attend to Reuben's injuries.

Reuben had a relatively uncommon blood type, and the small community hospital did not have any in supply. A cousin, "Red" Lanier, knocked on doors all over town, seeking a potential donor. Finally, a person was found who matched his blood type, and a direct transfusion from her saved his life. Still, his leg was so severely damaged that the family doctor made plans to amputate it. Fortunately, the specialist intervened, and through surgery, managed to save the limb, through as a result of the procedure, Reuben's right leg was shortened by two inches. Due to the extensive nature of his injuries, he had to be placed in a body cast for four months, enduring a sweltering Indiana summer. When the cast finally came off, there were still many more months of rehabilitation. The use of a cane would also be necessary before Reuben could regain independent mobility. While grateful that he would be able to walk, he would deal with a pronounced limp and pain for the rest of his life.

MINISTRY AND MARRIAGE (1950–1957)

After his accident, Reuben became active in the Lawrence County Youth Rally, a regional inter-congregational evangelistic ministry, even serving for a period of time as president. There he met preachers from various churches in the area, including Bill Blake, Ellis Wesner, and Gene Dulin. It was through their influence that Reuben determined to dedicate his life to something profoundly more meaningful than cement mixing or piano playing. He wanted to pour his life's energy into vocational Christian ministry. As a start, he made a visit to the Cincinnati Bible Seminary (now Cincinnati Christian University) where Bill Blake was a student. While there, Bill introduced him to Professor George Mark Elliott, who immediately identified Reuben's potential and encouraged him in his ministry goals. It was encouragement well spent.

In the late spring of 1951 Reuben moved with his mother and his brother to Cincinnati. For Vada, this was a return of sorts, given her own youthful days spent in the Cincinnati Conservatory of Music. For Reuben and Richard, however, it was a dramatic shift from rural Indiana to an urban environment. The family lived for a few months in an apartment building on Chateau Avenue. Neighbors in the building, including Wilkie Winter and Grayson Ensign, befriended them. These men would forever remain within their close circle of friends.

Reuben plunged into the academic environment. Given his disposition, he determined to study the Bible in an orderly way, beginning with the Old Testament. To that end, he signed up for his first course, Elementary Hebrew, in the summer of 1951. In the five years that followed he took many other courses, including courses in general education as well as Historical Geography, Christian Ethics, Hermeneutics, and studies of various books of the Bible. If this load were not enough, he also secured a full-time job and a series of weekend ministries. His full-time job was in the Control Laboratory of the Andrew Jergens Company, a vocation that continued throughout his years of schooling and beyond (1951–1969). His part-time ministries included positions with the Modest Church of Christ in Newtonsville, Ohio (1951–1954), and with the Lamb Union Community Church in Lamb, Indiana (1954–1956). Such a schedule left little room for sleep, or anything else for that matter. He pursued academics by day and his work by night. Still, in the midst of this busyness, there was a great surprise on his horizon.

She was a freshman from West Virginia studying at Cincinnati Bible Seminary (CBS). Reuben proudly introduced himself to Miss Lynn Maine as a fellow West Virginian. When she inquired how often he made trips back home, he was forced to confess that he now lived in Cincinnati and did not make regular trips back to West Virginia. While at school, both Reuben and Lynn signed up for Greek grammar, and somehow he found himself seated in the row behind her. Reuben privately and pleasantly took note that in Greek "spell-downs" she was often one of the last students standing. That same semester they both enrolled in a course focusing on the New Testament book of Acts. This was the beginning of a very long relationship.

May of 1956 would be memorable for Reuben, who was now twenty-eight years of age. During this month he was ordained to Christian ministry in the Tulip Street Christian Church in Mitchell, Indiana. The service was conducted by Tibbs Maxey. Tibbs was not only the minister of the congregation, he was also founder and president of the College of the Scriptures in Louisville, Kentucky. Reuben and Tibbs had been friends for some time, as the Tulip Street Church had been Reuben's home church in Mitchell. In fact, the Tulip Street Church began when Reuben, along with an aunt, an uncle, his grandfather, and others separated from the Disciples of Christ congregation in Mitchell to establish a new work with Maxey. On May 25th, 1956, Reuben graduated from the CBS with a Bachelor of Theology degree. Three days later, on the evening of May 28, he and Lynn were married in Follansbee, West Virginia. After their honeymoon, they returned to Cincinnati to take summer school classes. It was during that summer that discussions were held on the subject of creating a Bible College in Moberly, Missouri. The school opened and later became Central Christian College of the Bible. While Reuben never taught at this institution, he was instrumental in its founding, and was the designer of its seal.

In the fall of 1956, Reuben began a weekend ministry with the Lerado Church in Clermont County, Ohio. It would be his longest pulpit ministry, lasting almost five years. At the same time he began graduate work at CBS. His thesis was titled, "Maps of Palestine: A Pictorial and Cartographical Illustration of J. W. McGarvey's Lands of the Bible." Revealed in this thesis are his interests in history, geography, and photography. In May of 1957 he was awarded the degree of Master of Arts.

CLASSICS, CHILDREN, AND THE UNIVERSITY OF CINCINNATI (1958–1964)

Not content with his knowledge of the biblical world, Reuben entered a program of study in the Classics Department of the University of Cincinnati (UC). In his first year, he studied three foreign languages simultaneously: German, Latin, and Greek. French would come later. In November of that same year, his first son, Reuben, familiarly known as "Rick," was born. Throughout these events, he continued his weekend ministry with the church in Lerado, as well as his night job with the Andrew Jergens Company.

At this time, the Classics Department at UC was already a leading American center for the study of the ancient world. In the decade of the 1930s, Dr. Carl Blegin had investigated the site of Hissarlik, or Homer's Troy. Although Blegin was in his declining years by the late 1950s, his lectures and pictures stirred in Reuben a desire to participate in an archaeological excavation.

In his third and final year in the Classics program, Reuben was required to take a science course. In retrospect, many of his life-experiences prepared him for his choice: the scientific curiosity demonstrated as a child, the engagement with limestone and machinery in the cement plant, the geographical descriptions offered in his master's thesis, and the newly developed fascination with archaeology. All of these interests came together in his choice to study geology. This choice landed him in the classroom of Richard Durrell. Through Durrell's engaging lectures, the final piece of Reuben's academic pursuits was cast. Thus far, his work had been devoted to the study of God's word as special revelation. Durrell's lectures opened his eyes to yet another avenue, another order of revelation: God's world. For Reuben, the deeper reality of his "Father's world" was revealed in Romans 1:20: "For since the creation of the world His invisible attributes, His eternal power and divine nature, have been clearly seen, being understood through what has been made."[2] He began to understand that the study of the word of God and the world of God could complement each other.

Reuben's plan when entering UC had been to work through a program of classical studies to help him understand the biblical text more fully. While this quest was not yet completed, it would, take an unexpected trajectory. In June of 1961, he received his Bachelor of Arts in Classics. That fall, inspired in part by Durrell, he entered the Graduate School of the Geology Department.

In January 1961, Reuben was invited to teach ancient history at CBS. Now his hands were truly full. He taught a class in history, pursued graduate work in geology, worked nights in the Control Laboratory of the Jergens Company, and, all the while, helped in raising a young family. Lynn's role as wife, mother, and chief encourager can hardly be overstated. In August of 1961, a second son, Howard, was born. Three years later, in June of 1964, Reuben finished his thesis, "Philosophical Basis of Geology", and received a Master of Arts in Geology. The following month, Cathy, his first daughter was born. Whether measured by academic degrees or children, these were busy times!

Beyond his MA, Reuben continued his professional pursuit of geology at UC. As a doctoral candidate, he participated in an eight-week field camp that took him into the Rocky Mountains of Wyoming. This experience developed yet another passion that would last a lifetime: a love of the American West.

"THE ARCHAEOLOGICAL GEOLOGIST" (1965–1969)

For his doctoral thesis, Reuben sought to bring his multidisciplinary interests together in an archaeological excavation. Returning to his "old home" in the Classics department of UC, he inquired if there was any interest in having a geologist as part of a team being assembled to work on the Greek Island of Kia. His proposal was turned down. Undaunted, Reuben crossed Clifton Avenue to the neighboring Hebrew Union College-Jewish Institute of Religion (HUC-JIR), and made an appointment with the president of that school. Reuben had great admiration for Nelson Glueck, and knew of Glueck's pioneering work in the region that had only recently become the countries of Jordan and Israel.

2. This text is inscribed on Reuben's tombstone.

Reuben's own words relate the details of the encounter that took place on December 23, 1963 at 1:30 in the afternoon.

Reuben was welcomed into the president's office at the Klau library. Glueck asked, "How may I help you?" Appreciating Glueck's immediate directness, Bullard reponded

> "Dr. Glueck, I am a PhD track student in the University of Cincinnati Geology Department and I am casting about to determine the focus of my research. I want to apply scientific techniques of a geological nature to archaeological sites and their environments." [Glueck's] eyes began flashing warmly under those very dense eyebrows and I had scarcely spoken the last word when he burst out with "Ah! If you had been here two years ago you could have gone with me to the Negev!" He opened his desk drawer and took out a pad asking, "How much will you need? Will your wife want to go also?[3]"

Glueck described to him a new work being planned at Tel Gezer, near the modern city of Tel Aviv. The work would be done under the joint auspices of HUC-JIR and the Harvard Semitic Museum.

The first field season at Gezer in 1966 corresponded with a professional meeting of geologists (The 2nd International Clay Conference) scheduled in Jerusalem. Connected to this conference was a tour to introduce visiting scientists to the local geology. It was a dream come true for Reuben. If he were to do his doctoral thesis on the environment of Tel Gezer, participating in this meeting and its associated tours would be an invaluable way to familiarize himself with the region. His mentor and friend, Richard Durrell of UC, was already making plans to attend the conference, and he encouraged Reuben to do the same.

At the conclusion of the conference, Reuben and Lynn met the Gezer excavation team at the W. F. Albright Institute of Archaeological Research in East Jerusalem. This was the beginning of five summers of excavation for Reuben at Tel Gezer. During that time Reuben served in the role of geologist for the excavation. He also learned much about the archaeological process and archaeological photography. His pioneering role as an archaeological geologist on an excavation team is highlighted

---

3. Reuben G. Bullard, "A Biography of Nelson Glueck" in Gisela Walberg, *The Nelson and Helen Glueck Collection of Cypriot Antiquities* (Cincinnati, Jonsered: Paul Astroms Forlag, 1992) 57.

in the documentary film, *The Big Dig*,[4] and in the kind letters from his colleagues found in this volume. Throughout the 1966 excavations, Lynn carried their fourth child and second daughter. Suzanne was born in November of that year.

Reuben recorded a memorable event that took place very soon after the end of the Six Day War, June 5–10, 1967. He rode with Nelson Glueck to the Golan Heights along with two other members of the Gezer staff. He records how:

> We saw unexploded bombs still standing in the fields where they had fallen and ammunition scattered all along the side of the road. [Glueck] was so excited and intensely interested in the sights that he was experiencing in this area from which he had been forbidden for the last 20 years that he failed to realize, along with the rest of us, that he had made a turn that was taking us directly into the Syrian army cease-fire lines. Upon the advice of an Israeli soldier we turned from an area a quarter mile from that possibility in which all of us could have become Syrian prisoners, perhaps on a long term basis![5]

Reuben's fieldwork provided the data for his 1969 doctoral dissertation entitled, "The Geology of Tell Gezer, Israel, and its Excavations,"[6] and in June 1969, at the age of 41, Reuben received a PhD in Geology from the University of Cincinnati.

His academic preparation and work at Gezer, along with his development of personal relationships led to Reuben's appointment as trustee to the professional organization known as the American Schools of Oriental Research (ASOR). It was a position he would hold for four years (1970–1974). In 1971, George E. Wright of Harvard invited Reuben to co-direct with him the excavations at Idalion on the island of Cyprus. By the second year of the project, however, Reuben resigned from this position. It was simply too much to add this to the already delicate balance of responsibilities of being a churchman, teacher, chemist, excavator, husband, and father.

4. *The Big Dig*, a film directed by Art Swerdloff, produced by Televisual Productions (1973) and released by the Encyclopaedia Britannica Educational Corporation (1975). Originally produced on 16mm, this film describes the activity of the Gezer excavation. It was originally available in both a short (22 minute) and long (54 minute) version.

5. Reuben G. Bullard, "A Biography of Nelson Glueck," 58.

6. Reuben G. Bullard, "The Geology of Tell Gezer, Israel and its Excavations," Unpublished PhD Thesis (Cincinnati: University of Cincinnati, 1969).

DR. REUBEN GEORGE BULLARD, PROFESSOR (1970-2003)

By 1970, Reuben had been teaching for a decade at CBS. Within that period of time he rapidly progressed through the ranks of Instructor to Professor, and by 1972 he held the Chair of "Field II" in the Department of Arts and Sciences. In this role, his former teachers, R. C. Foster, George M. Elliott, and Wilkie Winter, now colleagues, were a constant source of encouragement.

In 1974, a new academic major appeared in the college catalog as a direct result of the collaborative efforts of Reuben and Wilkie Winter: A Bachelor of Arts degree in Ancient Near Eastern Studies. It would be a rigorous program, requiring that students study both Hebrew and Greek languages. It also outlined courses in Archaeological Techniques and Field Methods, New Testament and Old Testament Archaeology, and ancient history. In the ten years that this degree program stood (1978–1988), some seventeen students earned it. Of these, several would go on to earn doctorates. While classes in the area of Antiquities did appear in the Graduate School of the Seminary at that same period of time, it would take another five years before an MA program in Near Eastern Antiquities would be approved. Throughout this decade, Reuben and Wilkie provided vision and leadership. Eventually a third faculty member was added. A rising star in the field, Gerald Mattingly, joined the seminary faculty.

Of course, thousands of other students passed through the doors of Reuben's classroom. Courses such as Bible Survey, Ancient Near Eastern History, Classical Greek and Roman History, and Earth Science were among his teaching staples. In these venues the teaching was not always orderly, but it was always infectious. Discipline specifics were dramatically delivered to raw undergraduates, assisted by syllabi healthy enough to have a life of their own. All lectures were illustrated, if not by image, by personal narratives. Overnight field trips to Kentucky, Indiana, Ohio, and Michigan were organized to offer the opportunity to observe geological phenomenon first-hand; for some students, the experience of all-weather camping was a memorable first. Equally famous were Reuben's spontaneous exhortations. These were hard-hitting and wide-ranging, but tended to fall into one of three well-worn categories: general moral instruction, advice for successful relationships, and the importance of eating a healthy breakfast!

As might also be expected, his teaching responsibilities extended beyond the campus of CBS. While still part of the Core Staff of Tel Gezer, Reuben was invited to be an Instructor at the University of Cincinnati in 1968. A year later, he joined the faculty of UC as an Assistant Professor in Geology. He continued in this role through 1974. In 1975 he received an appointment in the College of Evening and Continuing Education (CECE) with the University of Cincinnati. In this capacity, he taught first for the Department of Geology, and later, for the Judaic Studies Department. He likewise had short-term teaching opportunities at two other Christian Colleges: Louisville Bible College (Kentucky), and the winter extension campus of Maritime Christian College (Prince Edward Island) in Antigua, British West Indies.

His work as churchman continued as well. He devoted himself, in turn, to the Chase Avenue Church of Christ (today known as LifeSpring Christian Church) in Cincinnati, the Banklick Christian Church in Covington, Kentucky, the Lystra Church of Christ in Williamstown, Kentucky, and the Nicholson Christian Church in Independence, Kentucky. Within the Nicholson congregation he served as deacon (1976–1978) and elder (1980–1982, 1984–1986, 1988–1992, 1994–1995, 1998–2001 and 2004).

Reuben worked as a geological consultant on many archaeological projects. Because of these associations, many laymen assumed he himself was an archaeologist. Given the opportunity, he would always correct this view, stating that he was a geologist with interests and field experience in archaeology; it was not the other way around. This careful distinction by Reuben and others eventually led to the creation of a new division within the Annual Meeting of the Geological Society of America (GSA) called "Archaeological Geology."[7] Reuben was instrumental in the formation of this division, but humbly credited it to Nelson Glueck's vision:

> The opening that [Glueck] gave to geologic studies at archaeological sites, which began in Tell Gezer, was imitated by both Americans and Israelis and others at other sites throughout the Near East. Specialized studies in petrology, sedimentation, topography, hydrology, stratigraphy, depositional structures and the development of the concept of archaeo-deposits and much

7. See the letter in this volume by George ("Rip") Rapp on the creation of the Archaeological Geology Division in the GSA.

more have developed. [Glueck's] quest for the fullest dimension of archaeological research provided one of the bases for the founding of a new unit of the Geological Society of American in 1976: The Archaeological Geological Division . . . This association has grown to have a membership of 500 scientists- a monument to [Glueck's] perception and that of others.[8]

Reuben's resume as a geological consultant includes many of the best-known American projects in the Mediterranean basin. In Israel-Palestine, his work was felt at the sites of Tell el-Hesi, Khirbet Shema, Tell Balata, Caesarea Maritima, and Tell Dan. In Jordan, his work extended to the sites of Hesban, Bab edh' Dhra', and Abila of the Decapolis. Reuben's expertise was sought after in other geographical areas as well. On the island of Cyprus, he worked with the excavations at Idalion, and the Kurion/Curium Excavations. In Greece he was a consultant on the work at Midea; in Italy he worked at Lugnano in Teverina. Reuben also spent a great deal of time in the country of Tunisia, investigating the site and harbor at Carthage.

Work in these distant places was not always easy, and was sometimes punctuated by moments of alarm. In June of 1970, Reuben agreed to visit the site of Hesban in Jordan to conduct a geological survey with the American team there. Soon after his arrival, however, a political crisis developed when a guerrilla organization clashed with the forces of the Jordanian government. With foreigners being targeted as hostages, Reuben and other American archaeologists went into hiding. Eventually they were rescued and airlifted to Athens by the United States government.[9] One year later, the U.S. State Department belatedly charged each of the archaeologists the sum of $126.00 for the evacuation effort![10]

8. Reuben G. Bullard, "A Biography of Nelson Glueck," 65.

9. Reuben Bullard recorded the following about his Hesban research of 1970 in his extensive vita: "This operation was aborted after a couple of days by a Palestinian attack and hostage taking of Americans in our area of Amman. We, along with the Bas van Elderen family, were subject to house arrest for 8 days. We were released to the international Red Cross after that time, to be flown to Beirut in a DC-6 @~ 4000' altitude {giving excellent sighting of the basaltic construction of towns and villages between Amman and Damascus—a special photographic record!}. Our final leg of evacuation was Athens from which we phoned our families. Thus ended our Jordanian research for that year."

10. This information was found in the diaries of Siegfried Horn, and was made available for this essay through the kindness of Larry Geraty.

Reuben used his geological knowledge closer to home as well. For many years he photographed the Banklick Creek in Kentucky as part of a geological study. He became increasingly concerned about the work of developers who were stripping away the area of trees and grass, and thus hastening erosion along the streambed. He was therefore eager to help a group of residents who suffered damage from a flood that came about because of this denudation. Insurance companies had been unwilling to fully compensate the owners, but his presentation on behalf of the residents helped them recoup their losses.

Reuben also organized several study tours to the Mediterranean basin from 1981–1999. These study tours focused on the geology, history and archaeology of the region. He led groups to places like Italy, Tunisia, Turkey, Greece, Egypt, Jordan, and Israel. He would often amaze the local guides with his knowledge. In Italy, for example, tour guides gathered to listen to his extemporaneous lecture on the provenance of various stones built into the walls and the floors of a monument. Many people went on these popular tours, which were both fun and educational. They provided an enriching experience for those wishing to become more familiar with Bible lands. Three couples also found each other as life mates on these tours!

An organization known as Christian Arabic Services (CAS) grew out of the first study tour that Reuben and Wilkie Winter took to Egypt in 1981. During post-trip lecture/visits to congregations and individuals, they linked up with Egyptian evangelical Christians hungering for biblical truth. Soon, four Egyptian men came to study in Cincinnati. Reuben encouraged their scholarship and the creation of CAS to facilitate evangelistic work in the Middle East. Reuben served as president of this organization from 1982–1985, and continued as an active member for the rest of his life.

Of course, CAS was only one organization with which Reuben was associated. Through the years Reuben held memberships in many groups and academic societies. These included the Ohio Academy of Science (Clay Minerals Society), Ohio Academy of History, the Society of Economic Paleontologists and Mineralogists, the Geological Society of America, the Archaeological Institute of America, the American Association for the Advancement of Science, the American Schools of Oriental Research, the National Geographic Society, the Cincinnati Museum of Natural History, the Cincinnati Historical

Society, the Smithsonian Institution, the American Association of University Professors, the Near East Archaeological Society, Sigma Xi at the University of Cincinnati, the Evangelical Theological Society, the Society of Biblical Literature, the Biblical Archaeological Society, and the National Historical Railroad Society.

He became an ambassador for the archaeological community to the local church by co-sponsoring, along with Wilkie Winter, "The Biblical Archaeological Exposition" (BAE) at the North American Christian Convention (NACC). Through individual and panel lectures, contemporary information from Mediterranean fieldwork could be presented to the public. These expositions grew rapidly in popularity; often the sessions were filled, with attendance reaching more than 150. Initially consisting of a only few sessions, in time they evolved into an all-day itinerary, well attended and described by those attending as "a convention within a convention." These sessions continued for twenty years until the NACC went through substantial refashioning.

Reuben experienced growth and change closer to home as well. The Cincinnati Bible Seminary expanded to become Cincinnati Bible College and Seminary, and eventually, as it is known today, the Cincinnati Christian University. After more than 40 years of service to this institution, Reuben retired in June of 2002. He continued as an adjunct for another two years in the College of Evening and Continuing Education (CECE) at the University of Cincinnati.

THE FINAL YEAR AND LEGACY (2004–PRESENT)

In January 2004, a former student helped to fulfill Reuben's life-long dream of visiting the state of Hawaii and seeing an active volcano on the Big Island. Here as elsewhere, Reuben climbed many mountains and overcame many challenges. He lived a full, rich, productive life until his last months when his health rapidly declined and he went to be with the Lord on July 3, 2004.

Reuben's legacy may be measured in many ways. First, it may be measured through his family. His wife, Lynn, was his closest companion and encourager for 48 years. Together, they raised four children: Reuben Jr. (Rick), Howard, Cathy, and Suzanne. These, in turn, married and gave him seven living grandchildren. Rick and Howard are ordained ministers. Rick is following in his father's steps, teaching Geology at Cincinnati Christian University and Northern Kentucky University. Howard ministers at Ben Davis Creek Christian Church in Rushville, Indiana. Cathy has a Master's degree in Computer Science, and home-schools her four children in Calcutta, Ohio. Suzanne and her husband, Brian Prichard, were former missionaries in the country of Belize, Central America. All are actively involved in local churches.

A second way in which Reuben's legacy may be measured is through those who experienced his infectious zeal for learning, namely, his students. Reuben integrated his many and various interests into ministry. He readily took on the hard questions of graduate students, yet equally embraced the opportunity to share with children the wonders of creation. He considered teaching a joy and a privilege. He expected excellence of himself, and encouraged the same of others. This is evident from the degrees and honors he was awarded throughout his life. Countless numbers of students at the Cincinnati Christian University and the University of Cincinnati were affected by his presence. The same might be said of many others who were touched, directly or indirectly, by his work through organizations such as the American Schools of Oriental Research, the North American Christian Convention, the Geological Society of American, or the Christian Arabic Services.

On the first day of any given semester, Reuben opened class with the same spirited declaration: "This course will change your life." On one occasion he was asked, "Why do you say that?" His response was, "Why would I waste my time if it weren't going to change you?" When studied deeply and presented clearly, God's word and world have the power to change. The life of Reuben George Bullard is testimony to this truth.

A young Reuben in the early 1940s

Reuben and his Buick convertible in 1948

Reuben and Lynn as newlyweds

Reuben (on the left) with Wilkie Winter at Gezer, summer 1968

Reuben teaching Earth Science in his classroom on the third floor
of "Old Main" at CCU ca. 1980

Examining a silver mine in Columbine Pass, Colorado, 1978

John Wineland (standing) assisting Dr. Bullard
while he examines a large monolithic column
from the church in Area D, Abila, summer 1984

Reuben with his sons Rick (on the left)
and Howard (in the middle)
at Petra, Jordan during the Book of Acts Tour (BOAT),
summer 1987

Reuben in the field at Lugano, Italy, summer 1991

Reuben in his Old Main office on the third floor, 1997

Son Rick (on the left) with Reuben presenting a lecture at
Cumberland Falls, KY during a Geology fall field trip, ca. 2000

2

Bibliography and Activities: Reuben G. Bullard, PhD

James Riley Estep Jr. and John D. Wineland

D URING HIS CAREER DR. Reuben Bullard published and presented numerous academic papers in the fields of archaeology, geology, Bible, and the integration of these subjects. He excelled in the classroom and in the academic community but he also shared his research with numerous congregations and Christian organizations. He endeavored to popularize the field of Biblical archaeology to a general audience by making it more accessible and relevant to the study of Scripture. To this end he organized and founded, along with Dr. Wilkie Winter the Biblical Archaeological Exposition (BAE) at the North American Christian Convention (NACC). He also made presentations to various congregations including Nicholson Church of Christ, Nicholson, Kentucky where he served as a long time elder. This bibliography and list of activities, includes both his contributions in the academic community, and to the general public.

THESES AND RESEARCH REPORTS

1. "Maps of Palestine: A Pictorial and Cartographical Illustration of J. W. McGarvey's *Lands of the Bible.*" M.A. thesis, Cincinnati Bible Seminary, 1957.

2. "The Philosophical Basis of Geology." M.S. thesis, University of Cincinnati, 1964.

3. "Armoured Pediments Along the Eastern Flank of the Central Big Horn Mountains, Wyoming." Field Research Paper, University of Cincinnati, 1967.

4. "The Geology of Tell Gezer, Israel and its Excavations." Ph.D. diss., University of Cincinnati, 1969.

ARTICLES IN JOURNALS

1. "The Archaeological Geology of Cyprus and the First Missionary Journey of Acts." *Near East Archaeological Society Bulletin* 47 (2002): 1–8.

2. "The Archaeological Geology and Seismic History of Kourion, Cyprus." In David Soren, "The Day the World Ended at Kourion." *National Geographic Magazine* 174, no. 1, (July, 1988): 30–53.

3. "Geological Study of the Heshbon Area, Jordan." *Andrews University Seminary Studies* 10, no. 2 (1972): 130–141.

4. "What Meaneth These Stones?" *The Seminary Review* 18, no. 1 (1971): 1–17.

5. with Dever, William G., H. Darrell Lance, Dan P. Cole, Anita M. Furshpan, John S. Holladay, Jr., Joe D. Seger, and Robert B. Wright. "Further Excavations at Gezer, 1967–71." *Biblical Archaeologist* 34, no. 4 (1971): 93–132.

6. "Geological Studies in Field Archaeology." *Biblical Archaeologist* 33, no. 4 (1970): 97–132.

FIELD REPORTS AND STUDIES

1. "The Archaeological Geology of Roman Carthage." In *Excavations at Carthage 2, 1975 conducted by the University of Michigan*, ed. John H. Humphrey. Tunis: Cérès, 1978.

2. "Lithic Analysis of an Opus Sectile Floor, Roman Carthage." In *Excavations at Carthage 2. 1975 conducted by the University of Michigan*, ed. John H. Humphrey. Tunis: Cérès, 1978.

3. "The Archaeological Geology of the Khirbet Shema' Area, Galilee." In *Ancient Synagogue Excavations at Khirbet Shema', Upper Galilee, Israel, 1970–1972*, eds. Eric Meyers, et al. 20–32. Durham: Duke University Press., 1976.

4. with Dever. William G., H. Darrell Lance, Dan P. Cole, and Joe D. Seger. *Gezer II: Report of the 1967–70 Seasons in Fields I and II.* ed. William G. Dever, Jerusalem: Hebrew Union College/Nelson Glueck School of Biblical Archaeology, 1974.

5. with Koucky, Frank L. "The Geology of Idalion." In *American Expedition to Idalion, Cyprus: First Preliminary Report 1971 and 1972*, eds. Lawrence E. Stager, Anita M. Walker and George Ernest Wright, 11–26. Cambridge: American Schools of Oriental Research, 1974.

CHAPTERS IN BOOKS AND REFERENCE ARTICLES

1. "Dr. W. Harold Mare, Professor and Archaeological Director: A Biography and Commentary on his Life." In *Beyond the Jordan: Studies in Honor of W. Harold Mare*, eds. Glenn A, Carnagey, Sr. et al., 5-31. Eugene: Wipf and Stock Publishers, 2005.

2. "The Berbers of the Maghreb and Ancient Carthage." In *Africa and Africans in Antiquity*, ed. Edwin Yamauchi, 180–209. East Lansing: Michigan State University Press, 2001.

3. "Roman Slavery." Standard Publishing's *Devotions Adult Quarterly*, June 2000.

4. "Geology." In *Oxford Encyclopedia of Archaeology in the Near East*, ed. Eric Meyers, vol. 2, 391–394. New York: Oxford Press, 1997.

5. "Magnetic Archaeometry." In *Oxford Encyclopedia of Archaeology in the Near East*, ed. Eric Meyers, vol. 3, 400–401. New York: Oxford Press, 1997.

6. "A Biography of Nelson Glueck." In *The Nelson and Helen Glueck Collection of Cypriot Antiquities, Cincinnati, Studies in Mediterranean Archaeology and Literature*, Pocket-book 11, with Gislea Walberg. Jonsered: Aström, 1992.

7. "Stones, Precious." In *International Standard Bible Encyclopedia*, ed. Geoffrey W. Bromiley, vol 4, 623–30. Grand Rapids: Eerdmans Publishing Company, 1988.

8. "Porphyry." In *International Standard Bible Encyclopedia*, ed. Geoffrey W. Bromiley, vol 3, 909. Grand Rapids: Eerdmans Publishing Company, 1988.

9. "Sedimentary Environments and Lithologic Materials at Two Archaeological Sites." In *Archaeological Geology*, eds. George Robert Rapp and John A. Gifford, 103–133. New Haven: Yale University Press, 1985.

10. "Geology in Field Archaeology." In *A Manual of Field Excavation: Handbook for Field Archaeologists*, eds. William G. Dever and H. Darrell Lance, 197-235. Cincinnati: Hebrew Union College, 1978.

PRESENTATIONS AND LECTURERS

1. "Hittite Presence in the Old Testament World." Presented at Biblical Archaeological Exposition, NACC, Indianapolis, IN., July 2003.

2. "Seminar on Archaeological Geology." Presented at Johnson Bible College, Knoxville, TN., March 2003.

3. "Churches of the First Christian Empire—Byzantium." Presented at Biblical Archaeological Exposition, NACC, Columbus, OH., July 2002.

4. "Punic and Roman Carthage." Presented at Covenant Theological Seminary, St. Louis, MO., Nov. 2000.

5. "Mycenae and the Philistines." Presented at Covenant Theological Seminary, St. Louis, MO., Nov. 2000.

6. "Abila of the Decapolis, the 2000 Field Season." Presented at NEAS Annual Meeting, Nashville, TN., Nov. 2000.

7. "Canaanite Infant Sacrifices." Presented at Andrews University, Berrien Springs MI., March 1999.

8. "The Cultural History of Carthage: Berbers, Phoenicians and Roman." Presented at Symposium on Africa for Africans, Miami University, Oxford, OH., Nov. 1998.

9. "CBC&S' Archaeological Research Consortium." Presented at Abila Archaeological Exposition, Cincinnati Christian University, Cincinnati, OH., Feb. 1997.

10. "From the Illegal to the Legal Church: Refusing to Render unto Caesar." Presented at Biblical Archaeological Exposition, NACC, Dallas, TX., July 1996.

11. "Petrographic Analysis of Pottery." Presented at ASOR Annual Meeting, Philadelphia, PA., Nov. 1995.

12. "The Origin of the Philistines." Presented at Biblical Archaeological Exposition, NACC, Indianapolis, IN., July 1995.

13. "Baptistery Architecture of Early Christian Churches." Presented at Johnson Bible College, Knoxville, TN., Sept. 1994.

14 "The Architecture and History of the Solomonic Gate, Tell Gezer, Israel." Presented at NEAS Annual Meeting, Washington D.C., Nov. 1993.

15. "The Building Stone Sources and Uses in Secular and Sacred Carthage." Presented at the GSA Annual Meeting, Boston MA., Oct. 1993.

16. "A Mineralogical Focus on Archaeology." Presented at Cincinnati Mineral Society, Cincinnati, OH., Sept. 1993.

17. "The City Gate: A Microcosm in the Time of Solomon in the Biblical World." Presented at Biblical Archaeological Exposition, NACC, St. Louis, MO., July 1993.

18. "Dr. Nelson Glueck, Archaeologist par Excellence." Presented at Cincinnati Museum of Fine Arts, Cincinnati, OH., April 1993.

19. "Geology and the Genesis One Record." Presented at Covenant Theological Seminary, St. Louis, MO., Feb., 1993.

20. "Canaanite Infant Sacrifices, as Illustrated at Carthage and Gezer." Presented at Covenant Theological Seminary, St. Louis, MO., Feb. 1993.

21. "The Building Stone Sources and Uses in Secular and Sacred Carthage." Presented at ASOR Annual Meeting, San Francisco, CA., Nov., 1992.

22. "The Archaeological Geology of Midea and Its Environment in the Argolid, Greece." Presented at GSA Annual Meeting, Cincinnati, Ohio, Oct., 1992.

23. "The Architectural Petrology of Abila Basilicas." Presented at Biblical Archaeological Exposition, NACC, Anaheim, CA., July, 1992.

24. "Use of Scientific Archaeological Data in Teaching," Presented at ASOR, Southeast Regional Meeting, Atlanta, GA., March, 1992.

25. "Environmental Geology of an Early Roman Empire Village [Umbria, Italy]." Presented at GSA Annual Meeting, San Diego, CA., Oct. 1991.

26. "Ancient Carthage." Presented at the McClellen Symposium: Africa and Africans in Antiquity, Miami University, Oxford, OH., March 1991.

27. "The Sediments Speak: The Story of Archaeological Geology," Presented at ASOR Southeast Regional Meeting, Atlanta, GA., March 1991.

28. "The Environmental Geology of the Tomb, Cave I-10A, Tell Gezer, Israel." Presented at the Cobb Institute of Archaeology, Mississippi State University, Mississippi State, MS., Nov. 1990.

29. "Canaanite Culture as Seen at Tell Gezer and Carthage." Presented at NEAS Annual Meeting, New Orleans, LA., Nov. 1990.

30. "Environmental Effects in the Archaeological History of Gezer." Presented at ASOR Annual Meeting, New Orleans, LA., Nov., 1990.

31. "Geological Research in Focus on Biblical Archaeology: Recent Studies at Tell Gezer." Presented at SBL Annual Meeting, New Orleans, Nov. 1990.

32. "Ancient Metallurgy on Cyprus." Presented at ASOR Southeast Regional Meeting, Charlotte, NC., March 1990.

33. "The Environmental Archaeology of Abila and the Decapolis." Presented at NEAS Annual Meeting, San Diego, CA., Nov. 1989.

34. "The Geological Environment of Biblical City/Sites in Palestine, Israel and Jordan." Presented at ASOR Annual Meeting, Anaheim, CA., Nov. 1989.

35. "Resurrection of a Christian Church Building at Abila, the Decapolis." Presented at Biblical Archaeological Exposition, NACC, Louisville, KY., July 1989.

36. "The Environmental Geology of Abila in the Jordanian Decapolis." Presented at ASOR Southeast Regional Meeting, Atlanta, GA., March 1989.

37. "The Late Bronze and Iron Age City Defenses." Presented at ASOR Annual Meeting, Chicago, IL., Nov., 1988.

38. "The Function of the Ancient City Gate Area." Presented at Johnson Bible College, Knoxville, TN., Sept., 1988.

39. "Biblical Archaeology and Backgrounds in the History of the Restoration Movement." Presented at Biblical Archaeological Exposition, NACC, Cincinnati, OH., July, 1988.

40. "The Environmental Archaeology of Abila of the Decapolis." Presented at Biblical Archaeology Exposition, NACC, Louisville, KY., July, 1986.

41. "Environmental Effects Upon the Destiny of Man as Seen in the Archaeological Record: Bab edh' Dhra', Tell Gezer, Curium and Carthage." Presented at Cincinnati Nature Center, Cincinnati, OH., Feb. 1987.

42. "The Archaeological Geology of the Area of Apollo Hylates, Kourion-West, *Kouion.*" Presented at the University of Arizona, Tucson, AZ., March 1986.

43. "Canaanite and Phoenician Infant Sacrifices at Gezer and Carthage." Presented at Transylvania University, Lexington, KY., Oct. 1985.

44. "Harbor-site Sedimentary Record of Occupational History of Carthage, North Africa." Presented at GSA Annual Meeting, Orlando, FL., Oct. 1985.

45. "Lithic Repertoire in Punic and Roman Carthage." Presented at GSA Annual Meeting, Orlando, FL., Oct. 1985.

46. "Historical Geography Is Essential to the Understanding of Biblical History." Presented at Biblical Archaeological Exposition NACC, Anaheim, CA., July 1985.

47. "Geology in the Service of Archaeology." Presented at Transylvania University, Lexington, KY., April 1985.

48. "ASOR Excavations at Punic and Roman Carthage: The Harbor and Tophet." Presented to the ETS Midwestern Section, Cedarville, OH., March 1985.

49. "The Environmental Geology and Lithic Repertoire of Abila, Jordan." Presented at ASOR Annual Meeting, Chicago, IL., Nov. 1984.

50. "The Geologic Setting of Abila, Jordan." Presented at ASOR Annual Meeting, Chicago, IL., Nov. 1984.

51. "Making the Bible 'Come Alive' Through Scientific Excavations." Presented at Biblical Archaeological Exposition NACC, St. Louis, MO., July 1983.

52. "The Environmental Geology of Tel Abila of the Decapolis, Jordan." Presented at ASOR Annual Meeting, New York, NY., Nov. 1982.

53. "The Punic Cemetery, Harbor Area, Carthage, Tunisia." Presented at SBL Midwestern Regional Meeting, Cincinnati, OH., March 1982.

54. "The Punic-Roman Lithic Repertoire of Carthage, in the Province of Africa." Presented at AIA Annual Meeting, San Francisco, CA., Dec., 1981.

55. "The Environmental Geology of Tell Gezer, Israel: New Discoveries." Presented at GSA Annual Meeting, Cincinnati, OH., Nov. 1981.

56. "Petrography and Provenance of the Lithic Repertoire of Punic and Roman Carthage, Tunisia." Presented at GSA Annual Meeting, Atlanta, GA. Nov., 1980.

57. "Lithic Repertoire of Punic and Roman Carthage." Presented at the Oriental Institute, University of Chicago, Chicago, IL., July 1980.

58. "Carthage, 1978: Punic Project, Geological Excavation Report." Presented at ASOR Annual Meeting, New Orleans, LA., Nov. 1978.

59. "Environment Geology in Archaeological Perspective: Highlights of Fourteen Years' Work." Presented at ASOR Annual Meeting, New Orleans, LA., Nov. 1978.

60. "Biblical Archaeology." Presented at NACC, Cincinnati, OH., July, 1977.

61. "The City of Sodom--Bab edh' Dhra', Southeastern Dead Sea Area." Presented at NEAS Annual Meeting, Philadelphia, PA., Dec. 1976.

62. "The Archaeological Geology of Roman Punic Carthage, Tunisia." Presented at AIA Annual Meeting, New York, NY., Dec. 1976.

63. with Leonard Larsen, "Low-Altitude, Aerial, Oblique Stereo-Slides and Variable Speed Movies for Geology Instruction." Presented at GSA Annual Meeting, Denver, CO., Oct., 1976.

64. "Environmental Geology and the Architectural and Lithic Repertoire of Tell Gezer, Israel." Presented at to the Georgia Chapter of the AIA, University of Georgia, Athens, GA., April 1976.

65. "The Archaeological Geology of The Commercial Harbor, Carthage, Tunisia." Presented at GSA Southeast Regional Meeting, Reston, VA., March 1976.

66. with Scott Thorton, "The Micro-sedimentology of Ancient Carthage and Its Harbor." Presented at the GSA Annual Meeting, Salt Lake City, UT., Oct. 1975.

67. with Frank Koucky, "Geology and Metallurgy at Idalion, Cyprus." Presented at GSA Annual Meeting, Dallas, TX., Oct. 1973.

68. "Archaeological Sedimentation and Stratigraphy at Tell Gezer, Israel." Presented at GSA Annual Meeting, Minneapolis, MN., Nov. 1972.

69. "Environmental Archaeology at Tell Gezer in the Shephelah of Israel." Presented at AIA Annual West Coast Lecture Series: University of Oregon, Eugene, OR., University of California, Berkeley, Berkeley, CA., University of California, Santa Barbara, Santa Barbara, CA., and University of California, San Diego, San Diego, CA., March 1972.

70. "Archaeological Illustration and Illumination of Biblical History." Presented at Maritime Christian College, Charlottetown, PE., CAN., Jan. 1972.

71. "Archaeological Geology of Tell Gezer, Israel." Presented at GSA Annual Meeting, Washington, D.C., Nov. 1971.

72. "Geology as an Archaeological Tool in Historical Research." Presented at the Harvard University Lectureship, Harvard Semitic Museum, Cambridge, MA., Jan. 1970.

73. "Terraces of the Bighorn Mountains along the Western Margin of the Powder River Basin, Wyoming." Presented at GSA Annual Meeting, Kansas City, MO., Nov. 1965.

3

Letters of Remembrance and Obituaries

Complied by Mark Ziese and John D. Wineland

LETTERS OF REMEMBRANCE

Gerald L. Mattingly

WHEN I ENROLLED AT Cincinnati Bible Seminary (CBS) for the Fall 1969 semester, Dr. Reuben G. Bullard ("Doc Rock") was widely regarded as one of the school's great treasures. Most students loved him and his classes, though a few did not fully appreciate what he was trying to accomplish through his life and teaching! All of my classroom experiences and post-college contacts with Reuben confirmed the more positive assessment, and I am grateful for the friendship we shared for almost thirty-five years. As I reflect on what Reuben meant to me, and to so many others fortunate enough to count him as friend and colleague, I think about three ways in which he made such an impact.

First, RGB (another nickname!) made a big impression on me in three of his courses: Earth Science; Archaeological Research, and Science and Christianity. Although he taught other courses that I did not have an opportunity to take, these three provided a venue for the initial, and still powerful, impact that Reuben had on me. That influence has persisted for almost forty years, since the content of those three classes (not to mention his enthusiasm for those subjects) shaped me as an impressionable student from Louisville, Kentucky. Though I came to CBS with some interest in history, archaeology, and science, Dr. Bullard focused my interest, and showed how my vague notions and curiosity about such things related to the study of the world of the Bible (i.e., its physical and historical contexts). Along with other good professors, he unleashed my curiosity. As a resident of the planet, teacher, and minister, Reuben provided a model for how we should study the world. For some of us, this meant that we should pay close attention to the subject-matter of those three courses, and those three in particular. *He* certainly did, and I acquired a special appreciation for the world, past and present, by watching him and by studying the content of those special classes.

Second, RGB taught me many lessons about how to study the world, and how to present the results of that study to others. When I reflect upon my experiences with Reuben in his classes and offices, in the library, and at the professional meetings, a number of very clear memories surface. All of Dr. Bullard's acquaintances knew that he loved books, including those big and expensive tomes related to archaeology and classical studies. I recall how every shelf of his office in "Old Main" was packed with books, journals, maps, and papers. He bragged about the rich holdings in the libraries of both the University of Cincinnati and Hebrew Union College and encouraged us to learn about those places. Though most of his career took place before the advent of computers, Reuben embraced the use of technology in his study of the world, especially in his work in chemistry, geology, and scientific photography. Contrary to the opinion of some, Reuben was not stuck in the past!

Professor Bullard's offices and labs also included significant collections of geological specimens and artifacts, and he made extensive use of this material in teaching. He was spellbound about the components of those geological specimens, and loved to talk about the processes that created those rocks and minerals. He also looked at archaeological artifacts, whether a magnificent monumental gate or a lowly clay pot, as the product of human ingenuity, and he spoke about those ancients as if he knew them personally! Time after time, our professor proclaimed, with an unforgettable gleam in his eyes, that *this* particular artifact or *that* particular rock would "change our lives." We did not know what he meant at the time, but we are starting to get the picture now! In addition to his own collections, Reuben used major museums for educational purposes. He introduced me to the joys of the Cincinnati Art Museum, where I remember my first encounters with Glueck's materials from Khirbet et-Tannur, and a wonderful relief from a mithraeum in Rome. Through slides and lively stories, he took us to the great museums in London, Paris, and Jerusalem, among other places. Dr. Bullard also promoted organizations, and encouraged our participation in the professional meetings, including the American Schools of Oriental Research, Near East Archeological Society, and Archaeological Institute of America. Although he had a pensive side, Reuben was gregarious, and he encouraged others to attend these gatherings and become acquainted with the work of a wide range of scholars. He delighted in hearing about what other students of the world had learned in their forays! Everyone who spent time with this memorable professor and friend knew Reuben's perspective on fieldwork; for him it was an absolutely indispensable aspect of geological and archaeological research. Whenever students or friends heard Dr. Bullard talk about field research, which he undertook regularly at home and abroad, we understood that this was an essential component of his *joie de vivre.*

Third, RGB provided me with an example of several important attitudes, an outlook that proved useful as I put together my own "philosophy of life." To put it in the simplest terms, he possessed a unique enthusiasm for learning, and an insatiable curiosity about Creation. This curiosity led (even *drove*) Reuben to think across the disciplines, rarely recognizing limits to what subjects he should take on. If a problem required knowledge from ancient history, or languages, or historical geography, Reuben relished the challenge. If a particular question called for data from chemistry or geology, this presented no barrier to his inquiry. Reuben integrated all of these fields into discussions about biblical and theological matters! He developed these skills because of his belief that anything worth doing was worth doing well. Like the illustrations in his classroom lectures, Dr. Bullard's research was integrated and thorough.

In addition to his outgoing nature, we will always remember Reuben because his life reflected a very strong sense of loyalty, and a devotion to friends, school, family, and church. His faithfulness in these dimensions of life flowed from his love for God, the study of whose world gave Reuben great pleasure.

Jon Weatherly

Reuben Bullard entered my life when I entered Cincinnati Bible College (now Cincinnati Christian University) as a freshman in 1977. I had no courses with him that year, but that didn't matter. "Doc Rock," as he was affectionately known, made it a point somehow to meet nearly every freshman.

He didn't just shake hands politely before moving on. He asked about my interests and my dreams. He encouraged me to learn everything that I could, and to set my sights high. Aware of how some Bible college students chafe at general studies requirements, he spoke with passion about learning from every discipline.

It was clear to me from that first conversation that Reuben Bullard was thirsty to learn everything that he could. It was also clear that his thirst to learn was an expression of what the Beatitudes call "thirst for righteousness." "All truth is God's truth," he told me then, and he told all students continually. Learning was one way that Reuben Bullard sought to honor God. And he shared his God-honoring passion to learn with everyone in a way that was infectious and compelling.

Nowhere was he more infectious for me than in the two-semester geology class that he taught. At the time our facilities were cramped, and barely adequate. But with passion Dr. Bullard brought the subject to life with slides, maps, specimens, and compelling lectures.

I can express the impression that the class made on me no better than with a rather personal revelation. In those days Dr. Bullard typically gave multiple choice questions that were phrased according to this formula: "You are on your honeymoon at [name of destination]. There you see [brief description of geological phenomenon]. You explain to your new husband or wife that this is _____, was caused by _____ [list of proposed answers follows]." Well, between the fall and spring semesters of that academic year, my fiancée and I were married. And throughout our honeymoon, starting on the trip from the airport to the hotel, and ending with the trip from the airport to our first apartment, I did that very thing. I explained to my bride every bit of rock and soil that I thought I understood. I was apparently in love with geology.

As a mentor of young scholars, Reuben Bullard was enthusiastic and gracious. My own interests developed toward exegesis and biblical theology rather than the sciences and archaeology that he pursued. But his interest in and encouragement for what I was doing were constant. While I was in graduate school, at Cincinnati and beyond, I could expect that he would inquire about my research interests, more than just politely, every time we met. I also learned to expect every summer an enthusiastic post card from him, sent from somewhere in the Mediterranean basin, a note that reminded me that my work in the library mattered to him even while he was up to his eyeballs in his own work on the field.

Eventually, my relationship with Reuben Bullard morphed from student-professor to colleague, as I joined the faculty of my alma mater where he continued to teach. Through those years, no one was more enthusiastic or appreciative of what I did than he. The same was true when I sacrificed twenty points from my IQ by becoming an administrator. Our relationship was the same: he sought constantly to encourage me in a way that strengthened my passion to learn, to discover, to teach, and to help others do the same.

Men like Reuben Bullard are rare. Few are as learned. Few are as wise. Few are as kind. So very few are all three. If rarity determines value, he was like a priceless gem. I can only hope to sparkle as brightly.

Dale R. Meade

I first met Reuben Bullard when I arrived on the campus of Cincinnati Christian University in the Fall of 1969. I heard stories of his boxes of rocks, and artifact collections in the attic museum of the building known as "Old Main." Being a rock hound and "archaeologist" myself (in truth, little more than collecting arrow heads as a Boy Scout), I was curious to see some exotic and genuine artifacts. I was also a very amateur photographer, and had been told that he had not one, but two Leica cameras! I was impressed. I braved my way up to the attic to meet Dr. Bullard. He was quick to welcome me and give me the tour. This whetted my appetite, and next year I signed up for my first class with him.

Being a child of the turbulent sixties, I had been infused with many of the ideals born in American scientific modernism. This had left me with some quiet doubts about the accuracy of the Bible and the scientific "proofs" that called it into question. For this reason I eagerly signed up for Dr. Bullard's Ancient History class. He immediately made his convictions clear, and set out to eliminate doubts such as the ones I uneasily harbored. He illustrated his lessons with artifacts and slides. He backed his profession of faith with his educational credentials and field research. He made history come to life, a difficult thing to do anytime, but especially at seven in the morning!

We shared many interests, and soon became good friends as well. I learned that students could legally "sneak" off campus at night if accompanied by a professor. I also learned that Dr. Bullard spent several nights a week in his office, and regularly studied till the wee hours of the morning. Thus began our ritual of the "five-way" at Skyline Chili, a nocturnal meal we always enjoyed. [1] Our shared interests also remained a life-long link as we worked together in study and ministry. I continued to "take classes" with him right up until the end, as I did guided research and helped him, just as he helped me.

Dr. Bullard inspired me to dream, to believe in God, and to believe in myself. He motivated me to finish my PhD through his example and constant encouragement. He was my teacher, but he became more than that; he was a friend and mentor during more than 30 years of missionary service.

Edwin Yamauchi

I am happy to reflect on my fond memories of a good friend and wonderful teacher/scholar, Reuben Bullard.

First, Reuben was a unique scholar, who combined his interest in the Bible and archaeology with his scientific training as a chemist and geologist. He had the distinction of being the first geologist to belong to the Core Staff of an archaeological dig in Israel, at the Tell Gezer excavations sponsored by Hebrew Union College (1966–73). He later served as an archaeological consultant in many other excavations in Israel, Jordan, Cyprus, and Carthage. It was this achievement that led me to invite him to participate in a conference on ancient Africa that I convened at Miami University in 1991. This resulted in his chapter, "The Berbers of the Maghreb and Ancient Carthage," published in *Africa and Africans in Antiquity* (East Lansing: Michigan State University Press, 2001), which I edited.

Second, our long relationship stemmed from our mutual involvement in the Near East Archaeological Society. Reuben was faithful in recruiting his students to participate in the society, many of whom became officers of the NEAS. He also served for many years on the NEAS nominating committee.

---

1. Skyline Chili, a local restaurant chain, began serving their unique "Cincinnati-style" chili in a section of town known as Price Hill. The original building opened in 1949 near the Cincinnati Christian University. This proximity, coupled with their night hours, has made it an enduring favorite for CCU students and professors alike. A "five-way" is a plate of spaghetti, covered with Skyline chili, cheese, and then loaded with beans and chopped onions.

Finally, I had the pleasure of having a number of his students continue their studies with me at Miami University, as they wrote their M. A. theses and doctoral dissertations under my direction. These have included:

Roger Chambers, PhD dissertation, "Greek Athletics and the Jews--165 B.C. to A.D. 70" (1980). Roger was the second of my seventeen doctoral students.

Robert W. Smith, MA thesis, "The Antipatrids and Their Eastern Neighbors" (1988); PhD dissertation, "'*Arabia Haeresium Ferax*?' A History of Christianity in the Transjordan to C.E. 395" (1994).

John Wineland, MA thesis, "The Region of the Decapolis" (1988); PhD dissertation, "Abila of the Decapolis: A Historical and Archaeological Examination from the Hellenistic Period to the Arab Conquest" (1996).

Adam Chambers, MA thesis, "Judaism, Hellenism, and the Greco-Roman Theater" (2002). Adam, who is the son of Roger Chambers, will be my final doctoral student.

I had the sad privilege of writing the obituaries for Reuben Bullard that appeared in *Biblical Archaeology Review* 30/6 (2004: 13) and in the *ASOR Newsletter* 54/2 (Summer, 2004: 5).

Keith N. Schoville

I first became aware of Reuben Bullard many years ago when I read his pioneering study of geological phenomena at Tel Gezer in Israel. I was beginning a career in Hebrew and Semitic Studies at the University of Wisconsin in Madison at the time. Because of my interest in biblical archaeology, I carefully read the issue of *The Biblical Archaeologist* that featured Reuben's research.[2] His study opened my eyes to the broader parameters of the archaeological enterprise, and his work continues to enrich me intellectually.

The paths of Reuben and myself first crossed as a result of our joint association with the Near East Archaeological Society (NEAS) a few years later. When I became a member of the organization (thanks to the recruitment efforts of Bastiaan van Elderen), Reuben and his colleague, Professor Willard ("Wilkie") Winter, were already on the Board of Directors. Both also served as faculty members of the Cincinnati Christian University. Besides our common interests in the archaeology

2. Reuben Bullard, "Geological Studies in Field Archaeology," *The Biblical Archeologist* 33 (1970/4: 98–132).

of the lands of the Bible, we were all three active in the Christian Church, so we bonded strongly. In time I became president of the NEAS, succeeding our long-serving colleague, Dr. Harold Mare. My acceptance of the responsibilities associated with that office were in large part due to the encouragement of Dr. Bullard, who was then and for many years continued as the chair of the nominations committee of the NEAS. Chair of the nominations committee in that (and most) organizations is a position that garners little in the way of kudos, but in my observations of Reuben Bullard, he did nothing for the sake of praise or personal glory. His efforts were solely focused upon the successful completion of the task at hand, be it the acquisition of knowledge and wisdom by his students in the field or classroom, or for the advancement of an organization's purposes.

I treasure memories of the pleasurable and interesting companionship of Reuben Bullard at the annual meetings of the NEAS. I recall chatting with him on the stairs in the Opryland Hotel in Nashville. If ever there was a worse place for an organization's annual meeting than that hotel, I have yet to see it! It is a fine location for individuals or for families on vacation (and we enjoyed the amenities of the hotel itself), but the location of meeting rooms was so disjointed and scattered, that we found ourselves spending as much time wandering the endless halls and riding the ubiquitous elevators in search of meeting rooms as we spent hearing the papers. Reuben and I enjoyed several comical interchanges about the situation during that meeting. But while it is human nature to complain now and then, Reuben never expressed anger as much as disgust. I remember him as an exemplary Christian scholar and gentleman.

The last time I saw Reuben was at the annual meeting of the NEAS and related societies in Toronto a number of years ago. His lovely wife, Lynn, accompanied him. They had flown into Toronto for the meeting while I had driven, so I was blessed to have their company as we drove into downtown Toronto for sessions hosted by the American Schools of Oriental Research and the Society of Biblical Literature. A focus of that meeting was the exhibit in the Royal Ontario Museum of the famous, or as some might say, "infamous," James Ossuary. The experience of visiting the exhibit and attending related lectures gave us opportunity to converse about the significance of it all. We both agreed that such material remains are interesting, but that our Christian faith is neither defined by, nor can it be denied by, the existence or lack of artifactual remains. I honor the honesty, conviction and consistency of my friend, Dr. Reuben Bullard. I am sorry only because I was never able to share his company on an archaeological excavation, such as Abila of the Decapolis, to which he contributed so much.

Joe D. Seger

Reuben Bullard burst onto the stage in Biblical Archaeology in the late 1960s at Tell Balatah-Shechem, and subsequently at Tell Gezer. As budding field archaeologists ourselves, some of us on the Gezer staff weren't certain what to make of this self-assured savant who had technical terms for all sorts of archeo-related phenomena. Now it was "colluvium," not just a downhill rock spill, and "vesicular basalt" for the stuff grinding stones were made of. The "New Archaeology" was sweeping over us in those years, forcing more attention to empirical details of all sorts, and Reuben was in the avant-garde. He instantly became a geological guru to us all. In time we learned from his lead, and could enter the dialogue. Often we were even able to wink at some of his more fanciful interpretations. But overall, he opened the way to many new and positive vistas of exploration and analysis.

We of course remember him well for that, but perhaps even more especially for his abundance of energy and optimism. Never challenge a man with a limp to an afternoon hike! While others napped, Reuben prowled, found clay sources, made ovens with volunteers, gathered dung for fuel, explored caves, and visited boundary markers. He was simply indefatigable. Always himself a constant learner, he was a wonderful teacher, and there was no one that didn't consider him a friend. In the parlance of the 1960s and 70s everyone "dug" Reuben Bullard.

After the Gezer years he moved on to work at Caesarea, Carthage, Kourion, and other sites. But it was my personal joy to continue working with him on Gezer publications, and we maintained the dialogue at numerous professional gatherings. Reuben was not quite a saint (with that twinkle in his eye you just knew that there was an imp in there somewhere), but he was most certainly one of the finest human beings one could hope to know. He was more than just a highly respected scholar and teacher, he was a very special individual. I was much honored to know him as a good friend.

George ("Rip") Rapp [deceased]

In 1971 I was on the Joint Technical Program Committee for the Annual Meeting of the Geological Society of America (GSA). Reuben Bullard submitted an abstract for a paper for this meeting on what was essentially an archaeological geology (orgeoarchaeology) topic. It was rejected because none of the sessions, each tightly focused on a given subdiscipline of earth science would take it. The paper did not fit with the perceived boundaries of any of the sub disciplines (e.g. geomorphology, sedimentology, or stratigraphy). Not only did geoarchaeology not fit into the organizational structure, geoarchaeology did not appear to qualify as a subdiscipline. It had no formal organization, no journal, no annual meetings, no university degree programs, or even university courses. I decided things had to change.

For the 1972 GSA meeting, as Technical Program Chair, I organized a session on geoarchaeology. The committee assigning rooms put the session in one of the smallest rooms. Before the first paper was well underway the audience had expanded into the hallway. I quickly put on my other hat as Co-General Chair of the GSA meetings, and moved us to a large room. For 1973 I was again on the Technical Program Committee, so I saw to it that geoarchaeology again got its foot in the door. I learned that to be guaranteed a place as a technical session, the session organizers must represent an associated society [e.g. the Mineralogical Society of America], or a division or section of GSA.

GSA was amenable to a division, so I wrote some bylaws, asked a few members for their active support, and made a formal proposal to the GSA Council for an Archaeological Geology Division. I chose archaeological geology, rather than geoarchaeology, because GSA was an association of geologists. The proposal was successful. I was surprised when over 400 GSA members joined the new Archaeological Geology Division.

Today archaeological geology is a thriving subdiscipline of earth science with established organizations, journals, worldwide meetings, university courses and graduate programs, and geoarchaeological faculty in many universities. It all started in 1971 when Reuben Bullard submitted an abstract. Thankfully, he lived to see his discipline of choice thrive.

Steven Bowman

Shortly after my appointment at the University of Cincinnati in 1980 I learned about a fascinating teacher/scholar, a geologist who had a degree in classics, and who was an experienced archaeologist. Here was someone, perhaps, who could answer one of my many sophomoric questions. I sought out Professor Reuben Bullard in the Geology Department's charming dugout (which no longer exists), and after he informed me of his contribution to the establishment of Judaic Studies at the University of Cincinnati (support that he avidly continued until his untimely death), I asked him if he could comment on, if not explain, all the zeros in the scientific dating of our cosmos. Reuben smiled and kindly invited me to sit in on his Environmental Geology class. Well, in the course of one year I learned about waves and sand, water and mud, and the vicissitudes of human intelligence with respect to the environment. I recalled during that year that the people of India had given the cipher zero to Muslim scholars during the Middle Ages with all of its ensuing contributions to mathematics and western mechanics. The question then arose over an evening soup whether a non-monotheistic tradition could answer a monotheistically based question. So we began a discussion of the relationship between faith and dirt, and I continued to teach my students William Foxwell Albright and Biblical Archaeology alongside the new discoveries and occasionally controversial interpretations of Israeli archaeologists for the next twenty-five years. Shortly after that course I joined Reuben's expedition to Egypt and Israel, an adventure that provided deep memories that augmented my subsequent teaching career. Reuben was a natural teacher whose scholarship sat lightly on his broad shoulders, and which he always delivered with an enticing smile. I know from our discussions that the recent tragedy at Virginia Tech would have elicited a confirming response to the comment that such an event was a terrible waste of life, talent, and potential, but then it has always been easier to destroy than to build. Perhaps that is one of the underlying contributions of the Mosaic revolution we both embraced: the hope that we can rise to the vision of social justice and its benefits as outlined in the texts we both studied.

Professor Reuben Bullard enjoyed teaching the next generation. He drew upon a vast repertoire of scholarship from science, religion, and classics. We never shared a dull moment over our periodic bowls of soup before our respective evening courses. *Ave et vale.*

Warren D. Huff

Reuben and I overlapped one another in our graduate careers at University of Cincinnati. I completed my dissertation in the early 1960s, and was asked to stay on as a junior faculty member. Reuben completed his degree a few years later. In those days all theses, as with all formal documents, needed to be typed with appropriate carbon copies. My typing skills were, at best, rudimentary, so I arranged with Reuben's wife, Lynn, to do my dissertation typing. I spent a number of very pleasant evenings in their home in Independence, Kentucky, proof-reading what Lynn had typed, and interacting with Reuben and their children.

Reuben was working hard to fulfill his degree requirements by combining his interests in geology and biblical history. At that time Hebrew Union College was directing archeological excavations at Tel Gezer in Israel. Gezer had been continuously occupied from the Bronze Age to the Hellenistic Period, and Reuben found he could apply many geological methods of field study to this important project. This experience led him to become actively involved in the field that was to become known as geoarchaeology, and he was to go on to inaugurate, in collaboration with George "Rip" Rapp at the University of Minnesota, this brand new subdiscipline in geology. In 1977 the Geological Society of America formally established the Archaeological Geology Division. In my view this is Reuben's finest legacy to geology.

Reuben was an avid photographer, as everyone knew, and he was perhaps my strongest influence when I decided to invest in some high-quality camera equipment. A senior member of the geology faculty at that time was Ken Caster, a paleontologist. Ken's lectures were very popular with the students, but he was also a very demanding instructor. He was quite artistic on the blackboard, and was fond of using various colored chalks to illustrate his lectures. He taught in a classroom that had one blackboard running the full length of the front wall, and another the full length of a sidewall. By the end of one of his lectures both boards would be full of highly organized text and numerous colored drawings of stratigraphic sections, outcrops, and fossils. Students would struggle to try to capture all of this information in their notebooks, but it was Reuben who found the solution. Using his photographic skills he would systematically photograph all of Ken's drawings and blackboard notes, and then make copies for whoever wanted them. If those photos still exist they would be a real treasure!

OBITUARIES

Reuben G. Bullard
by Rebecca Goodman, *Cincinnati Enquirer*
Reprinted with permission

Reuben G. Bullard Sr., an internationally known archaeological geologist and Christian scholar who taught at Cincinnati Bible College and Seminary and at the University of Cincinnati, died Saturday afternoon at his home here. He was 76.

"This field of archaeological geology is one that is relatively new," said UC professor of geology David Meyer. "Archaeologists are using more information about the rocks that are found at archaeological sites—determining how ancient people used stones in their cultures. He was one of the pioneers of the field."

Dr. Bullard worked on numerous excavations in Israel, Cyprus, Tunisia, Egypt, Jordan, Greece and Italy.

"As an archaeological geologist, his role would be to identify and interpret the environment in which a society, a culture, a city was located," said his son, Reuben "Rick" Bullard Jr. of Fort Thomas. That might involve the identification of quarries that were used to build walls or streets, or identifying the clay resources of the important ceramic industries.

"He would help unravel the complexities of the stratigraphy—or layers—within an archaeological context, helping the archaeologist properly interpret them," his son said.

Dr. Bullard's first project was at Tell Gezer, Israel, a site halfway between Jerusalem and Tel Aviv that has been occupied since prehistoric times. There, he worked with Nelson Glueck, former president of Hebrew Union College, and George Ernest Wright, former head of Semitic studies at Harvard University (both deceased).

Born in Wheeling, W.Va., Dr. Bullard moved to Mitchell, Ind., before his senior year in high school. He moved to Greater Cincinnati in his early 20s to study at Cincinnati Bible College.

"Geology was his great love," his son said. "He felt that this was the point that Bible history and science met. He could combine all of these things together—passion of history and science and a committed life to the Lord."

From Cincinnati Bible College and Seminary, Dr. Bullard received a bachelor's degree in theology and ancient Near East history, a master's degree in historical geography and a bachelor's degree in intertestamental studies. From the University of Cincinnati, he received a bachelor's degree in classics, a master's degree in the philosophy of geology, and a doctorate in geology.

He taught history, science and archaeology at Cincinnati Bible College from 1961 until 2001. He was in his 37th year teaching geology night classes at UC.

"He was a gentle man—a compassionate man—always looking for the beauty in creation," his son said.

In addition to his son Rick, survivors include his wife of 48 years, Lynn Maine Bullard; another son, Howard Bullard of Rushville, Ind.; two daughters, Cathy Bullard Morgret of Rome, Ohio, and Suzanne Bullard Prichard of Brandon, Fla.; a brother, Richard L. Bullard of Delhi Township; and six grandchildren.

Reuben G. Bullard, Archaeologist/Geologist
Passes Away at Home on July 3, 2004
Edwin Yamauchi

Reuben G. Bullard passed away at his home in Independence, Kentucky, on July 3, after bouts in the hospital with pleurisy and with bipolar chemistry. Bullard, who was born on March 18, 1928, in Wheeling, West Virginia, was 76 years old at the time of his death.

His sons praised their father at the funeral held on Thursday, July 8th at the church where he was an elder, as a devoted husband and father, and a bit of a renaissance man. Reuben lost his father at the age of 14. An auto accident when he was 20 cost him two inches from one leg, so he always walked with a limp thereafter. Inspired by his mother, Bullard trained as a classical pianist at Indiana University; he was also a gifted artist and a versatile handyman.

He first worked as a chemist at the Lehigh Portland Cement Company in Mitchell, Indiana, and served as a senior chemist at the Andrew Jergens Company in Cincinnati (1961–1968). He earned degrees in theology and historical geography from the Cincinnati Bible Seminary, and a degree in classics and his PhD. in geology/archaeology from the University of Cincinnati (1969).

He began a dual teaching career, teaching courses on geology, Bible, and ancient history as Professor of Geology & Archaeology at Cincinnati Bible College & Seminary in 1961, and from 1969 also teaching geology at the University of Cincinnati, first as an Assistant Professor in Geology and later as Lecturer in Biblical Archaeology & Environmental Geology at UC's College of Continuing Education. Even after his recent retirement from CBCS, he continued to teach at UC.

Bullard had the distinction of being the first geologist to belong to the staff of an archaeological dig in Israel, at the Tell Gezer Excavations sponsored by Hebrew Union College (1966–73). He served as a geological consultant at excavations in Carthage, Cyprus (Kourion), Israel (Khirbet Shema', Shechem, Caesarea Maritima, and Tell Dan) and Jordan (Heshbon, and Abila). He was president of the Cincinnati society of the Archaeological Institute of America (1974–79), and served as a trustee of the American Schools of Oriental Research and the Near East Archaeological Society.

Bullard contributed the chapters, "Geology in Field Archaeology," in *A Manual of Field Excavation*, edited by W. G. Dever and H. Darrell Lance (1978), "The Environmental Geology of Roman Carthage," in *Excavations at Carthage*, edited by J. Humphrey (1978), "Sedimentary Environments and Lithologic Materials at Two Archaeological Sites," in *Archaeological Geology*, edited by G. Rapp Jr. And J. A. Gifford (1985), and "The Berbers of the Maghreb and Ancient Carthage," in *Africa and Africans in Antiquity*, edited by Edwin Yamauchi (2001).

After earning PhD's, several of his students have followed in his footsteps, such as Robert W. Smith, who is teaching at Mid Atlantic Christian University, John Wineland at Kentucky Christian University and Sara Fudge a Cincinnati Christian University.

He is survived by his wife Lynn, two sons, Rick and Howard, two daughters, Cathy and Susan, and six grandchildren. Condolences may be sent to Lynn at Box 296, Independence, KY 41051, and gifts in his name to the Nicholson Christian Church, 1970 Walton-Nicholson Road, Independence, KY 41051.

Appeared in *The American Schools of Oriental Research Newsletter* 54.2 (summer 2004), and in the *Near East Archaeological Society Bulletin* 49 (2004). (Used with permission of the author).

Reuben G. Bullard
Christian Standard, September 19, 2004 p. 12
(Used with permission of *The Christian Standard*)

World-renowned archaeological geologist, scientific innovator, and Christian scholar Dr. Reuben G. Bullard, Sr. 76, died in his home in Independence, KY, on July 3. His geological expertise was first utilized at the archaeological site of Tell Gezer, Israel. Archaeologists consider that site as a major innovation in field and in laboratory research. To professionals in Near Eastern and Mediterranean archaeology, Dr. Bullard was a well-known, highly respected figure, and a pioneer in the application of geology to archaeology. In addition to Tell Gezer, he worked at other sites in Israel, Cyprus, Tunisia, Egypt, Jordan, Greece, and Italy. At the time of his death, he was serving as a consultant on the Karak Resources Project, directed by Dr. Gerald Mattingly, Johnson Bible College, Knoxville, TN.

Dr. Bullard used geology and archaeology in the classroom to shed light on the Scriptures. He had a deep appreciation for God's creation, God's general revelation (Romans 1:18–20), and the Bible, God's primary and specific revelation. His passion was passing on his knowledge and understanding to his students. He earned a Th.B. in theology and ancient Near East history, an MA in historical geography, and a BD in intertestamental studies, all from Cincinnati (OH) Christian University; and a BA in classics, an MS in philosophy of the science of geology and a PhD in geology from the University of Cincinnati.

He was an ordained minister and held preaching ministries in Mitchell, IN; Modest and Lerado, OH; Lamb Union Community Church in Indiana; and Lystra Church of Christ in Kentucky. He was an elder at Nicholson Christian Church, Independence, KY. He was involved with the start up of Central Christian College in Moberly, MO and designed the original seal for the college. He taught for 41 years at Cincinnati Bible College and Seminary and was in his 37th year teaching at the University of Cincinnati.

He married Lynn Maine in 1956; she survives. He also is survived by two sons, Reuben Jr. "Rick" of Fort Thomas, KY, and Howard of Rushville, IN; two daughters, Cathy Morgret of Rome, OH, and Suzanne Prichard of Brandon, FL; and six grandchildren. He was preceded in death by one grandson. Memorial contributions may be made to the Nicholson Christian Church stewardship campaign.

Reuben George Bullard, Sr. (1928–2004)
Ohio Journal of Science Dec 2005, Vol. 105 Issue 5, 144–45
Christopher Cumo
(used with permission from *The Ohio Journal of Science*)

Reuben George Bullard, Sr., age 76, professor of archaeology and geography at Cincinnati Christian University and adjunct professor at the University of Cincinnati in Cincinnati, OH, died 3 July 2004 at his home in Independence, KY. A pioneer in the field of archaeological geology, Bullard established the chronology of events at sites in the Mediterranean basin. His work coincides with the chronology of these sites within the narrative of the Bible. Bullard joined The Ohio Academy of Science 7 November 1986, affiliating with Section General Interest in Science.

Born 18 March 1928 in Wheeling, WV, Reuben George Bullard, Sr., was the son of Reuben George and Vada Bullard. By rights the appellation "Sr." belonged to the father, but his early death left the appellation free to devolve to Reuben Bullard, Sr., on the birth of his son, Reuben Bullard, Jr. In 1947 Reuben Bullard, Sr., received a diploma from Mitchell High School in Mitchell, IN; in 1956 a BA and in 1958 an MA in historical geography from Cincinnati Bible Seminary (now Cincinnati Christian University); in 1961 a BA in classics, in 1964 an M.S. in geology, and in 1969 a PhD. in geology from the University of Cincinnati. His M.S. and PhD. theses were entitled "The Philosophy of Geology" (1964) and "The Geology of Tell Gezer and Its Environs" (1969), respectively. While a graduate student he held the Fenneman Fellowship. In 1961 Bullard began teaching at Cincinnati Bible Seminary and was assistant professor at the University of Cincinnati (1969–1974). Although the novelty of his research prevented his receiving tenure, Bullard was later promoted to professor at Cincinnati Bible Seminary and adjunct professor at the University of Cincinnati. He taught ancient history, geology, archaeology, historical geography, a course on the relationship between science and Christianity, and courses on the Bible at Cincinnati Bible Seminary, and geology and geography at the University of Cincinnati. Bullard was chairman of Arts and Sciences at Cincinnati Bible Seminary.

His work in archaeological geology centered on pre-Roman and Roman antiquity. His principle research was at Tell Gezer, Israel, though he also conducted research in Libya, Cyprus, Tunisia, Egypt, Jordan, Greece, and Italy. "Archaeologists are using more information about the rocks that are found at archaeological sites, determining how ancient people used stones in their cultures," University of Cincinnati geology professor David Meyer told *The Cincinnati Enquirer*. "He [Reuben Bullard] was one of the pioneers of the field." Bullard identified the quarries from which ancient people took stones and the clay deposits for the crafting of pottery. He used stratigraphy to establish the chronology of events at ancient sites. His collaborators included Nelson Glueck, former president of Hebrew Union College in Cincinnati, OH, and George Ernst Wright, former head of Semitic studies at Harvard University in Cambridge, MA. "Geology was his great love," Reuben Bullard, Jr., told *The Cincinnati Enquirer* ."He felt that this was the point that Bible, history, and science met. He could combine all these things together: passion for history and science, and a committed life to the Lord."

In addition to being a member of The Ohio Academy of Science, Dr. Bullard was a founding member in the 1970s of the Archaeological Geology section of the Geological Society of America. He was also a member of the American School of Oriental Research, and about 1980 was president of the Cincinnati chapter of the Archeology Institute of America. His interests included photography, backpacking, traveling, and reading. Trained as a classical pianist, Bullard had been a music student at Indiana University in Bloomington, IN.

His wife Lynn Yvonne Bullard survives, the two having married 28 May 1956 in Fallonsbee, WV. Surviving also are sons Reuben George Bullard, Jr., of Independence, KY, and Howard Arthur Bullard of Rushville, IN; daughters Catherine Louise (Bullard) Morgret of East Liverpool, OH, and Suzanne Lynn (Bullard) Prichard of Tampa, FL; brother Richard L. Bullard of Delhi Township, KY; and six grandchildren. The family held visiting hours 7 July 2004 followed by a funeral service at Nicholson Christian Church in Independence, KY, and a memorial service 31 March 2003 at Cincinnati Christian University. Bullard was buried 7 July 2004 at Independence Cemetery in Independence. Friends may make donations to Nicholson Christian Church Stewardship Campaign, PO Box 5, Independence, KY 41051–0005 or to Cincinnati Christian University, 2700 Glenway Avenue, Cincinnati, OH 45204. The Ohio Academy of Science retains on file in its office an obituary published 7 July 2004 in *The Cincinnati Enquirer*.

4

The Labor of Animal Husbandry
in the Biblical World

Mark Ziese

THE UTILIZATION OF ANIMALS by man has both created and alleviated his work. Historically, this broad spectrum of labor investment
ranged from hunting to herding systems where, within the former,
animals were not only the prey, but oftentimes the means by which that
prey was tracked, pursued, or transported. In herding systems, care-
giving was directed toward preserving animal life for meat, milk, hair,
traction, trade, prestige, or a variety of other goals, ends, or products.
Labor intensity varied with time and task within these systems, although
the choice to utilize animal resources ultimately rested in the perception
that the quality of human life was somehow improved.

Galaty and Johnson have identified three critical areas for animal
husbandry study: land, livestock, and labor.[1] Given the limits of the present work, these three areas cannot, and indeed, need not be addressed
with equal weight. Adequate attention has been given to the Middle East
as a "marginal zone," "a land between," an area which forged subsistence
strategies empowered by diversity and mobility.[2] The second area, that

1. John G. Galaty and Douglas L. Johnson, *The World of Pastoralism: Herding
Systems in Comparative Perspective* (New York: Guliford, 1990) 3.

2. Additional information on this subject may be found in J. M. Wagstaff, *The
Evolution of Middle Eastern Landscapes: An Outline to A.D. 1840* (Totowa: Barnes and
Noble, 1985); Øystein S. LaBianca, *Sedentarization and Nomadization: Food System
Cycles at Hesban and Vicinity in Transjordan. Hesban 1* (Berrien Springs: Andrews,
1990); Rainey, Anson F. and R. Steven Notley, *The Sacred Bridge: Carta's Atlas of the
Biblical World* (Carta: Jerusalem, 2006); Daniel Hillel, *The Natural History of the Bible:
An Environmental Exploration of the Hebrew Scriptures* (New York: Oxford, 2006).

of livestock, continues to be addressed from a variety of perspectives, including the history of domestication and adaptation,[3] excavated faunal assemblages,[4] and the contemporary exploitation of livestock attributes.[5] The third dynamic, labor, has been addressed within the context of specific text corpora[6] and social development,[7] but remains to be more fully described from a tasking perspective.

Reasons for this are linked to the number and nature of the sources. The remains of labor are not easily extracted from the ground. Human behavior must be inferred from a variety of data, including excavated artifacts, ecofacts, artistic expressions, activity areas, and the like. As archaeological methods expand to gather non-traditional types of information, especially through regional survey, the ability to make and test such inferences will undoubtedly improve. Beyond archaeological excavation and regional survey, a second source of information on the subject of animal husbandry is ancient texts. Limits here, too, are well known. Preserved texts offer select windows into life in the past; windows that

3. Beginning points for reading on this subject include J. D. Vigne, J. Peters, and D. Helmer, eds., *The First Steps of Animal Domestication: New Archaeozoological Approaches* (Oxford: Oxbow Press, 2005); M. A. Zeder, "Archaeological Approaches to Documenting Animal Domestication," in *Documenting Domestication: New Genetic and Archaeological Paradigms*, M. A. Zeder, et al., eds. (Berkeley: University of California Press, 2006); M. A. Zeder, "Central Questions in the Domestication of Plants and Animals" in *Evolutionary Anthropology* 15.3 (2006) 105–17.

4. As just one example, consult Øystein S. LaBianca and Angela von den Driesch, eds., *Faunal Remains: Taphonomical and Zooarchaeological Studies of the Animal Remains from Tell Hesban and Vicinity. Hesban 13* (Berrien Springs: Andrews, 1995).

5. Gendrun Dahl and Andres Hjort, *Having Herds: Pastoral Herd Growth and Household Economy. Stockholm Studies in Social Anthropology 2* (Stockholm: University of Stockholm, 1976); Juliet Clutton-Brock, ed., *The Walking Larder: Patterns of Domestication, Pastoralism, and Predation* (London: Unwin Hyman, 1989).

6. See Gary Beckman, "Herding and Herdsmen in Hittite Culture," in *Documentum Asiae Minoris Antiquae*, ed. Erich Neu and Christel Ruster (Wiesbaden: Otto Harrassowitz, 1988) 33–44; Oded Borowski, *Every Living Thing: Daily Use of Animals in Ancient Israel* (Walnut Creek: AltaMira, 1998); Victor H. Matthews and Don C. Benjamin, *World of Ancient Israel, 1250–587 BCE* (Peabody: Hendrickson, 1993); Marek Stepien, *Animal Husbandry in the Ancient Near East: A Prosopographic Study of Third-Millennium Umma* (Bethesda: CDL, 1996); G. A. Klingbeil, "Agriculture and Animal Husbandry," in *Dictionary of the Old Testament: Historical Books*, Bill T. Arnold and H. G. M. Williamson, eds. (Downers Grove: Intervarsity, 2005), 1–20.

7. M. A. Zeder, *Feeding Cities: Specialized Animal Economy in the Ancient Near East. Smithsonian Series in Archaeology Inquiry* (Washington: Smithsonian Institution, 1989).

are often quite removed from the concern of the ordinary, rural, or long term. In this the biblical text is no exception. Finally (and fortunately), the study of husbandry relies on information gained through the observation of contemporary pastoralists in similar environments. While the drawbacks of leaning heavily upon analogy are well known, the value of this source for the study of labor can hardly be overestimated.[8] Hence, data for building a portrait of husbandry practices in the biblical world arise from three distinct sources: archaeological sites, ancient texts, and observed practice.

The dangers of compositing such a portrait are many. One keen difficulty concerns a lost sense of time. Throughout the biblical period, husbandry practices changed, shifted, and moved in conjunction with other dynamics. As one example, the social fabric of the patriarchal period, when Abraham, Isaac, and Jacob roamed the hill country with their flocks, was quite different from that of the time of David, or to pull even farther, than that of the contemporary *Bedu* of present-day Jordan. This obvious example clarifies the struggle of pumping an "ethnographic present" into the past. If, as suggested, it is possible to obscure the tremendous variability that exists among those who practice herding strategies today, how much deeper is the danger for those who work with more distant data?[9] If this was not enough, another danger to be contemplated is a reckless use of the biblical text. The topic of shepherding is a popular one with literally hundreds of biblical mentions. Analysis of these mentions can only be done with an awareness of literary devices such as generalization, idealization, and metaphor.

One way of dealing with these dangers is to discard the notion of a "single portrait." Rephrasing the present task as one of preparing "portraits" of animal husbandry suggests the multifaceted nature of the labor involved in husbandry, and allows for descriptive movement, complexity, and flexibility. "Portraits" by their nature are interpretive, and approach what could be termed caricature. Hence, the material presented here should not be viewed as an exact "map" of the past, but rather as a set of interpretations built upon factors viewed as constant, including physical

8. Roger Cribb suggests that "ethnographic settings provide an optimal environment in which to identify and study the behavior of key variables, refine measuring instruments, and isolate appropriate analytical units." See his *Nomads in Archaeology* (Cambridge: Cambridge University, 1991) 5.

9. Rada Dyson-Hudson and Neville Dyson-Hudson, "Nomadic Pastoralism," *Annual Review of Anthropology* 9 (1980) 15–61.

environment, animal physiology, and human needs. To limit exaggeration, frequent recourse is made to ancient texts and archaeological data. With these introductory thoughts in mind, two units of discussion follow. The first presents a profile of animal husbandry, noting definitions, stock selection, and cycles of labor intensity. The second section presents various portraits of husbandry practice arranged around types of labor.

I. ANIMAL HUSBANDRY IN PROFILE

A. Definitions

The term "animal husbandry" elicits many contexts; primary is the activity of personal subsistence. Animals digest agricultural products that cannot be eaten by humans. Such "live-stock" becomes, in essence, a mobile pantry; potential calories may be stored "on the hoof," converted, or consumed by man as time and needs demand. The virtue of mobility allows for the conveyance of resources from field to field, field to home, or field to market. This factor was indispensable for life in a marginal environment that lacked the technology of refrigerated transport and storage. Inedible animal products could be harvested and converted into needed items, either directly by manufacture, or indirectly by trade. Herd management operated fundamentally on the level of household (kin, clan, and tribe), although village-, temple-, and state-run enterprises were known in the biblical world (e.g. Nuzi). These dynamics have been plotted in several typologies that distinguish between degrees of mobility, specialized diet, or scales of production. As one helpful example, the summary of Wapnish and Hesse establishes twin poles of reference around mobile pastoralism and village-based pastoralism.[10] This paradigm overlies an older model, now viewed as obsolete, that drew a strict dichotomy between the lifeways of "the desert" (herder) and "the sown" (farmer). However, note Cribb's critical observation that agricultural systems are fundamentally different from and more stable than pastoral systems in terms of productivity, labor investment, and land requirements.[11]

10. Paula Wapnish and Brian Hesse, "Urbanization and the Organization of Animal Production at Tell Jemmeh in the Middle Bronze Age Levant," *Journal of Near Eastern Studies* 47.2 (1988) 83.

11. Cribb, *Nomads*, 24.

Hence, the practice of animal husbandry may be understood as an activity of subsistence commonly exercised at a household level. As one response to the risks of living in a marginal zone, the management of animal resources supplemented agricultural output and provided safeguards against its failure. To better understand the opportunities and limitations offered by the practice of husbandry requires a closer look at an inventory of animals.

B. Stock Selection

Much attention has been given to the domestication process as well as the ecological requirements for raising animals in Southwest Asia.[12] The questions of why or how certain animals came under the control of man need not be reviewed here. It is enough to note three broad, well-worn, and connected truths. First, the practice of husbandry extended subsistence/economic potential into regions where agriculturalism was not a viable option (too steep, too dry, too distant, too unstable, etc.). Second, as noted already, the careful coordination of agricultural and husbandry efforts offered efficiency, mobility, and diversity to people living in a marginal zone. Third, the practice of husbandry had "biological and social consequences for both tamed and tamer."[13] Key domesticates for the biblical world included the following:

1. Sheep. The most ubiquitous of herded stock, several breeds or classes of sheep are noted in Ancient Near Eastern records. However, not all of these are identified.[14] These breeds were developed specifically to maximize production of meat, milk, or wool. One of the most enduring breeds in the area is the *Awassi*, or "fat tailed" sheep (*Ovis orientalis*). Depictions of the *Awassi*, with its "ill-proportioned" tail reaching a size of 15 pounds, are readily identified.

Sheep appear as docile creatures, responsive to affection, but lacking initiative. Their perceived innocence made them a ready target for

12. Additional information on this subject may be found in Andrew N. Garrad, "The Selection of South-West Asian Animal Domesticates," in *Animals and Archaeology: 3. Early Herders and their Flocks,* ed. J. Clutton-Brock and C. Grigson (BAR International Series 202, 1984) 117–32. See, too, the broader presentation in Clutton-Brock, *The Walking Larder.*

13. Hesse, "Animal Husbandry," 206.

14. Such distinctions may not necessarily be breeds as such, but classes of animals determined by area of geographical origin or feeding methods. See Stepien, *Animal Husbandy,* 16–24, for an introduction to this discussion in the Ur III period.

literary metaphor or bloody sacrifice. In the biblical text, vocabulary that likely included both sheep and goats is the collective *ṣo'n* ("flock"). However, more specific terms are also found: *kebeś* ("sheep"), *rāḥāl* ("ewe"), *'ayil* ("ram"), *śeh* ("lamb").

2. *Goats.* Like sheep, goats (*Capra hircus*) were herded regularly in the biblical world, and were valued for milk, meat, hair, dung, and skins. Vocabulary and artistic representation also suggest various breeds of this hollow-horned ruminant were known. In general, goats were hardier, more mobile, and less selective in their diet than sheep; still, they were likely to be herded together with sheep and identified together. Biblically, these are known as a *ṣo'n* ("flock") or *miqneh* ("small cattle"). Ratio records of goat to sheep in a single herd are as much a reflection of practical concerns (see herding, below) as they are an indicator of environmental and/or market necessities.

The vocabulary of goats in the biblical text is diverse. Male (*tayiš* or *'attûd*) may be distinguished from female (*'ēz*). Ṣapir ("billy-goat"?), *śāpîr* or *gĕdî* ("young goat") also appear.

3. *Cattle.* The size and strength of bovids (*Bos taurus* and *Bos indicus*) were utilized chiefly in the biblical world for traction. Depictions of oxen pulling carts, wagons, sleds, threshers, and plows are familiar. Milk and dung would have also been managed, although young and old alike were certainly harvested for meat and hides. Due to a slow rate of herd increase (about 3% per annum), the more stringent environmental requirement for raising cattle, and the difficulty of processing/eating/storing large quantities of slaughtered meat, the value of a single animal was high. Cattle are well known as a measure of wealth or item of booty/luxury; this is particularly true of the stalled or fattened animal. Arguably, such value, coupled with the celebrated strength of bovoids, account for its frequent appearance in cultic settings.

Biblically, the language of *bĕhēmāh* and *bāqār* likely included cattle, but were not limited to such. *Šôr* and *ellûp* may narrow the field to simply bovine, while "bull" (*pār*) and "calf" (*'ēgel*) single out sex and age.

4. *Donkeys. Equus asinus* and other equid hybrids (such as the mule) were valued as pack transport and draft animals throughout the biblical period. Hardy and sure-footed, the donkey was well-suited for life in marginal zones, and appears to have been a popular choice. Donkeys and mules were used for threshing and pulling plows, carts, or wagons; other mentions suggest wild equids were hunted for sport, hides, and

possibly, food.[15] Some evidence suggests they were herded together with cattle at times.[16]

While playing a major role in textual sources, the physical remains of donkeys are infrequent in archaeological sites. A notable exception is the site of Tell Halif, where donkeys may have been bred for caravan use.[17] Biblically, the donkey and donkey hybrids are described by a family of terms including *ḥamôr, 'atôn, pere'*, or *'ārôd*. The two latter terms may refer to the wild oniger (*Equus onager*).

5. Horses. A late arrival to the inventory of domesticated stock in the biblical world, *Equus caballus* emerged as an animal of unchallenged speed and power. The horse (*sûs*) appears widely used by the end of the second millennium BC in cavalry and chariotry units. The extent to which it was used in non-military contexts is not known. It is likely that the labor investment required to maintain horses and their unsuitability for desert climes may have limited the application of these breeds to state-level enterprises. First millennium booty-lists from Egypt and Assyria frequently include horses.

6. Camels. The single-humped (*Camelus dromedarius*) and double-humped (*Camelus bactrianus*) camel provided milk, meat, and dung, but were primarily valued as animals of transport. The dromedary was particularly well adapted to the task, able to carry twice the load of donkeys while enduring the heat of desert zones with a minimum of water loss. Herding specialists who pushed the practice of husbandry out of the arena of mere subsistence into the forefront of interregional and international trade exploited these attributes. Camels also appear in tribute- and booty-lists, and on occasion, as military mounts.

Consistent with the Near Eastern record, the camel (*gāmāl*) appears in the biblical text as an animal of pack and transport. Its meat was considered unclean.

7. Pigs. Perhaps the most efficient meat producer in antiquity, the pig (*Sus scrofa*) had an exceptional rate of herd growth. It was managed apart from other herded animals on account of food needs and behavior.

---

15. See Juliet Clutton-Brock, *Horse Power: A History of the Horse and the Donkey in Human Societies* (Cambridge: Harvard, 1992) 94. Also see Borowski, *Every Living Thing*, 91–94.

16. See Stepien, *Animal Husbandy*, 62.

17. See Borowski, *Every Living Thing*, 95.

Correspondences between pig remains and periods of wetter climate, as well as conditions of political decentralization, have been drawn.[18]

While prohibitions against eating this animal were a part of some cultures and seem to be reflected in segments of the archaeological record,[19] folk from other corners of the biblical world had no qualms about consuming pork, and did so regularly.[20]

8. *Other.* The dog (*Canis familiaris*) played a supporting role in shaping subsistence patterns in the biblical world. As hunter, herder, scavenger, and pet, dogs are well represented in written texts, excavated remains, and artistic representations.[21] Other animals of mention include varieties of fallow deer and gazelle that were captured and managed. Birds such as geese, ducks, doves, pigeons, partridges, and quail were raised for meat and eggs. The domestic chicken (*Gallus domesticus*), too, played a role, although not possibly in a major way until the Persian period. Still other managed species of mention include the honeybee and some varieties of fish.

C. Cycles of Labor Intensity

The labor of animal husbandry in the biblical world cannot be understood apart from other lifeway cycles that varied in scale and intensity. Perhaps the most critical of these was climatic, as rainfall and temperature dictated the conditions against which all life was measured. Other factors that sketched the contours between the possible and the impossible included the biological "clocks" of key species, access to land and water, and the less perceptible, but equally real issues of attitude and belief. These "cultural" or "spiritual" limits effected patterns of stock selection and care, work habits, and minute details of life down to the level of what was eaten as a delicacy or rejected as inedible. This web of contour lines impacted the cycle of labor intensity, and strain present efforts

---

18. Hesse, "Animal Husbandry," 215.

19. M. A. Zeder, "The Role of Pigs in Near Eastern Subsistence: A View from the Southern Levant," in *Retrieving the Past. Essays on Archaeological Research and Methodology in Honor of Gus W. Van Beek*, ed. Joe D. Seger (Winona Lake: Eisenbrauns, 1996) 298.

20. Borowski, *Every Living Thing*, 141–44.

21. For more on canids in archaeological contexts, see Wapnish "Urbanization," 81–94.

to reconstruct patterns of behavior. Large-scale "husbandry-histories"[22] appear particularly vulnerable, given the present limits of knowledge.

On a smaller scale, a calendar of labor may be proposed for the sheep/goat herder of central Palestine. The arrangement of activity suggests periods of high and low labor intensity that may be tentatively plotted. The arrival of winter rains brought new life. Dry brown fields turned green, new shoots appeared, and the season of birthing began. Lactating ewes and does produced milk for their young; human managers could maximize and redirect that production for months to come. Patterns of herd movement were small or local, given ample winter pasturage and the periodic need of shelter from heavy rain or snow. As this period of precipitation drew to an end by early May, labor intensity reached its highest levels. Milking continued, wool and hair were cut, cleaned, and processed, and the young were butchered. As the hot summer set in, the search for pastures and water became increasingly more difficult. Milk production fell off, and migration to more distant regions was initiated. After cultivated fields were harvested under the summer sun, flocks moved in to clean the stubble. In this season of scarcity and movement, the management of breeding was a key activity. By late fall the rains returned, and the pregnant females began giving birth. Movement back to local winter pastures was accomplished, and a new cycle begun. The measure of the herdsman's days was complete.

II. THE LABOR OF ANIMAL MANAGEMENT

Several aspects of the labor of animal management may be surveyed. As indicated above, the intensity of these tasks varied according to duty, stock selection, timing, and perceived importance. Likewise, the application of animal muscle to specific tasks such as packing, pulling, and plowing was diverse. While it is tempting to follow these leads, such applications move beyond the present scope and are best explored elsewhere. For the moment, a strict survey of resource management in-

---

22. See Juris Zarins, "Pastoralism in Southwest Asia: The Second Millennium BC," in *The Walking Larder: Patterns of Domestication, Pastoralism, and Predation*, ed. Juliet Clutton-Brock (London: Unwin Hyman, 1989) 127–155; Israel Finkelstein, "Pastoralism in the Highlands of Canaan in the Third and Second Millennia B.C.E.," in *Pastoralism in the Levant: Archaeological Materials in Anthropological Perspectives*, ed. Ofer Bar-Yosef and Anatoly Khazanov (Madison: Prehistory, 1995) 133–42.

cludes the following categories: feeding, watering, protecting, breeding and birthing, milking, shearing, butchering, and marketing.

A. Feeding

The set of domesticated stock was almost exclusively herbivorous, requiring fodder, salt, and water. These needs were best met in the open pasture through supervised herding, although certainly at the level of household, limited numbers of stock could be restrained through corralling, tethering, or hobbling. Animals restrained and unable to forage for themselves, however, represented an increased labor investment; food and water had to be supplied.

As a beginning point for understanding herding strategies, unrestrained livestock may be categorized according to browsers and grazers. Browsers, like goats and camels, are more mobile and independent by nature, and tend to forage among low bush plants and trees. Grazers, like cows and sheep, move more slowly, less independently, and prefer grasses. These contrasts suggest that compatibility was possible in the instance of some species, although other issues such as mobility, water requirements, and need for human attention militate against quick conclusions regarding herd composition.[23]

The choice to combine browsers and grazers in the case of goats and sheep is a workable one. Given their "clumping" or "flocking" tendency, sheep are readily managed as they move in a loose, slow-moving front. The more independent and browsing nature of goats, on the other hand, is a liability if goats are herded in quantity, but an asset if scattered throughout the sheep. The goats keep the sheep moving by their own impulse, and consequently, help alleviate the problem of overgrazing and overeating. A picture of black goats moving ahead and among arterial lines of sheep is a scene readily captured in the lands of the bible today.

Beyond herd composition, the seasonality of rainfall, and consequently, pasture, affected feeding strategies. Pastures of the biblical

---

23. Thomas E. Levy notes that the ratio of sheep to goat is significantly different in the northern Negev (3:1) than it is in the more arid zones of central or southern Negev (approximately 1:9). See his "Transhumance, Subsistence, and Social Evolution in the Northern Negev Desert" in *Pastoralism in the Levant: Archaeological Materials in Anthropological Perspectives*, eds. Ofer Bar-Yosef and Anatoly Khazanov (Madison: Prehistory, 1995) 70.

world were hardly "natural." Well-worn patterns of grazing exerted selective pressure that modified the type and distribution of plant species. The effects of overgrazing were already in place by the biblical period, and suggest a limited vegetative set and the unchecked presence of toxic plants.[24] These trends created an agricultural crisis which was already recognized by the second and third centuries AD, given the pejorative attitude towards herders common to rabbinic writings: "No craft in all the world is held in greater contempt than that of the shepherd."[25]

To maintain herd sizes larger than the carrying capacity of a given region required both small- and large-scale movement. Small-scale movement was necessary on a daily basis; large-scale movement had to be seasonally directed. Foraging among the stubble of a harvested field aided both herder and farmer through the feeding of the flock, the removal of stubble, and the deposition of dung. This example of small-scale movement raises the issue of cooperation between two very different subsistence strategies; it also suggests the potential for tension and conflict should a herd track through a field not yet harvested. On a larger scale, movement between regions has been further isolated into vertical and horizontal patterns by Johnson.[26] Vertical patterns focus on the differences in moisture and temperature offered by elevation. Horizontal patterns focus on the seasonal contraction and expansion of pasture and the elliptical or pulsatory movements required, minimizing overgrazing. Pack animals such as donkeys or camels were also necessary to facilitate such seasonal, large-scale migrations. The hardship of outdoor living is suggested by the comment of Jacob, "The heat consumed me in the daytime and the cold at night, and sleep fled from my eyes" (Gen 31:40).

Effecting the movement of animals, especially that of sheep/goat herds required a variety of techniques probably known in the biblical

24. Cribb, *Nomads*, 28.

25. Moshe Aberbach, *Labor, Crafts and Commerce in Ancient Israel* (Jerusalem: Magness, 1994) 225. Aberbach also writes, "It was the shepherds and 'cowboys' who were often regarded with far more jaundiced eyes, and some people seem to have disliked them intensely. They were frequently guilty of allowing the animals entrusted to their care to graze in privately owned fields, thus robbing people and damaging their crops. That this was a real problem causing a great deal of anxiety and ill-will is indicated in the Midrashic stories" (*Labor*, 224). For other relevant comments, see Aberbach, *Labor*, 180–81, 224–31.

26. See Douglas L. Johnson, *The Nature of Nomadism: A Comparative Study of Pastoral Migrations in Southwestern Asia and Northern Africa* (Department of Geography Research Paper 118, Chicago, 1969).

world. The training of a flock leader involved the selection and castration of a male sheep or goat (bell-wether) that was taught to respond
to the commands of the shepherd. This training began at birth, and
was accomplished by a combination of punishments and rewards.[27] A
flock followed this single leader, who in turn followed the shepherd. For
maximum productivity, flock sizes likely numbered 30 to 50 head.[28] If a
herding dog -- as opposed to a guardian dog—was used to effect animal
movement, time and motion studies suggest the manageable flock size
could be extended to a number between 250 and 400 head.[29] However,
only one passage in all of the Old Testament (Job 30:1) mentions the
use of dogs in a shepherding context (*kalbê ṣōnî*, "dogs of my flock")
and here it seems to suggest the role of guardians rather than herders.
Without this canine assistance, and even with smaller herd sizes, strays
wandered off and had to be retrieved. Loss rates in the field may have
totaled between ten percent and thirty percent annually.[30] The imagery
of the "good shepherd" finding lost sheep was a common one and readily
incorporated as metaphor in biblical texts.

B. Watering

While water intake is critical for every living creature, the means by
which that water was obtained and the quantity/quality of water necessary for survival varied. Pregnant and lactating females had additional
moisture needs, as did large, active, working animals. Winter pasturage,
with its fresh, moist fodder, limited or eliminated the need to frequent
wells and springs, while dry summers with high ambient temperatures
and low humidity tied herders to the vicinity of water sources. Water

27. See Siegfried Hirsch, *Sheep and Goats in Palestine* (Tel-Aviv: Palestine Economic
Society, 1933) 27–28; Y. Tani, "The Geographical Distribution and Function of Sheep
Flock Leaders: A Cultural Aspect of the Man-Domesticated Animal Relationship in
Southwestern Eurasia," in *The Walking Larder: Patterns of Domestication, Pastoralism,
and Predation*, ed. Juliet Clutton-Brock (London: Unwin Hyman, 1989) 185–99.

28. At Nuzi, flock size averaged 38 head. Of these 90% were mature. See Matthews,
Social World, 57.

29. Cribb, *Nomads*, 28.

30. These figures, drawn from various Mesopotamian contracts, include losses
in the field due to old age, disease, wild animals, etc. Consider Martha A. Morrison,
"Evidence for Herdsmen and Animal Husbandry in the Nuzi Documents," in *Studies
on the Civilization and Culture of Nuzi and the Hurrians*, ed. M. A. Morrison and D. I.
Owen (Winona Lake: Eisenbrauns, 1981) 282.

needs also varied from species to species according to metabolism and the ability to tolerate temperature fluctuations and minimize water loss.[31] These factors may not have been quantified as such by husbandrymen in the past, but it is certain that they were acutely aware of these dynamics upon which their lives depended.

The task of watering animals was accomplished by leading the herd to an open water source such as a pool or stream, when available. Otherwise, water was obtained from wells, reservoirs, or small-mouthed cisterns dug into the ground. In these cases, it had to be drawn by means of a container attached to a rope, carried, and poured into a trough. This labor could have been substantial; a single camel may drink up to 27 gallons in ten minutes.[32] Deep grooves of rope wear radiating from the stone mouths of ancient systems are a witness to repeated pulls. A jar,[33] skin sack, or possibly a wooden bucket[34] may have been used as a drawing container attached to the end of the rope. This was a daily effort for much of the year; watering was a focal point of the herder's work and meetings.

Biblical stories describe significant meetings at watering points.[35] One text, Genesis 29:2–3, 8–10, suggests that the stone which covered the well or cistern was large enough that only by working together could several shepherds remove it and gain access to the water. This practice possibly fostered accountability and discouraged the waste or manipulation of a limited source by a single individual. Ironically, the first sight of Rachel coming with her flocks was enough to empower Jacob to move the stone single-handedly! Given the significance of water access in an arid land, it is not surprising that wells were closely guarded, and at times, contested. Resource negotiation was an important aspect of the labor of herding (Gen 21:25–34; 26:12–33).

31. For the unique physiology of the camel see Knut Schmidt-Nielsen, "The Physiology of the Camel," *Scientific American* 201.6 (1959) 140–51.

32. Schmidt-Nielsen, "The Physiology," 141.

33. As suggested by Gen 24:14.

34. Tsvika Tsuk, "Cisterns," in *The Oxford Encyclopedia of Archaeology in the Near East 2*, ed. E. M. Meyers (New York: Oxford University, 1997) 12.

35. See Genesis 24:11–22; Exodus 2:15–19.

C. Protecting

Not only did valuable resources such as fodder and water require protection, so did the animals themselves. Weather, predators, disease, and thieves threatened domestic livestock. Preventative measures included the use of enclosing structures, and weapons.

Caves and abandoned buildings were perhaps the most ubiquitous of animal pens in the hilly regions of Palestine, providing a sheltered and secure area with little effort. Enclosure walls, consisting of stacked fieldstones were also common. These walled areas were often subdivided into smaller units for animal separation. A single doorway allowed access (cf. John 10:1–10). Sometimes enclosures were built in conjunction with settlements, and at other times in isolated areas. Characteristic of the early Iron Age I, the circular arrangement of village houses created a large open courtyard where animals could be secured. Later, the three- or four-room house may have been designed around the housing of small stock. According to one proposal, low clearance "rooms" on the ground floor served as animal pens, while wooden ladders led to the human quarters above.[36] Such an arrangement not only provided security, but also a shared, odoriferous heat! Finally, on a different scale entirely, some large buildings like those at Megiddo in Cisjordan, or Jalul in Transjordan, may have served as "stables," or "docks" for the loading and unloading of pack transport trains.[37] Mangers and tethering holes attest to this use.

While such structures provided protection for some animals at specific times of the year, protection in the pasture rested in the hands of the herder. Campsites were established in the open field, or possibly in the ruins of abandoned structures where rudimentary pens could be fashioned. Sharp eyes, ears, and a strong back were combined with a rod and sling to form the shepherd's arsenal (e.g. 1 Sam 17:34–7, 40).

A final threat to the herd was disease. All profits earned by rapid breeding could be wiped out easily and quickly. According to Borowski,[38]

---

36. Ehud Netzer, "Domestic Architecture in the Iron Age," in *The Architecture of Ancient Israel from the Prehistoric to the Persian Periods*, ed. Aharon Kempinski and Ronny Reich (Jerusalem: Israel Exploration Society, 1992) 197.

37. Zeev Herzog, "Administrative Structures in the Iron Age," in *The Architecture of Ancient Israel from the Prehistoric to the Persian Periods*, ed. Aharon Kempinski and Ronny Reich (Jerusalem: Israel Exploration Society, 1992) 227.

38. Borowski, *Every Living Thing*, 67–68.

sheep and goats suffered from many diseases, including anthrax, anplasmosis, scabies, strongylosis (liverfluke), sturdy, brucellosis, contagious agalactic, enzootic virus abortion, foot-and-mouth disease, mastitis, sheep pox, tetanus, and virulent foot-rot. Beyond these was the problem of ticks, lice, flies, and parasitic worms that afflict both two- and four-legged creatures in the field!

What steps were taken to ward off these dangers in biblical Palestine is unknown. Protection against diseases of the hoof could be partially alleviated by regular trimming (yearly in the case of sheep, and monthly in the case of goats), and the avoidance of standing for long periods in mud. In the absence of antibiotics, little could be done to stave off infectious diseases apart from isolation. Herd recovery, particularly among the less reproductively resilient species such as cattle or camels, could have taken up to a decade. Only by striving for a maximal herd growth rate could disasters be offset.

D. Breeding and Birthing

Managed breeding of stock promoted herd growth, and stimulated the development of animals for specialized qualities or tasks. Breeding techniques were tied to specific biological and environmental cycles that were known and predictable. Herd growth potential through the careful management of these cycles was attractive in the case of some species, and undoubtedly played a role in the selection process. On the basis of modern observation, growth models for well-managed goat herds suggest an increase approaching 41 percent per year.[39] Sheep herd increases are less, approaching 26 percent,[40] while growth models for cattle, donkeys, and other large stock lag considerably behind. Camels, with a gestation period of more than a year, multiply slowly even under the best of conditions. While such figures hint that the labor of sheep/goat herding offered quick and easy rewards,[41] it must be borne in mind that droughts have reduced herd size by half at least once every decade in the modern Middle East.[42] Other catastrophic losses due to disease, theft, or, in a

39. Dahl, *Having Herds*, 103.

40. Dahl, *Having Herds*, 98.

41. Rabbi Johanan wrote in the third century, "He who wishes to become rich should engage in the breeding of small cattle," i.e. sheep and goats, see Aberbach, *Labor*, 179–80.

42. Dahl, *Having Herds*, 116; Cribb, *Nomads*, 31.

more likely scenario, a combination of adverse conditions, could initiate a downward spiral from which the herder could not escape.[43] However voiced in antiquity, the concept of "boom and bust" was well known.

Breeding techniques that promoted herd growth included the maintenance of male-female ratios, age management, castration or stud selection, isolation, and copulative supervision and assistance. In the case of *Awassi* sheep, the heavy tails that were undoubtedly the result of selective breeding proved to impede impregnation. Tupping required human help.[44] The cross-breeding of horses, donkeys, onagers and other equids is demonstrated by the hybrid remains and references across the biblical world; reproductive management was understood and practiced, at least selectively, no later than the early third millennium BC. This knowledge had a great impact on human thinking, and found expression in superstitious/religious acts intended to imitate or stimulate fertility. In the context of a subsistence economy, the significance of such expression is understandable. The curious behavior of Jacob described in Genesis 30:37–40 undoubtedly combined knowledge with superstition; his attempts to manipulate knew no bounds.

Births normally occurred in the winter or rainy season. Early births were preferred to late births, in order to take advantage of moisture for milk production. Multiple births were common with sheep, and especially with goats. In the recent past, newborns were kept inside the house/tent of the shepherd and allowed to suckle in the morning and evening. Only in the second week of their lives did they venture out to pasture.[45] Despite this close care, mortality rates undoubtedly remained high.[46]

E. Milking

While descriptions of milking activity are curiously absent from the biblical text, mentions of milk and milk-products imply widespread practice. Proverbs 27:27 suggests that goats' milk was a household staple, and that the responsibility of milking rested in the hands of the young

43. F. Barth, *Nomads of South Persia* (Boston: Little, Brown, 1961).

44. Palestinian shepherds use a stick to lift the ewe's tail to encourage the ram to mount.

45. Hirsch, *Sheep*, 59.

46. Larsa records suggest loss rates ranging from 25% to 79%. See Morrison, "Evidence," 156.

women, the *nĕ urôt*. This corresponds with the knowledge and practice of contemporary pastoral societies where the goat is recognized as an "animal of subsistence," i.e. a primary source of milk and meat.[47] Other biblical texts allude to the milking of cows,[48] sheep,[49] or possibly camels.[50] The management of these animals through the use of udder-bags, mouth-sticks, and techniques of stock separation and culling, demanded daily attention to maximize the period and quantity of lactation. Other significant factors, such as the arrival of rain and the timing of birth, could be anticipated, but not always controlled. While costly in labor intensity, such efforts yielded a ready and mobile source of protein.

The season of milk producing for does and ewes corresponded with the birth cycle.[51] Milk production began in the early winter months (December-January). By spring (March-April) the young animals were forcibly weaned, and milking became a daily chore performed twice each day. With the heat of late summer (July-August), the period of lactation was over. Milk yields varied according to the degree of management, breed, age and size of animal, litter, diet, and temperature, among other things, but may have averaged 18 gallons per season per doe and 13 gallons per ewe.[52] What percent of this yield was used for human consumption is difficult to ascertain. Obviously, the culling of young males for meat, and an aggressive weaning strategy would have increased milk yields for human consumption.

The activity of milking was likely accomplished in the field by using a long rope to tie two rows of lactating females head to head. Such an arrangement of animals was termed a *ribqâh*, reminiscent of the name Rebecca, the wife of Isaac.[53] With the animals thus immobilized, milkers would have had ready teat access from the flanks, and could move

47. Goats not only appear as more effective milk-producers than sheep, the milk that they produce more closely corresponds to human milk in fat, protein, and carbohydrate ratios. This makes goat milk more easily digested, a fact not lost on contemporary herders (See Dahl, *Having Herds*, 216 for statistics on goat and sheep milk). For more, note Dahl, *Having Herds*, 200, and David C. Hopkins, "Pastoralists in Late Bronze Age Palestine: Which Way did They Go?" *Biblical Archaeologist* 56.4 (1993) 207.

48. Deut 32:14; 2 Sam 17:29.

49. 1 Sam 7:9.

50. Gen. 32:15.

51. See Borowski, *Every Living Thing*, 52–53 for details.

52. Dahl, *Having Herds*, 212.

53. Borowski, *Every*, 53.

quickly around the group. Care to prevent strangulation was essential. Milking would have been done with the hands, and collected into containers. Such activity may be readily observed today among herding communities; a Mesopotamian cylinder seal depicts the antiquity of the practice.[54]

As a liquid, fresh milk or ḥālāb could be drunk directly[55] or stored in a skin-bag, like water or wine.[56] Modern pastoralists continue to use such bags not only as a transport container, but also as a suspended milk churn. ḥālāb could also be heated and eaten in conjunction with other foods, although the well-known prohibition against cooking a goat-kid in its mother's milk must be mentioned (Exod 23:19). Whether this taboo finds its origin in Canaanite sacrificial practice or in the area of an ironic, if not sadistic expression, is not known. Whatever the case, it is likely that the meat-milk taboo currently practiced is a late invention. Biblically, the combination of veal and ḥālāb was an appropriate meal for honored guests (e.g. Gen 18:8), and one that continues to find expression today in non-Jewish contexts.

The "shelf-life" of milk could be extended up to several months with processing. Curdling, congealing, draining, shaking, squeezing, or even drying activities transformed ḥālāb into products such as ḥemâh, or šĕpôt bāqār, "curds" or "yogurt," and gĕbînnāh, possibly "cheese" or "butter."[57] Such caloric resources could be stored or transported.[58]

From a literary perspective, milk and milk-products are frequent metaphors of luxury, abundance, or fertility. Common is the description of the land of Canaan as "a land flowing with milk and honey" (Exod 3:8, et al.). The simple richness of the flora that sustain both browser and bumblebee outstrip political vicissitudes (Isa 7:21–22), and tease the imagination with the anticipation of an eschatological age (Isa 55:1; Joel 3:18). For lovers, milk and honey euphemistically express physical pleasures (Cant 4:12; 5.1). Finally, from an NT perspective, milk symbolizes the most pure and basic doctrine, appropriate for the young (1 Cor 3:2,

---

54. J.M. Aynard, "Animals in Mesopotamia," in *Animals in Archaeology*, ed. A.H. Brodick (London: Barrie and Jenkins, 1972), 52.

55. Gen 18:8; Ezek 25:4; Prov 27:27.

56. Judg 4:19; cf. Gen 21:14, Josh 9:4; Matt 9:17.

57. Job 10:10; Prov 30:33.

58. Judg 5:25; 1 Sam 17:18; 2 Sam 17:29.

et al). As becomes obvious, the use of such metaphors finds a point of origin and understanding within the context of a pastoral lifeway.

F. Shearing

While goats provided a ready source of milk, meat, and hair, the primary value of sheep rested in their wool (*ṣemer*). Shorn wool was spun into threads, dyed, and woven into textile products,[59] or used as an item of trade or tribute.[60] These observations have prompted some to characterize goats as having a household, or subsistence orientation, while sheep have an orientation that is more market directed.[61]

The activity of shearing forms a backdrop for four biblical stories. First, it was the activity of shearing which took Laban away from home, giving Jacob the opportunity to flee, and Rachel the moment to seize the household idols.[62] Second, Judah was traveling to a sheep shearing when he became distracted by Tamar.[63] Third, Nabal was involved in shearing when he met and insulted David's envoys.[64] Fourth, a sheep-shearing party organized by Absalom became the site of the assassination of Amnon.[65] These texts prompt comments concerning the work of shearing.

First, in each case, shearing took place "somewhere else," presumably outside the village and in the field (however, note *bêt-ēqed*, possibly "house of shearing" in 2 Kgs 10:12, 14). Sheep owners ventured out to the herders to be a part of this event, which likely took place annually in the late spring. This timing placed the shearing activity beyond the spring rains, but before the summer heat. Even more interesting is the hint of a social system where mobile herders were tied to more sedentary owners on the basis of kin or contract. The event of shearing provided an opportune moment for owner and herder to confer, negotiate or renegotiate terms, tally and evaluate the livestock, and celebrate or terminate a relationship. Parallels for these dynamics are well known from Mesopotamian contexts, and have been explored.[66]

59. Ezek 34:3; Prov 27:26, 31:13; Job 31:20.
60. 2 Kgs 3:4; Ezek 27:18.
61. See Cribb, *Nomads*, 28 and Hesse, "Animal," 214.
62. Gen 31:19.
63. Gen 38:12.
64. 1 Sam 25:2, 3.
65. 2 Sam 13:23–24.
66. For additional information see Victor H. Matthews, *Pastoral Nomadism in the*

Second, shearing stories in the bible identify a specific group of people called "shearers" (*gōzzīm*), and suggest labor specialization. This is confirmed by documents from Ugarit where a class of workers identified as "shearers" (*gzzm*) worked in gangs, received deliveries, and worked certain fields.[67] Other information concerning this class of laborer is known from the Umma records.[68] These shearers may have washed the sheep in a preliminary way to remove dirt, fecal matter ("dags"), weeds, and other pollutants,[69] although a thorough job could only have been done by hand once the fleece was removed. This transformation from coat to fleece may have been accomplished with a sharp blade, iron scissors,[70] or by plucking. If one translates the *ne'ĕlāmāh* of Isa 53:7 as "bound" rather than "silent" (tongue-tied), it is possible that the animals' legs were immobilized during the process. According to Hirsch,[71] twenty to thirty head could have been sheared by a single man in a single day. Both ram (*'ayil*) and ewe (*rāḥāl*) were shorn, although Deut 15:19 prohibited the shearing of the firstborn. Whether the greasy lanolin or "wool wax" was used for soap, cream, or lubricant is not known. Bags would have held the sorted fleeces for transport to processing centers at home or market. Huge dye vats such as those excavated at Tell Beit Mirsim suggest the possibility of regional centers for this processing activity.

Up to a pound of hair may be cut from a goat in one season.[72] However, the coarser nature of goat hair undoubtedly demanded different prices, processes, and use. Sturdy ropes and bags could have been manufactured from goat hair. Black tents, as demonstrated by the familiar *bayt al-śa'ar*, or "houses of hair" of the modern Middle East, illustrate another possible use.[73]

Mari Kingdom, ca. 1830–1760 B.C. (Cambridge: ASOR, 1978); Morrison, "Evidence"; Martha A. Morrison, "The Jacob and Laban Narrative in Light of Near Eastern Sources," *Biblical Archaeologist* 46.3 (1983) 155–64.

67. M. Heltzer, "Labour in Ugarit," in *Labor in the Ancient Near East*, ed. Marvin A. Powell (New Haven: AOS, 1987) 241.

68. Stepien, *Animal Husbandry*, 91.

69. Cant 4:2; 6:6.

70. Borowski, *Every Living Thing*, 71.

71. Hirsch, *Sheep and Goats*, 29–30.

72. Hirsch, *Sheep and Goats*, 60.

73. cf. the "dark tents" of Cant. 1:5.

Third and finally, shearing stories in the bible suggest that the shearing day was not only a day of work, but also a day of joy.[74] Just as the day of harvest marked the successful end of an agricultural effort, so too the day of shearing brought closure to the husbandry cycle. Elements of feasting and drunkenness are noted.[75] In this light, the text involving Nabal is particularly interesting. First, it is interesting because the size and extent of the celebration is described as a *mišteh* ("feast")," or being *kĕmištēh hammelek* ("like the royal feast"). It could be possible that this feast not only involved Nabal's family, but also the entire shearing party. A second point of interest arises when Nabal suggests that "meat" (*tibḥāh*) has been butchered for his shearers.[76] While this meat may have been the main course of the feast, it may also have been a type of payment to the shearers (and herders?) for services rendered. Elsewhere, meat, milk, wool, and live animals were included in the terms of a herder's contract, possibly settled at shearing time.[77]

G. Butchering and Marketing

Butchering provided access to meat, skin, sinews, bone, and other animal products. These could be consumed, processed, sold, or traded. Unfortunately, information concerning butchering techniques and sites is difficult to obtain for a variety of reasons. Only one need be mentioned here: skeletal remains are typically disarticulated, as killing, bleeding, gutting, skinning, transporting, marketing, cooking, eating, and disposing of animal remains produced distribution patterns much wider than the zones of occupation typically sampled in excavation. Consequently, the archaeological record appears skewed in favor of the "meatier" portions of animals (hind limbs, fore-limbs, trunk); "non-meaty" remains (hooves, "wrists," "ankles," etc.) are not as well-represented. Still, butcher-marks on bone, harvest profiles, and certain installations demand attention in a discussion of human labor and society.[78]

74. 1 Sam 25:7–8.

75. 1 Sam 25; 2 Sam. 13.

76. 1 Sam 25:11.

77. J. N. Postgate, "Some Old Babylonian Shepherds and Their Flocks," *Journal of Semitic Studies* 20.1 (1975) 4–5.

78. See Brian Hesse and Paula Wapnish, "Pigs' Feet, Cattle Bones and Birds' Wings," *Biblical Archaeology Review* 22.1 (1996) 62. The authors describe areas that may have been used for carcass processing at Iron Age Ashkelon. Here, sheep/goat remains at this

The proposal that live animals were more valuable than dead ones[79] was certainly true for some segments of the pastoral spectrum. These segments were likely more mobile, more self-sufficient, and more focused on "secondary products" such as hair or milk. Within these segments, butchering was an alternative recourse, taken only in times of scarcity when all other resources were fully exploited, or when the survival of one animal threatened that of another deemed more valuable. For this reason, animals selected for butchering normally included the young or old, the unproductive, infertile, or injured. Slaughter patterns were likely seasonal and connected to the birthing cycle. Only special occasions such as feasts or sacrifices would have prompted the butchering of a healthy or fattened animal. Harvest profiles reflect this interest.[80]

Other segments of the pastoralist spectrum were more focused on meat production. Harvest profiles from the Early Bronze Age site of Yiftahel, for example, suggest that 80 percent of the pig population was slaughtered before two years of age, while a second peak was reached after three years.[81]

The butchering of large mammals such as pigs, cattle, or camels posed problems of preparation, storage, and transport. Processing four hundred pounds of meat or more was likely a communal effort; the same shared the immediate benefits of the kill. The scale of this problem was reduced considerably in the butchering of mature sheep and goats that dressed down to anywhere between 20 and 50 pounds, depending upon breed and condition. In the biblical text, the sheer number of butchering mentions (for the sake of eating) suggests a preference for young male goats. These were likely culled between three and 18 months of age, at a point when meat was still considered tender, investment remained small, and growth rates had not yet tapered off.

Wapnish and Hesse have outlined a three-tiered model of animal production that demands further investigation as it relates to butchering

site outnumber cattle by a ratio of eleven to one. Such proportions may not be site-wide, however, but a reflection of the specialized activity that went on in this area.

79. Thomas J. Barfield, *The Nomadic Alternative* (Englewood Cliffs: Prentice Hall, 1993) 5.

80. Wapnish and Hesse, "Urbanization," 84.

81. Eliot Braun, *Yiftahel: Salvage and Rescue Excavations at A Prehistoric Village in Lower Galilee, Israel,* Israel Antiquities Authority Reports 2 (Jerusalem: Israel Antiquities Authority, 1997) 161.

and marketing systems.[82] In the first tier, animals are raised and harvested locally in a self-contained system. It is anticipated that all ages of animals are represented in the total set of sites. In the second tier, animals are largely purchased from outside pastoralists. For this group of consumers, it is expected that faunal remains reflect a high proportion of animals at market age, *e.g.* between 18 and 30 months. Finally, the third tier represents a producing economy where market age animals are sold elsewhere. Correspondingly, only the very old or young animals are well represented in the harvest profile. Wapnish and Hesse do not underestimate the difficulty in applying these generalizations, and recognize that multiple production interests (meat, milk, or hair) complicate the task. Still, this proposal is a useful beginning point for analyzing single sites within larger site contexts.

CONCLUSION

While the face of subsistence labor remained constant throughout the biblical period, the use of animal resources undoubtedly relieved a deep strain. Animal muscle broke hard ground for planting, transported people and goods, and facilitated armed conflict and escape. Animal products filled the stomach, clothed the back, and provided necessary tools, equipment, shelter, and resources for trade. The power of these dynamics was immense and attractive. The successful exploitation of the unique set of animals known in the biblical world was never easy; in truth, the task of husbandry created labor. Yet, despite the demands of living in a marginal zone, or perhaps even because of them, the choice to utilize animal resources created a unique lifeway path. As suggested here, the consequences of this choice for shaping the biblical world, its heirs, and its students have only begun to be explored.

---

82. Wapnish and Hesse, "Urbanization," 84.

5

Archaeological Insights into the Crucifixion of Jesus

James Riley Estep Jr.

"**Y**OU FOOLISH GALATIANS! WHO has bewitched you? Before your very eyes Jesus Christ was clearly portrayed as crucified" (Gal 3:1). For the Galatian Christians the image of crucifixion needed no further description since it was readily recognized. However, for Christians twenty centuries later the image has been lost. The earliest Christian icons depicting the crucifixion appear nearly two hundred years after the practice was banned in the Roman Empire.

Christian fascination with the cross is obvious throughout the twenty centuries of the church's existence. The alleged discovery of the one true cross of Christ by the Empress Helena generated the initial interest and adoration of the cross-image in Christianity. Heightened by the Roman Catholic practice of venerating relics, the medieval church claimed to possess fragments, or even splinters, of the cross of Christ. These were of sufficient number to build a small house! Over the last four decades, renewed interest in the cross and crucifixion was sparked by the discovery of the first physical remains of a crucified man near Giv'at ha-Mivtar, Israel in 1968, with the nail still piercing his right heel. While Christian scholarship has primarily focused on the theological significance of the crucifixion, historical and archaeological information can provide keen insight into the practice of crucifixion, and as such inform our understanding of the crucifixion of Jesus Christ.

What was crucifixion really like? What can we say about the crucifixion of Christ? This chapter will attempt to accomplish three tasks: to briefly summarize the practice of crucifixion in Roman civilization, primarily based on literary sources; to introduce the reader to the only known physical remains of a crucified man, and the scholarship surrounding this discovery; and to assess the possible implication of the historical and archaeological record of crucifixion for our understanding of the crucifixion of Jesus Christ.[1]

THE PRACTICE OF CRUCIFIXION

Most of our knowledge about crucifixion in the ancient world comes from literary sources from the Greco-Roman world, including Christian authorities.[2] While Rome may have mastered the art of crucifixion, the practice of using a cross (Lat. *crux* and Gk. *stauros*) was older, and widely practiced by the ancient cultures in the Mediterranean world and ancient Near East. It was practiced by the Persians, Phoenicians, Indians, Assyrians, Greeks, northern Europeans (e.g. Germans and Britons), and Carthaginians. Typically it was reserved for slaves and criminals convicted of severe crimes. Rarely were a nation's nobility subjected to it, especially Roman citizens, although there are some notable exceptions.[3] Literary evidence exists for its practice in connection with the Qumran community, as well as the whole of ancient Palestine.[4] In short, crucifixion was virtually a universal practice as an accepted punishment for criminal behavior.[5] However, the Romans did indeed perfect it. Though it was practiced for centuries prior to the rise of Rome, crucifixion was adopted as official punishment for non-Romans in the first century BC. Cicero called it *"summum supplicium"* ("most extreme punishment").[6] Literary sources mention crucifixion several hundred times, with victims often numbering in the thousands.[7]

---

1. The next chapter is written in conjunction with this one, addressing the more specific issue of crurifragium, the practice of breaking of the legs during crucifixion. This chapter will focus on the orthoarchaeological evidence for the practice of crucifixion.

2. For the most comprehensive history of crucifixion in the ancient world, see Martin Hengel, *Crucifixion: In the Ancient World and the Folly of the Message of the Cross* (Philadelphia: Fortress Press, 1977).

3. Gerald G. O'Collins, "Crucifixion," *Anchor Bible Dictionary*, Volume 1: 1207–1208.

4. Cf. Joseph A. Fitzmyer, "Crucifixion in Ancient Palestine, Qumran Literature, and the New Testament," *Catholic Bible Quarterly* 40 (1978) 493–513; David W. Chapman, "Perceptions of Crucifixion Among Jews and Christians in the Ancient World," *Tyndale Bulletin* 52 (2000) 313–16.

5. Martin Hengel. *Crucifixion: In the Ancient World and the Folly of the Message of the Cross* (Philadelphia: Fortress Press, 1977).

6. Cicero, *Verr*, 2.5.168.

7. Cf. O'Collins (1992).

Today most Christians would readily recognize a standard cross shape, and they might assume that this design was typical of all crosses. In actuality, evidence from the ancient world attests to various forms of crosses (See Figure 1). The simplest form of a cross was the *crux simplex*, which consisted of a single stake. Most typically used was a t-shaped cross, the *crux commissa*. The cross-shape most typically associated with Christianity (☦) was the *crux immissa*, and is by tradition the form upon which Jesus was crucified.[8] More infrequently used was the *crux decussate*, which was shaped like an X. Hence, to determine how a human was positioned during crucifixion, one must first determine which type of cross was used for the crucifixion.

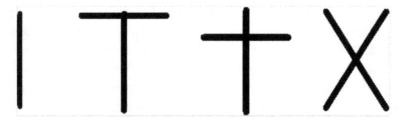

Figure 1: Types of Roman Crosses

The second and third forms of crosses typically consisted of three parts: the *patibulum,* or cross-beam, usually carried by the victim across the nape of the neck; *stripes* or *staticulum,* the upright post to which the cross-beam was attached, and which was typically permanently stationed at the cite of executions; and the *sedile,* which was a peg or seat that supported the victim's weight, but which was not always used.

In addition to the literary references to crucifixion, some material remains also add to our knowledge of the subject. A supply of Roman nails, dating to AD 78, and typical of those used in crucifixion, were discovered at Pinnata Castra, a Roman fort located at Inchtuthill in eastern Scotland. These nails date to the period of Agricola's withdraw from his reconnaissance mission. The nails, ranging from 15–23 cm (6–9 inches) in length, were heavy-headed, sharp tipped, quadrilateral, and made of iron.[9]

---

8. Irenaeus, *Heresies*, 2.24.4.

9. E. M. Blaiklock. "Crucifixion," in *Dictionary of Biblical Archaeology*, 140.

JEHONANAN: THE ONLY REMAINS
OF A CRUCIFIED MAN

The remains of a crucified man were unexpectedly discovered by Vassilios Tzaferis in 1968 during the excavations at Giv'at ha-Mivtar. Located in Tomb 1, Chamber B, Ossuary 4 were the skeletal remains of a 5'5" adult male, along with the remains of a small child. The ossuary bore the inscription, "Jenonanan, son of HGQWL." Buried nearby were his wife, Martha, two children, and fourteen other members of his family.[10] Jehohanan appears to have lived in Jerusalem, and died between the ages of 24–28, around AD 30. The tomb was a typical familial Jewish burial site from the first century AD. In short, the tomb was typical for the region, and would have been excavated with little public notice had it not been for the discovery of Jehonanan's remains. What makes his remains unique is that they represent the total physical evidence from the ancient world for crucifixion: a right *calcaneum* (heel bone), still pierced by an 11.5 cm (4.5 inches) iron nail similar to those found in Scotland, with traces of wood at both ends, acacia wood near the head and olive wood near the point of the nail.[11]

Oddly, the nail piercing Jehonanan's ankle was bent,which prevented it from being removed from his ankle, thus allowing his remains to be identified as those of a crucified man. But how was the nail bent? Zias and Sekeles speculate about the accident that occurred some 2000 years ago, which inevitably resulted in this archaeological discovery.

> After affixing the right foot to the upright . . . the nail . . . may have accidentally struck a knot in the upright, thus bending the nail downwards. Once the body was removed from the cross, albeit with some difficulty in removing the right leg, the condemned man's family would now find it impossible to remove the bent nail without completely destroying the heel bone. This reluctance to inflict further damage to the heel led to the eventual discovery of this crucifixion.[12]

10. N[ico] Haas, "Anthropological Observations on the Skeletal Remains from Giv'at ha-Mivtar," *Israel Exploration Journal* 20 (1970) 38–59; V[assilios] Tzaferis, "Jewish Tombs at and Near Giv'at ha-Mivtar, Jerusalem" *Israel Exploration Journal* 20 (1970) 18–32; Vassilios Tzaferis, "Crucifixion – The Archaeological Evidence," *Biblical Archaeology Review* 11 (1985) 52–53.

11. Haas (1970): 55–56; Y[igael] Yadin, "Epigraphy and Crucifixion," *Israel Exploration Journal* 23 (1973) 19–22.

12. Joseph Zias and Eliezer Sekeles. "The Crucified Man from Giv'at ha-Mivtar: A

Others have suggested that the nail was intentionally bent to more securely affix the feet to the cross,[13] although this seems unlikely since if bending the nail was indeed intentional, part of the common practice of crucifixion, more remains than this single example would have been discovered.

Prior to this discovery, only speculative discussion could occur in regard to the positioning of a human on the cross.[14] The discovery of Jehohanan provides at least one glimpse into the enigma of the positioning of a human during the act of crucifixion. Since discovery of the Jehohanan remains there have been three distinct interpretations of the nature of his crucifixion, all reappraising the affixing of the feet and upper extremities to the cross. The remains of Jehohanan were initially examined in 1970 by Nico Haas of Hebrew University's Hadassah Medical School in Jerusalem, and Vassilios Tzaferis, the archaeologist who discovered the burial site and skeletal remains.[15] Three years later, their interpretation was challenged by Yigael Yadin, although his reinterpretation was not widely acknowledged or accepted.[16] In 1985, yet another interpretation of Jehohanan's remains was proposed by Joseph Zias of the Israel Department of Antiquities, and Eliezer Sekeles of Hebrew University, challenging both of the previous interpretations.[17] Any further reassessment will have to be done with the information already obtained from the remains as they were returned to their original tomb in 1986, except for the heel bone.

Affixing the Feet to the Cross

Four prevailing theories have been offered to explain the positioning of the feet on a cross, three directly in relation to Jehohanan. In 1932, Hewitt made the astonishing assertion that nails were not used to affix

Reappraisal," *Israel Exploration Journal* 35 (1985) 27.

13. Cf. Yadin (1973) 19–22.

14. For example, William D. Edwards, Wesley J. Gabel, and Floyd E. Hosmer, "On the Physical Death of Jesus Christ," *Journal of the American Medical Association* 255 (1986) 1455–1463 provides a purely speculative portrait of Jesus' crucifixion which bares little resemblance to the remains of Jehohanan's.

15. Haas (1970); Tzaferis (1970); Tzaferis (1985).

16. Yadin (1973); cf. also Fizmyer (1978) 486–99.

17. Zias and Sekeles, *Israel Exploration Journal* (1985); cf. Joseph Zias and Eliezer Sekeles, "The Crucified Man from Giv'at ha-Mivtar—A Reappraisal," *Biblical Archaeologist* 48 (1985) 190–91; Cf. Joe Zias, "Crucifixion in Antiquity: The Anthropological Evidence," www.joezias.com/CrucifixionAntiquity.html; Joseph Zias, "Death and Disease in Ancient Israel," *Biblical Archaeologist* 54 (1991) 155.

feet to a cross, arguing that the only reason for believing such an idea was "the strength of tradition" and "supposed messianic prophecy."[18] Of course, this was presented 37 years prior to the discovery of Jehohanan's remains, and thus he did not have the advantage of this discovery.

Haas and Tzaferis argued that both feet were pierced by a single nail through the *calcaneum*, first the right heel then the left. Haas claimed to have found traces of the left heel bone attached to the right heel.[19] He assumed that the nail was 17–18 cm long (6¾ -7 inches), when in fact it was only 11.5 cm The problem with this view, as noted by Yadin[20] and Zias and Sekeles,[21] is that the nail was not long enough to penetrate a one-inch block of acacia wood, both *calcaneum*, and still affix the feet to the olive wood upright post, thus leading them to challenge Hass and Tzaferis' interpretation of the remains.

Yadin responded by suggesting that the feet were actually nailed to a separate plaque, and that the plaque was then affixed to the cross. Thus, the feet themselves would have never actually been nailed to the cross, but rather the feet would have been affixed together by an acacia wood plaque, with the nail bent intentionally to further secure the heel to the wood, forming a loop, and then simply hung over the top of the cross.[22]

However, Zias and Sekeles later responded that the nail pierced just the right *calcanis*, meaning that the feet were not together when nailed to the upright post. Since the actual length of the nail is only 11.5 cm., it would have only been long enough to pierce the one-inch piece of acacia wood, the right *calcanis*, and enter the olive wood upright post. Hence, each foot required nailing to the cross, possibly on the sides of the upright.[23]

Affixing the Upper Extremities to the Cross

Three prevalent theories exist regarding how the arm was positioned on the cross (See Figure 2). First, the arms were tied to the cross-bar. Hewitt supported the theory based on the fallacy that nails were not necessarily used in the practice of crucifixion. This is supported by the fact that

18. J. W. Hewitt, "The Use of Nails in Crucifixion," *Harvard Theological Review* 25 (1932) 41.

19. Haas (1970) 42, 49, 55–56; Tzaferis (1985) 52–53.

20. Yadin (1973) 20.

21. Zias and Sekeles, *Israel Exploration Journal* (1985) 24.

22. Yadin (1973) 19–21.

23. Zias and Sekeles, *Israel Exploration Journal* (1985) 26–27; Zias and Sekeles, *Biblical Archaeologist* (1985) 190.

if the victim had to carry the cross-beam, it may well have been tied to the upper arm and across the back while on route to the execution site.[24] Zias and Sekeles affirmed the rope hypothesis in their model of Jehohanan's crucifixion.[25]

Secondly, the wrists were pierced by a nail. Haas and Tzaferis noted that Jehohanan's right radius (one of the two bones in the forearm) had an abrasion, presumably from the nail which supported the body.[26] The pierced-wrist theory was popularized by French physician Pierre Barbet, who, after experimenting on amputated arms, concluded that the palm could only support about 88 pounds before tearing through the fingers, far less than the weight of an adult human.[27] As expected, Zias and Sekeles maintain that the radius marks are inconsequential and should not be directly associated with a nail, hence dismissing it as being evidence for piercing the wrist, favoring instead the rope alternative.[28]

Thirdly, the hand/palm was pierced by a nail. Jehohanan's remains do not give any indication, even theoretically, that the nail was placed in the hand. Physician Frederick Zugibe, Chief Medical Examiner for Rockland County, New York, determined that the palm of the hand could support the weight of a human when properly placed.[29] Additionally, if a peg or seat were provided for the victim, the full body weight would not necessarily be suspended by the nails in the hands and/or the feet. However, once again, Jenohanan's remains are in effect mute on this option.

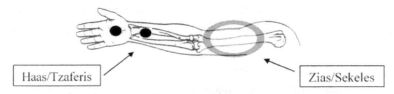

Haas/Tzaferis   Zias/Sekeles

Figure 2: Affixing the Upper Extremities

24. Hewitt (1932) 29–45.

25. Zias and Sekeles, *Israel Exploration Journal* (1985) 27; Zias and Sekeles, *Biblical Archaeologist* (1985) 190; Zias, *Biblical Archaeologist* (1991) 155.

26. Haas (1970) 51, 57; Tzaferis (1985) 52.

27. Pierre Barbet, *A Doctor at Calvary* (Garden City, New York: P. J. Kennedy, 1953).

28. Zias and Sekeles, *Israel Exploration Journal* (1985) 24; Zias and Sekeles, *Biblical Archaeologist* (1985) 190.

29. Frederick T. Zugibe, "Two Questions about Crucifixion: Does the Victim Die of Asphyxiation? Would Nails in the Hands Hold the Weight of the Body?" *Bible Review* 5 (1989) 41–43.

Proposed Positions of Jehohanan's Crucifixion

As previously noted, following the discovery of Jehohanan's remains in 1968 three basic interpretations have been developed regarding his position on the cross. The original interpretation was advanced by Haas and Tzaferis in 1970, and later reasserted by Tzaferis in 1985 (see Figure 3). Note the peculiar position of the legs, which reflects the conclusion as to the placement of a single nail through both feet. Likewise, note that the arms are shown pierced just above the wrists, based on their understanding of the marks on the radius.

Figure 3: Haas (1970) and Tzaferis (1985)[30]

Yadin's proposal suggested a complete re-interpretation of the remains. Fitzmyer accurately summarized Yadin's theory that "the heels were pierced and fixed together to be attached to two plaques of wood, . . . and

30. Tzaferis, *Biblical Archaeology Review* (1985) 52–53. Image Used with permission of the *Israel Exploration Journal*

the nail was then bent backward to secure the attachment. The man then was fixed to the cross by being hung by his parted legs over the top of the cross; the legs with knees apart but with heels securely fastened together to form a loop over the top to prevent the body from sliding down."[31] This position gains support from Yadin's contention that the inscription of Jehohanan's ossuary appears to describe him with the title "the one hanged with knees apart." Yadin concluded, "Thus, both the inscription [on the ossuary] and the skeletal remains point toward the same solution [to the question of positioning of the feet]."[32] Yadin never furnished a diagram depicting this proposed position.

The most recently reappraised position, formulated by Zias and Sekeles in 1985, is represented in Figure 4. Immediately, one may notice the difference between their positioning of the legs as well as the arms from that of Haas and Tzaferis' interpretation. Zias and Sekeles maintain that the nail was far too short to have pierced both feet simultaneously, and hence were pierced individually, requiring two nails to affix the feet.[33] This would likewise find support from Yadin's contention that Jehohanan died "with his knees apart," rather than Haas and Tzaferis' depiction.[34] Since they also rejected the notion that Jehohanan's radius evidenced the use of nails in the wrist, they depicted him as being tied to the cross-beam rather than nailed to it.

31. Fitzmyer (1978) 497. Cf. Yadin (1973) 20–23.

32. Yadin (1973) 22.

33. Zias and Sekeles, *Israel Exploration Journal* (1985) 27. Cf. Zias, "Crucifixion in Antiquity."

34. Zias and Sekeles, *Biblical Archaeologist* (1985) 191.

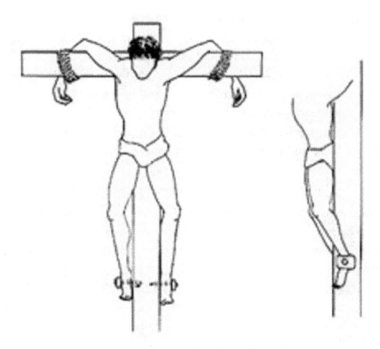

Figure 4: Zias and Sekeles (1985)[35]

These three proposed models of Jehohanan's crucifixion contain speculation, evidence, and interpretation of orthoarchaeological data. Figure 4.5 contains a summation of these three interpretations, noting the distinctive elements of each.

	Haas/Tzaferis	Yadin	Zias/Sekeles
Body Direction	Head up	Head down	Head up
Arms	Wrist-Pierces	????	Arm-tied
Legs	Together, bent	Bowed, bent	Straddle, straight
Body	Seated	"Standing"	"Standing"
Feet/Heels	Nailed together	Nailed separate	Nailed separate
Seat/Peg	Yes	No	No
Nails	3 (2 wrist, 1 feet)	2 (2 feet, ??)	2 (2 feet, 0 arms)
Cross	*Crux commissa*	*Crux immissa*	*Crux immissa*

Figure 4.5: Summation of Interpretations

35. Zias and Sekeles, *Israel Exploration Journal* (1985) 27; Zias and Sekeles, *Biblical Archaeologist* (1985) 190; Zias, *Biblical Archaeologist* (1991) 155. Image used with permission of the *Israel Exploration Journal*.

One option that has not been asserted is that perhaps Haas and Tzaferis were correct about the affixing of the arms, i.e. wrist-nailed to the cross-beam, and that Zias and Sekeles were correct about the affixing of the feet, i.e. separately nailed straddling the upright. This would represent the majority of the insights provided by Jehoanan's remains. In this instance, Jehohanan would have been crucified in a head up position, using four nails, two piercing his wrists, and a nail piercing each heel as he straddled the upright post on either a *crux commissa* or *crux immissa*.

IMPLICATIONS FOR JESUS RESEARCH

While the discovery of Jehohanan is indeed phenomenal and insightful, it must be remembered that he is but one of thousands crucified by the Romans in Palestine alone. To suggest that his remains represent the definitive model of Roman crucifixion is optimistic. This is especially true since ancient authorities mention the Romans using a variety of forms when crucifying criminals. For example, Seneca wrote, "I see crosses there, not just one kind [of cross] but many different ways [victims are crucified]."[36] Similarly, Josephus, when describing the aftermath of the destruction of Jerusalem in AD 70 wrote, "The soldiers themselves through rage and bitterness nailed up their victims in different postures as a grim joke, til owing to vast numbers there was no room for the crosses and no crosses for the bodies."[37] However, it must be acknowledged that it appears that this crucifixion was not part of a mass execution of prisoners, but simply one of the individuals crucified under the reign of Pontius Pilate, as was Jesus. While the discovery of Jehonanon's remains confirm general elements of the account of the crucifixion of Jesus Christ, e.g. that the practice of crucifixion was performed in Roman Judea using both nails and wooden beams, more specific issues may also be informed by this discovery.

Shape of the Cross

Graffiti from the Palatine hill in Rome satirically depicts Christ on a t-shaped cross, but with a donkey's head and the caption reading, "Anaximenos worships his god."[38] Two rare catacomb inscriptions seem

36. Seneca, *Dialogue*, 6.20.3.

37. Josephus, *J.W.*, 5.449–51.

38. The date of this graffiti is debated, with some holding to the first century AD,

to insert the t-shaped cross into the names of two crucified Christian martyrs, e.g. Dionysion (Διονψσιον). Another inscription has the letter M with what may be a symbol of a cross-beam in some martyr's names, e.g. through the M of VERIC M VNDVS (Vericundus), possibly representing the cross-beam of a *crux*.[39] The earliest depictions of the crucifixion of Jesus with the traditional shape of the cross comes from the late fifth century, almost 200 years after crucifixions were legally abolished in the Roman Empire by Emperor Constantine, thus no living witness could attest to any crucifixion, let alone that of Jesus. Jehohanan's crucifixion was in all probability performed on a t-shaped cross as part of an execution in Jerusalem under the governorship of Pontius Pilate, meaning it likely was the shape of Jesus' cross.

Horror of Death by Crucifixion

It is commonly thought that flogging was atypical, and hence Jesus' treatment was more severe than that of a typical criminal. However, flogging was, in fact, quite common, and was standard procedure in the Roman practice of crucifixion. Seneca comments to Lucilius, that one "would have many excuses for dying even before mounting the cross."[40] The position of Jesus on the cross is, of course, speculative at best, and does not fully match any of the proposed models mentioned previously. Realizing that his hands/wrists were pierced, as were his feet, and reflecting on the images created by Haas/Tzaferis, Yadin, and Zias/Sekeles, we can begin to more accurately visualize the physical suffering of Christ on the cross. Without belaboring the point, death by crucifixion was a result of either exhaustion asphyxia, i.e. suffocation due to fatigue, or shock due to the traumatic treatment of the body.[41]

Broken Legs

Jehohanan's legs had been broken to hasten death, as had been the crucifixion companions of Jesus (John 19:32). Tzaferis comments that this "also provides evidence for a Palestinian variation of Roman crucifixion

---

while others place it in the third century AD. See Blaiklock, 140–141. Cf. George M. A. Hanfmann, "The Crucified Donkey Man: Achaios and Jesus," *Studies in Classical Art and Archaeology* (Locust Valley, NJ: J. J. Augustin, 1979) 205–7, Plate 55.

39. Ibid, 141.

40. Seneca, *Epistles*, 101.

41. Cf. Zugibe, (1989) 34–41; Edwards, Gabel and Hosmer (1986).

– at least as applied to Jews. . . . In Palestine the executioner would break the legs of the crucified person in order to hasten his death and thus permit burial before nightfall."[42]

Burial of Crucified "Criminals"

According to all four canonical gospels, Jesus received a proper Jewish burial.[43] Yet, there are those who voice the argument that the resurrection accounts were obviously fictitious, since no criminal who had been executed by crucifixion would have received a customary Jewish burial, i.e. being placed in a tomb rather than a mass grave or left on the cross to physically decompose. For example, John Dominic Crossan maintains that Jesus' body would have more likely have been devoured by animals and/or birds, and hence "there might be nothing left to bury at the end."[44] However, Jehohanan's remains, which do indeed attest to his having been crucified, were given a proper burial in a Jewish tomb, even among family members. Crossan suggests that Jehohanan is an anomaly, that the proper Jewish burial of a crucified criminal was a rarity, since literally thousands were crucified in Roman Judea, and yet only a single set of crucified human remains have been discovered.[45] The only reason this particular set of skeletal remains was identified as those of a crucified man was due to the anomaly of the nail. It is possible that other crucified individuals were properly buried, but without any physical evidence indicating crucifixion. Yet, Jehohanan's remains are unique, an anomaly, because he is the only skeletal remains to indicate crucifixion was the cause of death.

CONCLUSION

The discovery of the skeletal remains of Jehohanan provides the contemporary Christian with a portrait of a crucifixion that may bear similarity to that of Jesus Christ's. With this simple phrase, "even a death on the cross," Paul emphasized to the Philippian Christians the full extent of Christ's devotion and obedience to fulfilling the Father's will (Phil 2:5–

---

42. Tzaferis (1985) 53.

43. Matthew 27:57–61; Mark 15:42–47; Luke 23:50–56; John 19:38–42.

44. John Dominic Crossan, *Jesus: A Revolutionary Biography* (New York: Harper Collins, 1994) 126.

45. Ibid., 125–26.

8). Even with the hundreds of references to crucifixions, the thousands of icons, the preserved remains of a crucified man, and the description offered in the pages of the New Testament itself, we can still only begin to reflect on and imagine the suffering of Christ. Yet, more importantly than anything discussed in this chapter is the reason for Jesus' crucifixion, dying not for any crime of his own, but for us. "God made him who had no sin [Jesus] to be sin for us, so that in him we might become the righteousness of God" (2 Cor 5:21).

6

Crurifragium: An Intersection of History, Archaeology, and Theology in the Gospel of John

Brian Johnson

THE GOSPEL OF JOHN has long been regarded as a *theological*, as opposed to a *historical* work.[1] There is much, however, to commend the historical accuracy of at least some parts of the Gospel of John.[2] Two features of the Gospel of John that commend its historical accuracy are the archaeological confirmation, particularly of topographical features of the Gospel of John,[3] and eyewitness statements within the Gospel of John itself which claim that the document is based at least in part upon the first-hand testimony of an eyewitness to the events that it narrates.[4] John 19:31–37 provides an interesting nexus for examining both the

1. In one sense this distinction can be traced as far back as Clement of Alexandria who is cited by Eusebius as calling the Gospel of John a "spiritual Gospel" (*Hist. eccl.* 6.14.7). It is far from clear, and I would also add unlikely, that Clement was making the same distinction modern scholars are making in regards to the Gospel of John's reliability.

2. I personally accept the historicity of the entirety of the Gospel of John, but it would be a large task to prove that, given the constraints and methods of historical research.

3. On this see particularly Urban C. von Wahlde, "Archaeology and John's Gospel," in *Jesus and Archaeology*, ed. James H. Charlesworth (Grand Rapids: Eerdmans, 2006) 523–86.

4. On the issue of eyewitness and the Gospel of John see Richard Bauckham, *Jesus and the Eyewitnesses: The Gospels as Eyewitness Testimony* (Grand Rapids: Eerdmans, 2006); Martin Hengel, "Eye-Witness Memory and the Writing of the Gospels," in *The Written Gospel* ed. Markus Bockmuehl and Donald A. Hagner (Cambridge: Cambridge University Press, 2005) 70–96; and Samuel Byrskog, *Story as History—History as Story* WUNT 123 (Tübingen: Mohr Siebeck, 2000).

eyewitness claim and the archaeological background. One of the three possible explicit eyewitness statements in the Gospel of John is contained here (19:35).[5] Also, the practice of *crurifragium* (the breaking of the leg bones of crucified individuals) is mentioned in this passage, and this act has possibly been confirmed archaeologically. What is additionally interesting is that alongside these two potentially historical features, this passage contains two elements that can and have been frequently understood *theologically*: the "fulfillment" formula in reference to Jesus' bones not being broken (19:36), and the flow of blood and water as a result of the thrust of the soldier's spear (19:34). Taken together these items make this passage a prime location to examine questions of the historicity of the Gospel of John and the way the author draws connections between history and theology. This chapter will examine the way these elements work together within the narrative in an attempt to understand the author's use of historical detail, eyewitness testimony, and theological interpretation in his presentation of the death of Jesus. This examination will in turn perhaps suggest a way forward in understanding how history and theology should be understood within the Gospel of John as a whole.

THE POSSIBILITY OF ARCHAEOLOGICAL CONFIRMATION OF THE PRACTICE OF *CRURIFRAGIUM*[6]

In 1968 at Giv'at ha-Mivtar, an area of Jerusalem, several ossuaries were discovered. The remains of several people were discovered in these tombs.[7] But most amazing and significant of all was the discovery of the skeleton of a man whose ankle bone had been pierced by an iron nail.

---

5. The other two are John 1:14, and John 21:24–25.

6. I am grateful to have the opportunity to express a kind remembrance of the man who first introduced me to the formal study of archaeology, Dr. Reuben Bullard. Much to my wife and children's chagrin, I'm not able to pick up a rock, to drive through a highway cut, or to sit around a campfire without thinking about what I am told about God's world by what I am seeing. This is due to the continuing influence of "Doc Rock" (as he was affectionately called by his students) on my life.

7. For the original reports see Nico Haas, "Anthropological Observations on the Skeletal Remains from Giv'at ha-Mivtar," *IEJ* 20 (1970) 38–59 and Vassilios Tzaferis, "Jewish Tombs at and near Giv'at ha-Mivtar, Jerusalem," *IEJ* 20 (1970) 18–32. See Joseph Zias and Eliezer Sekeles, "The Crucified Man from Giv'at ha-Mivtar: A Reappraisal," *IEJ* 35 (1985) 22 fn. 3 for a thorough listing of the studies on this discovery up through the writing of their article.

This was taken as evidence to indicate that this man had been crucified.[8] By pulling together information from the inscriptions and the material remains, this burial was dated to a time prior to AD 70, and more specifically to a time roughly contemporary to the time of Jesus' crucifixion.[9] There are several elements of this discovery that are of interest to the student of the Scriptures.[10] For the purpose of this essay, I want to focus upon one aspect of the state of the crucified man's remains. The initial reports indicated that the crucified man's leg bones had been broken.[11] This fact could perhaps be suggestive of an archaeological confirmation of the practice of *crurifragium*.[12]

There were several obstacles to a thorough and effective study of this find. First, this was an accidental discovery by a construction crew building in the Northeast area of Jerusalem in the aftermath of the Six Days War.[13] While these types of accidental discoveries are frequent, the construction project and the unplanned nature of the dig often bring challenges. Tzaferis, for example, describes being "called in" on this discovery after it had been made.[14] Secondly, there was a short time frame for examining the material remains before re-internment took place. Haas describes having only four weeks to examine the material remains of thirty-five individuals.[15] Focus was placed upon the crucified individual because of the unique nature of the find. Haas also focused

---

8. See Haas, 44; Tzaferis, "Jewish Tombs," who calls this "undoubtedly a a [sic] case of crucifixion," 31. Heinz-Wolfgang Kuhn, "Die Kreuzesstrafe Während der frühen Kaiserzeit. Ihre Wirklichkeit und Wertung in der Umwelt des Urchristentums," in *ANRW* II 25.1: 713 calls the evidence that this man was crucified "eindeutig" (unambiguous), and even though Zias and Sekeles question several elements of the original studies, they do not call into question that this find represents a crucified man.

9. Vassilios Tzaferis, "Crucifixion—The Archaeological Evidence," *BAR* 11 (Jan/Feb 1985) 44.

10. See James Estep's essay in the present volume for several good examples of the significance of this find.

11. Haas, 57; Tzaferis, "Jewish Tombs," 31.

12. This was the immediate evaluation of Haas who stated about the force necessary to break the legs, "This direct, deliberate blow may be attributed to the final 'coup de grâce.'" Haas' statement has been quoted or alluded to in virtually every study of this find since.

13. See Tzaferis, "Crucifixion," 44 for an engaging first-hand description of the find.

14. Tzaferis, "Crucifixion," 44.

15. Haas, 38–39.

more narrowly upon the specific bones of this individual which were related to the crucifixion.[16] Thirdly, the bones were fragile and in a poor state of preservation.[17] This is especially problematic because evidence of *crurifragium* is based upon the breaking of bones. The bones of this individual could have been broken at a time subsequent to his crucifixion.[18] Fourthly, I would contend that the unique nature of this find also contributed to difficulties in evaluating its significance. There are two parts to this. On the one hand, because this is the *only* example of a crucified individual that has been identified to the present, there is no other data against which to compare and to evaluate this finding. Other examples of the remains of crucified individuals would help in better understanding certain features of this find. For example, ancient literary sources tell us there was a great deal of variation in the manner of crucifixion.[19] Simply reflecting on the Gospel of John's description of Jesus' death shows variation among the three crucifixions mentioned there. Two of the *crucaria* undergo *crurifragium*, while Jesus does not. Presumably, Jesus' side was pierced. On the other hand, the uniqueness of this discovery also resulted in intense interest and scrutiny of the findings. In particular, it is possible that a desire for this discovery to illuminate the most well-known crucifixion in history may have led the initial researchers to leap to some conclusions that were not well-supported by the evidence. Fitzmyer argues against this, saying that because this came from "non-Christian team-work, it cannot be thought to be conditioned or prejudiced."[20] One certainly understands Fitzmyer's point, but it could be stated that Christian or not, information regarding Jesus' crucifixion is fairly widely known, particularly among historians and archaeologists living in and connected with museums and other organizations in Jerusalem. I am not suggesting that the original report *fabricated* evidence in order to "prove" or provide background for Jesus'

16. Haas, 51.

17. Haas, 51. See also Zias and Sekeles, 24–25.

18. Zias and Sekeles, 24–25.

19. Martin Hengel, *Crucifixion in the Ancient World and the Folly of the Message of the Cross* (Philadelphia: Fortress Press, 1977) *passim*, and also Joe Zias and James H. Charlesworth, "Crucifixion: Archaeology, Jesus, and the Dead Sea Scrolls," in *Jesus and the Dead Sea Scrolls*, ed. James H. Charlesworth (New York: Doubleday, 1995) 284–85, and the evidence from Josephus, *J.W.*. 5.451.

20. Joseph A. Fitzmyer, "Crucifixion in Ancient Palestine, Qumran Literature, and the New Testament," *CBQ* 40 (1978) 498.

crucifixion, but it is possible that the well-known accounts of this most famous crucifixion may have unintentionally provided a lens through which the material remains were interpreted.

After the initial flurry of excitement and activity surrounding this discovery had died down, scholars began to question, critique, and re-examine the evidence. One part of this reexamination was in regard to the supposed *crurifragium* of the crucified man. Zias and Sekeles had the opportunity to examine the remains before they had been reburied.[21] On the basis of their examination, they questioned nine of Haas' original findings. The sixth item they mentioned was Haas' contention that the breaking of the leg bones constituted evidence for *crurifragium*. Zias and Sekeles label the evidence for this "inconclusive." They level three arguments against Haas' interpretation. First, as was mentioned previously, the material was poorly preserved. This, say the authors, "led to numerous breaks which were obviously post-mortem."[22] Secondly, they show that Haas has mislabeled two photographs of leg bones which he used to make his case.[23] Thirdly, they show that if the two lower left leg bones of the individual are aligned "it is evident that the breaks are situated at different angles."[24] This leads Zias and Sekeles to the conclusion that the breaks of the left leg which Haas took as evidence of *crurifragium*, "must have occurred after the death of the individual, and were not related to the time of crucifixion."[25]

Zias and Sekeles raise several significant issues with Haas' initial examination and interpretation of the evidence. This they attribute, almost entirely, to the speed with which the examination necessarily took place.[26] As mentioned above, however, this may also be partly explained by a desire to gain details that would give insight into Jesus' crucifixion. Particularly with reference to *crurifragium*, it may be that Haas was led to this conclusion by literary reports of crucifixion rather than the evidence itself. That having been said, Zias and Sekeles' interpretation of the evidence is also speculative. The forensic scientist, Frederick T.

21. Zias and Sekeles, 22. See also Herschel Shank's summary of their article, "New Analysis of the Crucified Man," *BAR* 11 (Nov/Dec 1985) 20–21.

22. Zias and Sekeles, 25; see also, Zias and Charlesworth, 280.

23. Zias and Sekeles, 25.

24. Ibid.

25. Ibid.

26. Zias and Sekeles, 22.

Zugibe, who has done extensive research into crucifixion, concludes Zias and Sekeles may not be correct. Zugibe says, "Forensically, [the evidence] is more consistent with the victim's receiving more than one blow at different angles."[27] J. F. Strange interprets the data of the broken legs to be connected with removal of the body from the cross. He writes, "The lower leg bones reveal evidence of violent removal from the cross. The left leg had been severed by a single blow while the bones of the right leg had been splintered, probably by the same blow."[28]

Because there are differing interpretations of the evidence of the broken leg bones, perhaps it is safest to accept Zias and Sekeles' original statement that the evidence is inconclusive. While there appears to be problems with Haas' initial analysis in this case, Zugibe makes clear there are other ways to see the evidence that would still be consistent with *crurifragium*. Unfortunately in this case, because of the state of the remains and their unavailability for further research, no definitive statement can be made. Care should be taken not to generalize from this one case, nor to make direct correlation between these remains and evidence of the precise method of Jesus' crucifixion. The possibility of further archaeological evidence should be awaited before strong connections are made. Strange's article can be taken as an example of drawing perhaps too much from this evidence. He presents the three major ways this crucifixion has been reconstructed, but then says that any of these views "alters the traditional view of Jesus' crucifixion."[29] While this find certainly brings helpful information, and adds to our picture of crucifixion in the first century, Strange clearly overstates the significance for reconstructing Jesus' crucifixion. This evidence may still prove to be valuable in two ways. First, if subsequent discoveries of crucified individuals are made, then the evidence of the broken leg bones could be compared to those of others, and become part of a set of data that will provide a clearer picture of the practice. Secondly, it has been said that these remains were only identified as a crucified individual because of the random circumstance which led to the nail being left in his ankle, rather than being removed.[30]

27. Frederick T. Zugibe, *The Crucifixion of Jesus: A Forensic Inquiry* (New York: M. Evans and Co., 2005) 106.

28. J. F. Strange, "Crucifixion, Method of," in *IDBSupp* (Nashville: Abingdon, 1976) 199.

29. Strange, 199.

30. See James H. Charlesworth, *Jesus with Judaism*, Anchor Bible Reference Library (New York: Doubleday, 1988), 122 and Zias and Sekeles, 27. On the other hand, Yigael Yadin understood the bending of the nail not as a coincidence at all, but as a deliberate

It has been suggested that while the literary record mentions thousands of crucifixions during this period, sometimes hundreds at a time (for example, Josephus, *J.W.* 2.75, 5.449–51, *Ant.* 13.379–80), it is unusual that archaeological evidence of only one crucified individual has been discovered. To be somewhat speculative, perhaps this find suggests it would be useful to reexamine already exhumed human remains, and those that are discovered subsequently, in order to identify those where the leg bones seem to have been deliberately broken in a fashion similar to this discovery. An examination of the ankle bones of individuals with legs broken like this might turn up additional evidence of crucifixion. However, this type of study might confirm Zias and Sekeles' suspicions that similar breaks can occur when the bones are placed in ossuaries, or when they are recovered by archaeologists, or as a result of further deterioration. Such a study may not be feasible or helpful, but it could provide a way of collecting data with which this find could be compared.

The initial point to be made here is that while it is tempting to use the evidence from the discovery of this crucified man to bolster the credibility of the Gospel of John's account of Jesus' crucifixion, care must be taken. The evidence for *crurifragium* is inconclusive in this case. However, this evidence should not be dismissed out of hand either. If there are literary statements regarding *crurifragium* in connection with crucifixion, and if additional archaeological discoveries help give context to the discovery at Giv'at ha-Mivtar, then this evidence might show that a detail of Jesus' crucifixion that is unique to the Gospel of John accords well with what we know of the historical practice.

THE GOSPEL OF JOHN AND THE PRACTICE OF
CRURIFRAGIUM

Because of the uniqueness of the detail regarding the *crurifragium* in the Gospel of John, commentators typically give some very specific interpretations of the act. Köstenberger's approach is typical: "In order to hasten death, the victim's legs (and sometimes other bones) would be smashed with an iron mallet, a practice called *crurifragium* (breaking of the shinbone). This prevented the person from prolonging life by pushing himself

---

way of attaching the crucified man's ankles together, "Epigraphy and Crucifixion," *IEJ* 23 (1973) 21. One argument against Yadin's reconstruction that I have not seen raised is that if intentionally bending the nail tip was a common practice in crucifixion, we might expect to find more nails still embedded in the ankle bones of *crucaria*.

up with his legs in order to breathe. Arm strength soon failed, and as-phyxiation ensued."[31] Raymond Brown's approach, in his magisterial com-mentary, is likewise very specific. He writes, "The *crurifragium* was done with a heavy mallet; usually only the legs were broken, but occasionally other bones as well. Originally a cruel capital punishment in itself, the *crurifragium*, despite its brutality, was a mercy when it accompanied the crucifixion, for it hastened death."[32] Brown then cites the example of the recently discovered (at the time of his writing) remains of the crucified man, saying that both of his legs were broken.

It is interesting that when one begins to survey the literary refer-ences to *crurifragium* there is not nearly as much specificity, and the vast majority of these references do not refer to a connection between the breaking of the legs of the individual and crucifixion![33] Some references refer to the breaking of the legs in connection with capital punishment, but not crucifixion. For example, Polybius 1.80.13 refers to prisoners' hands being cut off, legs being broken, and then the prisoners being thrown *alive* into a trench, presumably to die there from their wounds (see also Ammianus Marcellinus 14.9.8). Other references do not seem to be referring to death at all, but the breaking of the legs of slaves or others, or a mutilation of their legs as a punishment, or perhaps with the purpose of ensuring that they do not run away (see Plautus *Poenulus* 886 and *Truculentus* 638). Another example of the breaking of legs not con-nected with death would be Suetonius' description of Tiberius breaking the legs of an acolyte and "sacred trumpeter" who objected to Tiberius' sexual assault of them (Suetonius *Tiberius* 44). As Koskenniemi, Nisula, and Toppari write, "*Crurifragium* [was] widely used as a horrible deter-rent punishment among the Romans, especially for slaves."[34]

There are few literary examples of connection between *crurifragium* and crucifixion. One of the clearest is from the *Gospel of Peter* 4.14 in which it is said that Jesus' legs would not be broken because the officials

31. Andreas Köstenberger, *John,* Baker Exegetical Commentary on the New Testament (Grand Rapids: Baker, 2004) 551–52.

32. Raymond E. Brown, *The Gospel According to John XIII-XXI,* Anchor Bible 29A (New York: Doubleday, 1970) 934.

33. For these parallels see Erkki Koskenniemi et al., "Wine Mixed with Myrrh (Mark 15.23) and *Crurifragium* (John 19.31–32): "Two Details of the Passion Narratives," *JSNT* 27 (2005) 379–91. However, these authors do not seem to consider the connec-tion between *crurifragium* and crucifixion, but only explicit mentions of *crurifragium* as a punishment.

34. Koskenniemi et al., 388.

wished to punish him more severely. The language used in the *Gospel of Peter* is different than in the Gospel of John's account, as is the time-frame (i.e. before or after Jesus' death), causing Brown to speculate that the *Gospel of Peter* potentially draws upon "an independent source."[35] However, the *Gospel of Peter* 4.12 also mentions the Johannine detail of the dividing of Jesus' garments. This suggests the *Gospel of Peter*'s dependence upon the account of the Gospel of John.[36] More to the current point, it should be noted that this reference does not provide the kind of specificity of practice that the commentaries suggest. Crossan mentions the account of Andrew's martyrdom in which the order is given not to break Andrew's legs in order to increase the torturous element of his death.[37] Crossan draws on the similarities between this account and the account of the *Gospel of Peter*, but both cases here are literature that post-date the Gospel of John. Both of the passages in these documents do seem to confirm that *crurifragium* was intended to speed the death of the person being crucified, but the account of the Gospel of John itself seems to imply this as well, so there is little new information that can be gathered from these accounts.

Cicero provides an account that predates the Gospel of John, and which seems to *implicitly* tie together *crurifragium* and crucifixion. It is interesting that this is quite a vague reference, but the vagueness suggests that *crurifragium* may have been a widely known practice to Cicero's readers. Cicero is writing about the ironic fulfillment of prophecies. In one particular case he mentions the death of a pirate, Icadius, who is killed after his legs are broken in a rock fall.[38] The irony seems to be that Icadius could be expected, as a pirate, to suffer death by crucifixion accompanied by *crurifragium*, but instead his *crurifragium* comes in an unexpected way. Harrison writes, "By suffering a death of 'crurifragium' by the accidental means of a rock-fall in a cave, Icadius was pre-empting the 'crurifragium' in crucifixion as inflicted on pirates by Roman justice."[39] This suggests that *crurifragium* would be well-known as a pun-

35. Brown, vol. 29A, 934. See also Raymond E. Brown, *Death of the Messiah* vol. 2 (New York: Doubleday, 1994) 1176.

36. See John A. T. Robinson, *The Priority of John*, ed. J. F. Coakley (Oak Park, IL: Meyer-Stone Books, 1987) 279–80.

37. John Dominic Crossan, *The Cross that Spoke: The Origins of the Passion Narrative*, (San Francisco: Harper & Row, 1988) 164.

38. Cicero, *De Fato* 5. My treatment is based on the interpretation of S. J. Harrison, "Cicero and 'Crurifragium,'" *CQ* 33 (1983) 453–55.

39. Harrison, 454.

ishment inflicted upon pirates, perhaps in connection with crucifixion, and therefore there would be no need of explanation for Cicero's readers. Harrison adds two further references that seem to imply crucifixion and *crurifragium* in Cicero (*Philippics* 11.14, 13.27). If Harrison's argument is accepted, this would show that the practice of *crurifragium* was widely known prior to the writing of the Gospel of John, and would have been associated with execution of criminals.

This would perhaps make the Gospel of John the first *explicit* statement of *crurifragium* in connection with crucifixion that remains to this day.[40] Rather than seeing this as some sort of "defeat," or argument for the Gospel of John's lack of credibility, it might be better to consider the reference in the Gospel of John as a part of a trajectory of thought. This type of pattern would be expected, namely to begin with vague statements predating the Gospel of John, followed with more explicit statements within the Gospel of John itself, with the later statements such as in the *Gospel of Peter* being even more specific, and perhaps relying in part on the Gospel of John.[41]

What should be more carefully considered, however, is the specificity with which the practice is described in commentaries, and the failure to cite ancient passages which would support this specificity. The descriptions of the practice seem to stem from quotations of Lactatius, a third century Christian, who is clearly influenced by the Gospel accounts, and who would not have had immediate access to the prevailing practice of the first century.[42] This seems to be an example of commentaries citing commentaries without going back to do research of the original sources.[43] Until such a study is done, perhaps the descriptions of *crurifragium* in commentaries should be somewhat less exact.

40. More research needs to be done on this. In fact, a full treatment of the literary evidence is warranted.

41. This follows the proposal of Adele Reinhartz in "John and Judaism: A Response to Burton Visotsky," in *Life in Abundance: Studies of John's Gospel in Tribute to Raymond E. Brown, S.S.* ed. John R. Donahue (Collegeville, Minn.: Liturgical Press, 2005) 109, that it may be fruitful to see the items in the Gospel of John as a part of the texture of the trajectory of practices and beliefs in this period of time rather than trying to mine doubtful pieces of background.

42. See, for example, Leon Morris, *The Gospel According to John*, NICNT (Grand Rapids: Eerdmans, 1971) 818 fn. 84 who cites Plummer's citation of Lactantius (!).

43. More work needs to be done in order to trace these specific elements, and the traditions and texts which gave rise to them.

EYEWITNESS TESTIMONY AND THE *CRURIFRAGIUM*

When considering the historical accuracy of this passage, the issue of eyewitness testimony should be considered as well. This context is one of only three places in the Gospel of John where what seem to be eyewitness statements are made, and it is the *only* such statement within the narrative itself. It is worth considering the connection between this eyewitness statement (19:35), and the mention of *crurifragium*. According to the narrative, the Jews wanted the bodies removed because of the special Sabbath. This is likely a reference to the ordinance of Deut 21:22–23 which stated that those executed as criminals are not to be left hanging overnight because this would cause the land to be "desecrated."[44] So the request is made that the legs of those on the cross be broken (19:31). The soldiers then break the legs of those crucified on both sides of Jesus (19:32), but when they come to Jesus they find that he is already dead, so his legs were not broken (19:33). Instead, we find a soldier piercing Jesus' side, which brings a flow of blood and water (19:34). At this point the eyewitness statement is made in order to confirm what was seen (19:35).

Eyewitness statements often occur at the beginning and the ending of a narrative which is purporting to be an eyewitness document in order to keep from disrupting the narrative flow. There seem to be two exceptions to this general rule: "either to underline some special source, or to win credence for something unusual (at times, marvelous)."[45] Of these two uses, the one which seems most to apply to this situation is the latter. That is, the author here inserts a note of eyewitness testimony and credibility in order to confirm for the reader what might otherwise seem to be a hard-to-believe detail of the account. This possibility becomes even more likely if the author tends to use another literary feature to "underline special source." In the case of the Gospel of John, the author seems to use the figure of the Beloved Disciple to indicate when and how he had first-hand information to some of the material he recounts.[46]

Marincola writes further of these uses of eyewitness statements to bolster a hard-to-believe account: "In these, the author steps out of the mimetic narrative to guarantee (in reality the only way possible in a his-

44. Brown, 29A, 934.

45. John Marincola, *Authority and Tradition in Ancient Historiography* (Cambridge: Cambridge University Press, 1997) 80.

46. See Bauckham, 397–99 and Derek Tovey, *Narrative Art and Act in the Fourth Gospel*, JSNT Supp. Ser. 151 (Sheffield: Sheffield Academic Pres, 1997) 140.

torical narrative) that what will seem unbelievable to the reader actually took place."[47] The statement of John 19:35 then could be taken to apply to the flow of blood and water. Treatments of the detail of the flow blood and water have varied radically. On the one hand, there are authors who have asserted this was a detail included by the author to show the reality of Jesus' death. In this case it would have been understood by a typical reader that a flow of blood and water indicates the pouring out of blood and pericardial fluid that would indicate death.[48] These studies are often done by, or in conjunction with, medical professionals.[49] What is difficult to understand is that the typical reader would have been familiar with these medical phenomena in order to understand that the author here is confirming that Jesus is dead. Other scholars, however, suggest that this flow of blood and water is miraculous. If this is the case, it would accord much better with an understanding that the author here is confirming something that the reader may have had difficulty believing: that blood and water flowed from the side of Jesus after he was pierced.

I would like to make one further suggestion that the eyewitness statement may also apply to the *crurifragium* as well. The *crurifragium* itself would not need to be confirmed if it was a commonly known part of crucifixions.[50] But it should be noted that what the author is here witnessing to is that Jesus' legs were *not* broken. This leads to the spear piercing the side of Jesus and the flow of blood and water, but also *itself* becomes grist for the author's interpretive mill as well, as will be seen in the next section. The hard-to-believe part of the *crurifragium* is that it did not need to be applied to Jesus because he was already dead. Notice that in the account itself there is an expectation among the Jews that Jesus would still be alive. This accords with the statement in Mark 15:44 that Pilate was surprised to hear that Jesus had already died (*ho de Pilatos ethaumansen ei ēdē tethnēken*).

If the eyewitness statement applies to both the flow of blood and water, and the lack of need for Jesus' legs to be broken, this also makes more sense of the structure of the narrative as we have it. It should be

47. Marincola, 82.

48. One example would be John Wilkinson, "The Incident of the Blood and Water in John 19.34," *SJOT* 28 (1975) 149–72.

49. For example, John J. Collins, "An Exegetical Note: The Crucifixion of Our Lord and Some Medical Data," *CBQ* 12 (1950) 171–72.

50. This would be the case if we accept Harrison's argument mentioned above.

remembered that following the eyewitness statement (19:35), there is a double fulfillment formula. The author cites the Scriptures, by which he likely means the Passover regulations of Exodus 12: "not one of his bones shall be broken." This is clearly a reference to the absence of *crurifragium* being applied to Jesus. Then the author cites Zech 12:10 "They will look on the one they have pierced," referring to the spear thrust into Jesus' side. The author presents these items as fulfillment of Scripture, but it is important to him that these things are understood by the reader as having *actually* occurred. The author, therefore, inserts an eyewitness statement in the middle of this narrative to confirm the validity of what he had witnessed.

THE *CRURIFRAGIUM* AND THEOLOGY

The two details in the Johannine account of Jesus' death, that Jesus' legs were not broken, and the flow of blood and water, were *both* connected to the eyewitness statement of John 19:35. Both of these details are also interpreted by the author to be fulfillment of Scripture. It is clear that the author of the Gospel of John is making a theological point with these details, and tying them to the prophetic expectation regarding God's redemptive plan.[51] The author is showing that the death of Jesus was foretold, even in its details, and this prophecy has effective meaning for those who become Jesus' disciples ("believing, you may have life". . . 20:31).[52] What is at issue here, however, is whether the author of the Gospel of John has *invented* these details to theological purpose.

The foregoing analysis has suggested that, even given some problems of detail, the Gospel of John's mention of *crurifragium*, though unique to this Gospel, seems to accord very well with our knowledge of the first century practice of crucifixion. Further, it is also *precisely* at this place that the author "breaks the fourth wall" to address the reader, and to highlight the reliability of what is being reported, even if it is unusual or hard to believe. This suggests that while the author may be using these details to theological purposes, the events themselves are not invented, but actually occurred. J. A. T. Robinson came to a similar conclusion.

51. See Tom Thatcher's treatment of the author's use of Scripture, witness, and memory in *Why John Wrote a Gospel: Jesus—Memory—History* (Louisville: Westminster John Knox, 2006) 24–32.

52. Notice that this applies to the slightly earlier account of the soldiers "casting lots" for Jesus' clothing (19:24), another detail unique to the Gospel of John.

He concludes that the passion narrative in John's Gospel has an eyewitness source, but he is not so naïve as to think that the author is not interested in theology. Instead, the author chooses to record the details he does *precisely* to make a theological point. In doing so the author has not neglected the historical. On this issue, Robinson writes, "To [the author] the faith is the truth *of* the history, what *really* happened, from the inside."[53] For the author it is crucial that his theological understanding of Jesus' death is based upon the reality of the events, and he wants his readers to form their theological information on the same basis. Keener says of the *crurifragium*, "That his bones were in danger of being broken likely reflects the genuine historical practice of some crucifixions, but John also derives theological mileage from this as from other traditions he employs."[54]

CONCLUSION

This account provides an interesting place to examine the connection in the Gospel of John between archaeology, historical background, and theology. There seem to be clear connections between all three of these areas in this place. This is suggestive for the way the Gospel of John should be understood as a whole. Perhaps there are other places where this connection between archaeology, history, and theology can be examined in order to gain a clearer picture of the author's aims and his purposes in his presentation of Jesus. The account at Cana may provide one such location with the ongoing archaeological work at Khirbet Qana,[55] the discovery of stone jars like those mentioned in the account of John 2,[56] literary information regarding the practice of ceremonial cleansing in Galilee, and further reflection on how the cleansing motif functions with the Gospel of John's narrative.[57] Other sections of the

53. John A. T. Robinson, "'His Witness is True': A Test of the Johannine Claim," in *Twelve More New Testament Studies* (London: SCM Press, 1984) 113.

54. Craig S. Keener, *The Gospel of John: A Commentary* vol. 2 (Peabody, Mass.: Hendrickson, 2003) 1150.

55. Peter Richardson, "Khirbet Qana (and Other Villages) as a Context for Jesus," in *Jesus and Archaeology*, ed. James H. Charlesworth (Grand Rapids: Eerdmans, 2006) 120–44.

56. Charlesworth, 105–8; Thomas Kazen, *Jesus and Purity* Halakah: *Was Jesus Indifferent to Impurity?* Coniectanea Biblica NT Ser. 38 (Stockholm: Almqvist & Wiksell, 2002) 84.

57. See, for example, my paper from the International Meeting of the SBL in July

Gospel of John will likely prove fruitful for this kind of examination as well. However, there is further work remaining to be done. Further work also needs to be done on the practice of *crurifragium* in the ancient world. Before assessment of the Gospel of John's historical accuracy, and how widespread the practice was, the specifics of the practice need to be researched more thoroughly. Further, until additional evidence comes to light, the example of the bones of the one crucified victim we have remains inconclusive. What this short study has suggested, however, is that the Gospel of John will stand up to the united scrutiny of these areas of inquiry, and that such study will be fruitful in leading toward a greater understanding of the Gospel of John

2007, "'Already You Are Clean': Cleansing in the Gospel of John."

7

Population, Architecture, and Economy in Lower Galilean Villages and Towns in the First Century AD: A Brief Survey

David A. Fiensy

IN A PREVIOUS ERA of scholarship, we were dependent on Josephus and the Mishnah to describe life in Galilee in the time of Jesus. Sometimes these sources created an almost utopian view of the region. More recently, other scholars have turned to the social sciences to inform their understanding of Galilee in the New Testament period. This approach tends to picture a society in tension with exploited peasants, widespread indebtedness, and a people on the brink of revolution. However, in the last thirty years, more and more archaeological work has been done in the region. This work sometimes confirms the older views; at other times it leads to a reassessment. The survey below relies on material remains from recent archaeological work in Galilee to draw a picture of village life in the Herodian period. Three questions organize this study. First, how large were villages and towns in Galilee? Secondly, what was in a village or town of Galilee? Finally, what did the inhabitants of Galilee do for a living?

I. HOW LARGE WERE VILLAGES AND TOWNS OF GALILEE?

Most residents of Lower Galilee lived in villages. Josephus wrote that there were 204 cities and villages in all of Galilee.[1] Whether this figure represents an actual administrative count, or is merely his estimate is unclear, but the unevenness of the number might suggest the former. At

---

1. Josephus, *Life* 235.

any rate, if we calculate the population of first century Galilee at 175,000 persons,[2] and if we calculate the populations of the two cities, Sepphoris and Tiberias as 8,000 to 20,000 persons each,[3] then that leaves between 135,000 and 160,000 persons living in villages and towns in both Upper and Lower Galilee.

In defining ancient Galilean village sizes, we must first deal with the Greek and Hebrew terms for village and city. The two Greek terms which, in the main, are found in Josephus and the Gospels, *polis* and *kōmē*, seem to have been used in a confusing way. Technically, a *polis* had its own constitution, coinage, territory, and *boulē*.[4] But these texts often seem to refer to villages as cities and cities as villages. A. N. Sherwin-White suggested that the solution to the problem was to consider the city (*polis*) in both Josephus and the Gospels as a capital of a toparchy, even if the place was not technically a city.[5]

2. See E. M. Meyers, "Jesus and His Galilean Context" in D. R. Edwards and C. T. McCollough, eds., *Archaeology and the Galilee* (Atlanta: Scholars, 1977) 59; and H. Hoehner, *Herod Antipas* (Cambridge: Cambridge University, 1972) 53. Hoehner prefers the figure 200,000 and Meyers prefers 150,000 to 175,000. Meyers accepts Josephus' figure of 200 villages in Galilee, and multiplies this number by 500 residents per village. That number, plus the populations of the two cities, gives his final population figure. C. C. McCown cites an older figure of 400,000 for Galilee ("The Density of Population in Ancient Palestine," *JBL* 66 [1947] 426. His own estimate was 100,000 (p. 436) based on an estimate of 150 persons per square mile. He derives this estimate from comparing with other population densities in the modern period.

3. The figures of J. Reed, *Archaeology and the Galilean Jesus* (Harrisburg, PA: Trinity, 2000) 117, are 8,000 to 12,000 in each city. Meyers suggests 18,000 for Sepphoris and 24,000 for Tiberias ("Jesus and his Galilean Context", 59). J.A. Overman, "Who Were The First Urban Christians?" *SBL SeminarPapers* (1988) offered 30,000 to 40,000 for Tiberias and 30,000 for Sepphoris. R. Horsley, *Archaeology, History and Society in Galilee* (Valley Forge, PA: Trinity Press International, 1996) 45, maintained that both cities together had a population of 15,000. If we adhere to the general rule that 10% of the population in the ancient world lived in the cities, then a population of 175,000 for Galilee needs around 10,000 in each of the two cities. But see the calculation below.

4. See E. Schürer, G. Vermes and F. Miller, *The History of the Jewish People*, (Edinburgh, T. and T. Clark, 1973–87) II, 86f; A.H.M. Jones "The Urbanization of Palestine" *JRS* 21(1931) 78–85; V. Ehrenberg "Polis" *OCD*.

5. Sherwin-White, *Roman Society and Roman Law in the New Testament* (Oxford: Clarendon, 1963) 129f. Cf. Schürer, et al. *History of Jewish People*, II, 188. The term *komopoleis* in reference to the villages of Galilee may indicate (Mark 1:38) the same as the phrase *poleis kai komai* (Matt 9:35). See M. Goodman, *State and Society in Roman Galilee* (Totowa, NJ: Roman and Allenheld, 1983) 27. The term *polichne*, which Josephus used frequently (*J.W.* 1.22, 41, 334, 3.20, 134, 430, 4.84, etc.), seems to be a word for town or large village.

The rabbinic terms for cities, towns, and villages are as follows: *kĕrak*, *ʿiř*, *ʿirah*, *qiryah*, and *kāpār*. The middle three terms appear to have been roughly equivalent in size, representing a median between *kĕrak*, the large walled city, and *kāpār*, the small un-walled village. An *ʿiř* could also be a very small hamlet. S. Krauss, followed by S. Dar, affirmed that the *kĕrak* was the equivalent of the *polis* in the technical sense.[6] S. Applebaum affirmed that the *ʿiř* was not only a medium-sized town, but also could mean an isolated farm (similar to a Roman villa).[7] This position has been accepted by S. Safrai and Dar, but received with skepticism by M. Goodman.[8] Applebaum further asserts that the terms *ʿirah* and *qiryah* referred to settlements linked to large administrative centers, either in a tenurial relationship to the center of a vast estate, or to an urban center.[9] So much of this seems speculative that we would have to agree with Goodman to be cautious in giving consent.

The simplest procedure is to refer to the three most common usages in the rabbinic literature: the *kĕrak*, the *ʿiř* and the *kāpār*.[10] Of these three terms, the most frequently used in the Mishnah is *ʿiř*.[11] Thus, it could be concluded that most peasants lived in the Mishnaic period in a town or large village in population midway between the small village, *kāpār*, and the city, *kĕrak*. But whether that conclusion is appropriate for the Herodian period must be determined on the basis of the material remains.

The number of inhabitants of a typical town and village is only now being clarified by archaeologists. Z. Yeivin[12] discussed ten towns in

6. S. Krauss "City and Country" *He-Atid* 3 (1923) 50–61; cited in S. Dar, *Landscape and Pattern* (Oxford: BAR, 1986) 21.

7. S. Applebaum, "Economic Life in Palestine" in S. Safrai and M. Stern, *Compendia Rerum Iudicarum* (Assen/Amsterdam: Van Gorcum, 1976) I.2, 643; and Applebaum, "The Settlement Pattern of Western Samaria from Hellenistic to Byzantine Times" in S. Dar, *Landscape and Pattern*, 263.

8. S. Safrai, "The Jewish City in Eretz Israel" *City and Community*, 227–236 (Heb.) cited in Dar, *Landscape and Pattern*, 21f; Goodman, *State and Society*, 28. See M. Erub 5:6 and t.BB 3:5 on selling an *ʿir*.

9. Applebaum, "Economic Life", 644.

10. M. Erub 5:1, 5:3, 5:6; m. Shek 1:1, m. Meg 1:1, 1:2, 1:3, 2:3, 3:1. m. Ket 1:1, m. Arak 9:6, m. Kelim 1:7. See Schürer, et al., *History of the Jewish People*, II, 188f.

11 Goodman, *State and Society*, 28, affirms that the term *ʿir* is used in the Mishnah over one hundred times, *kĕrak* only eleven times, and *kāpār* twelve times.

12. Z. Yeivin, *Survey of Settlements in Galilee and the Golan from the Period of the Mishnah in Light of the Sources* (Hebrew University: PhD diss., 1971) VI.

Galilee and the Golan, falling mainly into the following categories: large towns (22 to 25 acres), and middle-sized towns (10 to 17 acres). He also listed one town with 2.5 acres.

D. Urman's[13] survey of the Golan discovered one site over 175 acres; four sites from 30 to 50 acres; 14 sites with 10 to 30 acres; 28 sites which were 5 to 10 acres; 54 sites which were 2.5 to 5 acres; and 33 sites with less than 2.5 acres. Those 87 sites of 5 acres or less were either small villages/hamlets or single farms. The distinction cannot be determined without excavation.

S. Dar[14] gives the measurement of six villages in Samaria at 4 to 5 acres, 3.5 acres, 6 acres, 6 to 7.5 acres, 2.4 acres, and 10 acres. The team of R. Frankel has made a survey of Upper Galilee recently.[15] Although the survey identified settlements from the Neolithic through the Ottoman periods, we can select out the settlements that are relevant to our study.[16] The survey indicates that of the 74 sites that relate to our inquiry, 37 were less than 2.5 acres, 27 were 2.5 to 5 acres, seven sites were 5 to 10 acres; and three sites were 10 to 30 acres.

Finally, we might add a few sites from Lower Galilee that have been excavated, some of them some time ago, others more recently. Nazareth, Jesus' hometown, is difficult to measure since the ancient village lies underneath two modern churches. J. D. Crossan and J. Reed[17] suggest that the village covered 10 acres, but that much of it was empty space because of gardens, orchards, and places for livestock. S. Loffreda calculates the size of Capernaum to have been between 10 and 12 acres.[18] P. Richardson has likewise estimated that Cana (8 to 9 acres), as well as

13. D. Urman, *The Golan* (Oxford: BAR, 1985) 87f, 93.

14. Dar, *Landscape and Pattern*, 51, 53, 42, 47, 36, 231.

15. R. Frankel, N. Getzov, M. Aviam and A. Degani, *Settlement Dynamics and Regional Diversity in Ancient Galilee* (Jeruslaem: Israel Antiquities Authority, 2001).

16. I have selected only settlements that include Hellenistic and/or Roman occupation, and that did not continue past the Byzantine period.

17. Crossan and Reed, *Excavating Jesus* (San Francisco: HarperSanFrancisco, 2001) 34. On the other hand, J. Strange ("Nazareth" *ABD* IV, 1050) surmises that it covered an area of 60 acres.

18. Loffreda, "Capernaum" *NEAEHL* I, 292. But Crossan and Reed, *Excavating Jesus*, 81, suggest 25 acres was the size of Capernaum, and that it had a population of 1000. In another publication, Reed (*Archaeology and the Galilean Jesus* [Harrisburg, PA: Trinity Press, 2000] 83) suggests that the population of Capernaum was 1,700. See my calculation below.

Yodefat (10 acres), were in this same size-range.[19] The site of Shihkin (Asochis) has now been identified (see below). The survey team of J. F. Strange, D. E. Groh, and T. R. Longstaff estimate the occupation area of this important industrial town at 27 acres.[20] Finally, Crossan and Reed estimate the size of Sepphoris at 100 to 150 acres.[21]

It appears from these findings that most peasants lived in towns or villages less than 10 acres in size. The ten towns examined by Yeivin may not then be typical of Galilean peasant life, at least for the Herodian period. We presume that the same conditions that prevailed in Upper Galilee, the Golan, and Samaria, also existed in Lower Galilee, as our brief survey of a few villages and towns seems to confirm.

The population of these towns and villages may be figured by counting the number of houses, and multiplying by five (for five inhabitants on average to a room), then subtracting 25 percent to allow rooms for storage and animals. Yeivin has, in this manner, estimated the population of several cities in Galilee and the Golan:

Table 1 Yeivin's Population Estimates[22]	
Site	Population
Juhadr	5250
Mazraat Kuneitra	900
Khirbet Shema	1250
Arbel	5000
Usha	3000

Most of these towns appear to have flourished in the Mishnaic period, and thus we must be cautious in affirming that they give us an appropriate sample in size of a typical Herodian peasant village or town. Further, the method of counting dwellings is not always appropriate since many villages are not preserved enough to identify the living quarters.

19. P. Richardson, *Building Jewish in the Roman East* (Waco,TX: Baylor University Press, 2004) 81.

20. Strange, Groh, and Longstaff, "The Location and Identification of Ancient Shikhin (Asochis)" *IEJ* 44 (1994) 216–227; 45 (1995) 171–87 available on-line at http://www.colby.edu/rel/archaeology/Shikhin.html.

21. Crossan and Reed, *Excavating Jesus*, 81.

22. Yeivin, *Survey of Settlements*, VI.

Another method of determining population is to multiply the number of acres of the site times the supposed number of people that on average lived on one acre in antiquity. The figure accepted by both M. Broshi and Y. Shiloh is 160 to 200 people per acre.[23] The higher number seems too many persons per acre since there must have been in most villages spaces for threshing floors, perhaps gardens, and even areas where nomadic folk and travelers stayed in tents.[24] I incline, therefore, toward the lower number of 160 persons per acre.

Thus, using the lower number, Yeivin's towns ranged from 3520 to 4000 for large towns, 1600 to 2720 for medium-sized towns, and lists one village of 400 people. Likewise, according to Urman's figures, the Golan had one city with over 28,000 people (Caesarea Philippi), four towns or cities with 4800 to 8,000 people, 14 towns with populations ranging from 1600 to 4800 people, 28 villages with populations of 800 to 1600, 54 villages with populations of 400 to 800, and 33 villages with populations less than 400 people. The four Samaritan villages had populations of 640–800 people, 560 people, 960 people, 960–1200 people, 384 people, and 1600 people, respectively.[25] The survey of Upper Galilee indicates that 37 villages had less than 400 persons, 27 villages had 400 to 800 persons, seven villages had 800 to 1600 persons, and three towns had 1600 to 4800 persons. The four villages listed from Lower Galilee would all be between 1,280 and 1920 persons.[26] The larger town, Kfar Shikhin, would number 4320 persons. Using this calculation method, Sepphoris would have numbered around 16,000 persons.[27] But since Sepphoris had

23. Broshi, "The Population of Western Palestine in the Roman-Byzantine Period" *BASOR* 236 (1979) 1–10; Shiloh, "The Population of Iron Age Palestine in the Light of a Sample Analysis of Urban Plans, Areas, and Population Density" *BASOR* 239 (1980) 25–35.

24. See the work on a modern village in the Middle East: L. Sweet, *Tel Toqaan: A Syrian Village* (Ann Arbor: University of Michigan, 1974) 52.

25. Dar often estimates the population, however, at more than these amounts. For example, the population of Hirbet Hajar would be, at most, 1000 people using Broshi's method, but Dar estimates the population at 1500 to 2000. See Dar, *Landscape and Pattern*, 51. The average village in Egypt may have been somewhat larger. Cf. N. Lewis, *Life in Egypt Under Roman Rule* (Oxford: Clarendon, 1983) 68.

26. But Crossan and Reed (*Excavating Jesus*, 34) estimate the population of Nazareth at 200 to 400 persons in spite of their suggested 10 acre size for the village. Strange (*ABD* IV, 1050) calculates the population of Nazareth at 480 or less. Richardson (*Building Roman*, 76) suggests that Yodefat had a population of 1,000.

27. Compare the calculation given at the beginning of this essay. This figure is closer

more open spaces than most villages, a market place, wide streets, much larger houses for the same number of family members as a village house, perhaps we should estimate it even lower. Thus, a range of 10,000 to 12,000 seems more feasible.

Table 2: Villages in Galilee, Golan and Samaria		
	Site in Acres	*Population Estimates (160 person/acre)*
Yeivin	22–25	3520–4000
	10–17	1600–2720
	2.5	400
Urman	1 site, 175	28,000
	4 sites, 30–50	4,800–8,000
	14 sites, 10–30	1,600–4,800
	28 sites, 5–10	800–1,600
	54 sites, 2.5–5	400–800
	33 sites, less than 2.5	Less than 400
Frankel et al.	3 sites, 10–30	1.600–4,800
	7 sites, 5–10	800–1,600
	27 sites, 2.5–5	400–800
	37 sites, less than 2.5	Less than 400
Dar	4–5	640–800
	3.5	560
	6	960
	6–7.5	960–1,200
	2.4	384
	10	1,600
Lower Galilee Sites	3 sites, 10	1,600
	1 site, 5–10	800–1,600
	1 site, 10–30	4,320
	1 site, 100 to 150	16,000–24,000 (10,000–12,000)

to that of E. Meyers (note 2). The size of Tiberias is yet to be determined since most of it now lies under the modern city.

Most of the villages cited by Dar date from the Hasmonean through the Herodian (one through Byzantine) period. The towns in the Golan range from the early Roman to the Byzantine periods. All of those selected from the Upper Galilee survey are Hellenistic or Roman. All of those listed from Lower Galilee are Herodian (or Early Roman= 30 BC to AD 70). Thus, it appears that most peasants in the two Galilees, the Golan, and Samaria, during the Roman period, lived in villages from around a couple hundred in population to around 2000 inhabitants.

A. Ben David has attempted to define the Hebrew terms for town in the Mishnaic period, assigning to each a population figure:

1. A hamlet (ʿiř)—50 inhabitants or less

2. A village (kāpār)—400 to 600 inhabitants

3. A country town (ʿiř)—600 to 7500 inhabitants

4. A large city (kĕrak)—10,000 to 60,000 inhabitants[28]

His figures seem to harmonize roughly with what we have discussed above. It is interesting that Ben-David's four categories also fit with the depictions of towns and cities in the Madaba Map. Small villages are depicted as buildings having two towers, larger villages with three towers, small cities with four or five towers (e.g., Jericho, Azotus), and large cities are represented much like in an aerial photograph showing actual walls and buildings (e.g., Jerusalem, Jamnia, Ascalon).[29]

Therefore, I suggest the following categories based on Ben David:

Table 3: Categories of Villages, Towns, and Cities in Galilee in the Herodian Period				
Village	kōmē (Gk)	kapār (Heb)	2000 inhabitants or less	e.g. Nazareth, Cana, Yodefat, Capernaum
Town	kōmē (Gk)	ʿiř (Heb)	2000 to 6000 inhabitants	e.g. Shikhin
City	polis (Gk)	kĕrak (Heb)	Over 6000 inhabitants	e.g. Sepphoris

28. A. Ben-David, *Talmudische Ökonomie*, (Hildesheim: Georg Olms, 1974) 49.

29. See M. Avi-Yonah, *The Madaba Mosaic Map* (Jerusalem: Israel Exploration Society, 1954) 21f.

Thus, although Josephus states that even the smallest village in Galilee had over 15,000 inhabitants,[30] the archaeological data indicate that most folk in Samaria, Golan, and Upper and Lower Galilee lived in villages (*kĕparim*) that numbered between a few hundred to 2000 persons.

II. WHAT WAS IN A VILLAGE OR A TOWN OF GALILEE?

Next, to describe a typical Galilean small town or village we will compare the hypothetical "medium-sized town" of the Mishnaic period, which Z. Yeivin has constructed, with an actual peasant village of the Herodian period described by Dar. Yeivin has put together a composite of an ʿiř bānônît, or town of medium size, based on the plans of Khorazin and Einan in Galilee, Nahef and Naaran in the Golan, and Horvat Susia in Judea. Although these towns flourished in the late second century AD, they do not seem to differ markedly from the Herodian village (first century AD) described by Dar as far as their layout and the type of buildings are concerned.

Yeivin's composite town indicates no street planning. The streets were haphazardly determined, often leaving open areas which became public domain. This arrangement can be observed in several of the villages in Lower Galilee, particularly Capernaum,[31] and is often noted by observers of modern Middle Eastern villages.[32] (Contrast this with Sepphoris, which had streets running parallel and perpendicular in an orthogonal grid pattern.) The town had no gates or fortified walls, but the houses were often built touching each other so that they formed a kind of *de facto* protective outer wall. Yeivin's hypothetical town has a synagogue. Nearby is the cemetery (*bayit haqqibrôt*).[33] According to Yeivin's previous estimates, a "medium-sized town" would have an area of ten to seventeen acres, and thus a population of 1600 to 2720 people. Although the composite village is Mishnaic, the buildings and their ar-

30. Josephus, *J.W.* 3.43.

31. Crossan and Reed, *Excavating Jesus*, 81.

32. See J. W. McGarvey, *Lands of the Bible* (Nashville: Gospel Advocate, 1966) 105, 108; L. Sweet, *Tell Toqaan,* 51, 54 (The streets are mere "cow paths."); A. M. Lutfiyya, *Baytin: A Jordanian Village* (London: Mouton, 1966) 20. For open areas as public domain, see also Sweet, 55.

33. Z. Yeivin, "On the Medium-Sized City," *Eretz Israel* 19 (1987) 59–71 (Heb. with Eng. summary).

rangement surely did not change that much from the Herodian to the Mishnaic period.

The village in Samaria known as Khirbet Karqush will serve as our example of an actual village from the Hasmonean-Herodian period. This village, although not in Lower Galilee, is a helpful model because so many of its structures are well preserved. Dar[34] was able to date the village from the tombs in the nearby cemetery. The village covers an area of 3.5 acres, and thus would have had a population of from 560 to 700 people, according to Broshi's method of computing population, a typical size for the Herodian period. Dar used Yeivin's method of determining the population, and concluded that the village held around 600 people. Dar divides the village structures into two main blocks: A and B. Block A, which may be a later (Byzantine) section of the village, contained several courtyard houses. Across the street from Block A (in Block B) were several more courtyard houses. Dar believes that one of the buildings was a water reservoir. Another building had an unknown function, and was built in the Hellenistic period. There were also several parts of an oil press found in the village which were not *in situ*.

Dar believes that two of the buildings were public buildings. He found several other examples of such buildings in Samaritan villages,[35] and from other evidence we know that most villages in Syria, even small ones, had public buildings of some sort.[36] The buildings were not evidently financed from taxes, but from donations of wealthy families when such families lived in or near the village, and perhaps also from the revenues of village owned land.

The one public building we cannot be sure existed in first century AD Galilean villages was the synagogue. Certainly synagogues existed in the Herodian period, but that most villages had a separate building for them is unproven. Most of the remains of the oldest synagogues are from the end of the second century or beginning of the third century AD.[37] Probably many of the towns also had commercial buildings.[38]

---

34. Dar, *Landscape and Pattern*, 42–46.

35. Dar, *Landscape and Pattern*, 49.

36. M. Harper, "Village Administration in the Roman Province of Syria," *Yale Classical Studies* 1 (1928) 105–168; and A. H. M. Jones, *The Greek City From Alexander To Justinian* (Oxford: Clarendon, 1940) 286.

37. See H. Shanks, *Judaism in Stone* (Jerusalem: Steinmatzky, 1979) 17–30.

38. Such as the building found at Nabratein by E. Meyers, J. Strange, and C. L.

Southeast of the village of Khirbet Karqush lay the cemetery, with both the Kukh type of burial and open cist graves. Dar found sixteen systems of Kokhim tombs, and twenty dwelling units in the village. Thus, he concludes that most families had a hypogeum. Evidently, however, the poorer families did not.

There was some evidence that one family was wealthier than the others. Dar found an ornamental tomb in the cemetery, and a larger than usual courtyard house. Yet, the difference in economic status must have been small, argues Dar, so that this family was only *primus inter pares*. In other words, this family probably did not own the village.

Just north of the supposed water reservoir was a large open square. One wonders if this area had a specific purpose such as a village market place, which would have been the center for exchange in ancient Palestine.[39] The Synoptic Gospels indicate that most small towns and villages had markets[40] in addition to major market centers such as what existed in Jerusalem, Sepphoris, Shechem, Lydda, and Antipatris.[41] It is possible that such open areas served as temporary market places in villages on the market day.[42] Alternatively, open areas may have been tent cities for seasonal nomadic visitors. Such village areas are known in modern Middle Eastern villages.[43]

The hypothetical medium-sized town of Yeivin, and this actual village in rural Samaria described by Dar, indicate common patterns. Most villages of any size had not only residences, but public and commercial buildings, agricultural structures (oil or wine presses), cemeteries outside the village, and open spaces which were perhaps used on market days as temporary markets. They also had narrow, unpaved streets arranged in haphazard patterns, and they had no gates or walls.[44]

Meyers. See "Second Preliminary Report on the 1981 Excavations at en-Nabratein, Israel," *BASOR* 246 (1982) 35–54.

39. The market place was called *šūq* in the rabbinic literature (see Jastrow) and *agora* in the Gospels (Mk 6:56). See also Goodman, *State and Society*, 54.

40. See Mk 6:56, 7:4, 12:28, Matt. 11:16=Luke 7:32, Matt. 20:3, Matt. 23:7=Luke 11:43.

41. Applebaum, "Economic Life", 687.

42. The pre-Mishnaic market day was Friday. See Applebaum, "Economic Life," 687, and Goodman, *State and Society*, 54.

43. L. Sweet, *Tel Toqaan: A Syrian Village*, 52.

44. See, e.g., Capernaum (Crossan and Reed, *Excavating Jesus*, 81); and Nazareth (Reed, *Archaeology and the Galilean Jesus*, 131).

By way of contrast, the cities of Sepphoris and Tiberias were planned constructions with streets in a grid pattern. In each is found a Cardo, or main street over 40 feet wide. Tiberias had a stadium for athletic games, a monumental gate, and possibly a gymnasium. Sepphoris had a large basilica (115 x 130 feet), i.e. a building used for government purposes (administration or law courts).[45] Finally, there may have been a theater built in Sepphoris in the first century AD, but the date of this structure is debated.[46] The cities had spacious streets, market places, large public buildings, large domestic quarters, and more comforts of life such as entertainment. To go from village to city was to cross into a new subculture.

III. WHAT DID THEY DO FOR A LIVING IN GALILEE?

Most villages were supported by agriculture.[47] If Dar's findings in Samaria are typical, the individual farm plots (one for each nuclear family) were marked off in the fields surrounding the village. The farmer, then, did not reside on his farm plot, but walked out to it from the village to work it. The village residents huddled together in close quarters in the village. A good example of this arrangement can be seen in the village of Qawarat Bene-Hassan in Samaria, described by Dar. There the village and surrounding farm plots, marked off by stone walls, are still well preserved. Similar farm plot systems were discovered by Dar's survey team in several other villages.[48]

45. See Crossan and Reed, *Excavating Jesus*, 60–67; M. Dothan, *Hamath Tiberias* (Jerusalem: Israel Exploration Society, 1983) 16. See on the basilica in Sepphoris: J. Strange, "The Eastern Basilical Building" in Rebecca M. Nagy, Carol L. Meyers, E. M. Meyers, and Z. Weiss, eds., *Sepphoris in Galilee* (Winona Lake: Eisenbrauns, 1996) 117–21. The building consisted of rows of offices or shops, all with floor mosaics. One room had a stepped pool.

46. For a date in the early first century (thus the time of Antipas and Jesus) see J. Strange, "Six Campaigns at Sepphoris" in L. I. Levine, *The Galilee in Late Antiquity* (New York: Jewish Theological Seminary, 1992) 342; and R. Batey, *Jesus and the Forgotten City* (Grand Rapids: Baker, 1992) 83–103. For a date of late first century or early second century for the theater see: Z. Weiss and E. Netzer, "Hellenistic and Roman Sepphoris: The Archaeological Evidence" in Nagy, C. Meyers, E. Meyers, and Weiss, eds., *Sepphoris in Galilee*, 32; C. L. Meyers and E. M. Meyers, "Sepphoris" in E. Meyers, ed., *OEANE* IV, 533; and E. M. Meyers, "Jesus and His World: Sepphoris and the Quest for the Historical Jesus" C. G. den Hertog, U. Huebner, and S. Muenger, eds., *Saxa Loquentur: Studien zur Archäologie Palästinas/Israels* (Münster: Ugarit, 2003) 198–90.

47. See M. Avi-Yonah, *The Holy Land* (Grand Rapids: Baker, 1966) 188–89.

48. E.g., see Dar, *Landscape and Pattern*, Figure 45, (Hirbet Burqa). See also Ben-David, *Talmudische Ökonomie*, 49. Compare also the results of the survey of the Golan by Urman, *Golan*, 93, who notes that most of the villages and towns had an agricultural

But the agricultural base does not mean that there was no industry in Herodian Palestine, especially in Lower Galilee. As a matter of fact, there may have been more industry in Lower Galilee than elsewhere in Palestine. Y. Magen's work on stoneware production has brought to light, for example, two quarry workshops in Lower Galilee, one in Bethlehem of Galilee (just southwest of Sepphoris), and the other in Kefar Reina (just east of Sepphoris). These were major producers of stone cups and other vessels. Stoneware has been discovered throughout Galilee as well (in 12 villages and cities).[49]

Further, the pottery of two villages, Kefar Hananya and Kefar Shikhin, already well known from the rabbinic sources (m.Kel 2:2; b.BM 74a; b.Shab 120b), has now been discovered archaeologically. D. Adan-Bayewitz and I. Perlman have established that the tiny village of Kefar Hananya (located on the border between Lower Galilee and Upper Galilee) exported its common pottery up to 24 kilometers away into Galilee and the Golan. The pottery manufactured in this village has shown up in Nazareth, Capernaum, Kefar Kanna, Tiberias, and Magdala in Lower Galilee, and in Meiron, Khirbet Shema and Tel Anafa in Upper Galilee, among other sites. It also appears in the ruins of Gentile cities such as Acco-Ptolemais, Hippos, Pella, and Scythopolis.[50] Further, it is clear that 75 percent of the first century common table wares (so far only cooking bowls) excavated at Sepphoris were made in Kefar Hananya. In addition, 15 percent of the storage jars, or kraters, discovered thus far in Sepphoris originated in the nearby town of Shikhin. As a matter of fact, the Shikhin storage jars account for the majority of pottery of that type in Galilee.[51] Two conclusions are usually drawn from these data. First, the cities with their rich people must not have completely exploited the peasants who lived in the villages, but rather must have given them opportunities for marketing their goods

economy. Cf. Lewis, *Life in Egypt*, 65.

49. Y. Magen, *The Stone Vessel Industry in the Second Temple Period* (Jerusalem: Israel Exploration Society, 2002) 160.

50. Adan-Bayewitz and Perlman, "The Socio-Economic and Cultural Ethos of the Lower Galilee in the First Century: Implications for the Nascent Jesus Movement" in L. I. Levine, ed., *The Galilee in Late Antiquity*, 53–91.

51. J. Strange, D. E. Groh, and T. R. Longstaff, "Excavations at Sepphoris: The Location and Identification of Shikhin" *IEJ* 44 (1994) 216–27. The process by which these conclusions were made is called neutron activation analysis. The scientific test allows the excavators to determine the chemical content of the clay used in making the pottery. The clay content of many of the wares found in the villages and cities of Galilee indicates that much of the pottery came from the area of Kefar Hananya, and that many of the large jars came from the town of Shikhin (1.5 kilometers from Sepphoris).

and thus increase their economic situation. Second, the villages not only engaged in farming, but had industries as well. [52]

Shikhin (Asochis) was a town spread over 27 acres. Today the ruins do not allow a good analysis of housing types since so many of the stones have been cannibalized by successive occupations, and since the entire site is now an olive orchard. But from the meager ruins one can detect evidence of some well-constructed buildings. One was 32 feet long with walls from 2.6 to 3.25 feet thick. A second one was 27.6 feet long. A third was 20 feet long with walls 1.6 feet thick. A fourth was constructed of cut stones, 1.8 feet thick, and preserved to a length of 8.7 feet. [53] These are huge buildings for this period which would indicate that they are either industrial buildings or a dwelling for a family with an above average amount of wealth.

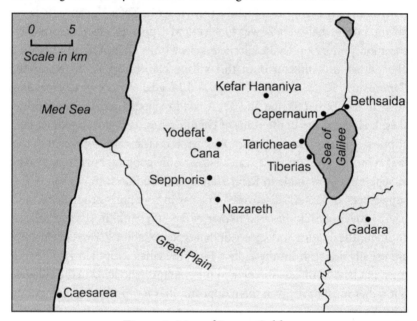

Figure 1: Map of Lower Galilee

52. See D. Adan-Bayewitz, *Common Pottery in Roman Galilee* (Ramat-Gan, Israel: Bar-Ilan University Press, 1993) 23–41, 216–236; idem., "Kefar Hananya, 1986" *IEJ* 37 (1987) 178–179; D. Adan-Bayewitz and I. Perlman, "The Local Trade of Sepphoris in the Roman Period" *IEJ* 40 (1990) 153–172; J. Strange, "First Century Galilee from Archaeology and from the Texts" in D. R. Edwards and C. T. McCollough, eds., *Archaeology and the Galilee*, 41; D. R. Edwards, "First Century Urban/Rural Relations in Lower Galilee: Exploring the Archaeological and Literary Evidence" *SBL 1988 Seminar Papers*, 169–182; E. Meyers, "Jesus and His Galilean Context" in Edwards and McCollough, *Archaeology and the Galilee*, 57–66.

53. Strange, Groh, and Longstaff, "The Location and Identification of Ancient Shikhin (Asochis)" *IEJ* 44 (1994) 216–27; 45 (1995) 171–87 available on-line at http://www.colby.edu/rel/archaeology/Shikhin.html.

Further archaeological evidence as to the economies of the villages in Lower Galilee comes from the excavations of five villages. The first two villages, Khirbet Qana (probably the Cana of the New Testament), and Yodefat (or Jotapata) were somewhat more prosperous than the other three. The results of excavating these two villages have been collected by P. Richardson.[54] What he found was that Cana had some small industry. Two *columbaria* (dove cotes) have been found, and a wool dying installation has been identified. Further, at Khirbet Qana there were three types of houses, representing evidently three tiers of economic prosperity in the village. But most residents lived in the simple terrace houses which shared walls with one another. The houses were made of un-hewn stones, and had mud floors. Their roofs were of sticks and mud.[55]

Likewise, the houses of Yodefat were one or two stories of rough masonry. The walls were filled with mud plaster, and the floors were beaten earth. There was little evidence of public buildings in Yodefat. There were some large cisterns and two large open pools, evidently for community use. This village was walled. One large house in Yodefat had rather elaborate frescoes in a style similar to those in the Herodian palace at Masada, as well as in the houses of the wealthy in Jerusalem.[56] Thus, at least one family there had attained a measure of wealth. Near Yodefat was a cave that had an "industrial-scale double press olive oil station." This installation would seem to indicate more olive oil production than was necessary simply for private use. There was, therefore, an olive oil business in Yodefat. The most important industry in Yodefat, however, seems to have been pottery making, since several kilns are evident among the ruins.[57]

We might also compare these two villages with three others: Nazareth, Capernaum, and Bethsaida (the last of which was not technically in Lower Galilee). Nazareth was exclusively an agricultural village. So far, the excavations under the two churches in modern Nazareth (Church of St. Joseph and Church of the Annunciation) have revealed granaries, pits, vaulted cells for storing wine and oil, and oil presses.[58]

---

54. Richardson, *Building Jewish in the Roman East* (Waco, TX: Baylor University Press, 2004) 57–71.

55. The other two types of houses were side courtyard houses (the second tier) and central courtyard houses (the upper tier). Richardson, *Building Jewish*, 103–4.

56. M. Aviam, "Yodefat" *Hadashot Arkhelogiyot* 112 (2000) 18–19.

57. Richardson, *Building Jewish*, 57–71.

58. B. Bagatti, "Nazareth, Excavations" *NEAEHL* III, 1103–105.

Only slight traces of the houses have been left, leading one archaeologist to suggest that the houses must have been made of fieldstones and mud.[59] In addition, many of the houses were constructed around caves (that is, the caves were used for dwellings). These villagers do not seem to have been as prosperous as those at Yodefat and Khirbet Qana. Nor do they seem to have had any industry or way to make a living beyond farming.

Capernaum was a medium sized fishing and agricultural village. The private houses were built of undressed basalt field stones stacked without mortar. Small house-rooms (in *insula* fashion) surrounded large courtyards (the largest is 24 x 19.5 feet).[60] The walls are so weak that V. Corbo surmised that they could never have held a stone slab roof. The roofs must have been sticks and mud. Finally, there are no houses such as those of the upper tier at Khirbet Qana, and certainly none discovered thus far with elaborate and expensive frescoes such as the one at Yodefat.

Finally, Bethsaida was a small town, perhaps slightly larger than Capernaum, with fishing persons and farmers. The excavator describes the residential quarter from the Herodian period as a "humble community of country people who lived in poor dwellings and were occupied in fishing, viticulture, and livestock raising."[61] The houses were constructed similarly to those in Capernaum. Although Bethsaida lay in antiquity just outside the boundaries of Lower Galilee, its houses and economy were similar to what we find in the other villages.

59. Reed, *Archaeology and the Galilean Jesus*, 132.

60. V. Corbo, *The House of Saint Peter at Capharnaum* (Jerusalem: Franciscan, 1972) 35–52; J. F. Strange and H. Shanks, "Has the House Where Jesus Stayed in Capernaum been Found?" *BAR* 8/6 (1982) 26–37; S. Loffreda, "Capernaum" *NEAEHL* I, 291–95.

61. R. Arav, "Bethsaida Excavations: Preliminary Report, 1994–1996" in Arav and R. Freund, eds., *Bethsaida* (Kirksville, MO: Truman State University Press, 1999) II, 3–113.

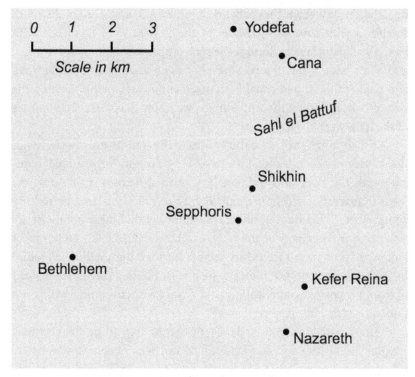

Figure 2: Map of Sepphoris and Vicinity

So, most residents of Lower Galilee in the first century AD would have lived in a village with a few hundred to 2000 inhabitants, and would have been engaged in agriculture, though some would have been involved in industry. It was not uncommon for entire villages to be devoted to one type of industry[62] such as the villages mentioned above which were devoted to pottery or stone ware vessels.

By way of contrast, if one lived in one of the two cities of Lower Galilee, Sepphoris or Tiberias, life would have been quite different. Many of those living in the cities were either the richest of the rich, or were their "retainers," those hired to meet the administrative needs of the rich. The houses of some of these wealthy persons may have been discovered in Sepphoris in the domestic quarter on the western slope of the acropolis. E. Meyers, one of the excavators of Sepphoris, believes that it was inhabited by "well-to-do aristocratic Jews."[63] The houses in

62. See J. Klausner, *Jesus of Nazareth* (New York: MacMillan, 1925) 178; Avi-Yonah, *The Holy Land*, 193.

63. E. Meyers, "Roman Sepphoris in Light of New Archaeological Evidence and

this quarter date from the early first century AD, and were multi-room dwellings with courtyards. Many of the houses were furnished with fresco wall paintings of floral scenes (no animals or human depictions), and a few had mosaic floors. Several of the houses were multi-storied, and many of them had ritual bath installations (stepped pools). By the size of houses and by the furnishings, we know that these were houses of the well-off.[64]

Yet, although they were the houses of the well-to-do, they were not the houses of the extravagantly rich. They do not, for example, compare with the large and elaborately furnished mansions found in the Jewish Quarter of old Jerusalem[65] dating to the same time period. By comparison of the houses alone, we would say that these are modestly rich persons. They may be the richest in Lower Galilee, but not in all of Palestine/Israel in the Herodian period. Further, the small items found inside the houses do not indicate great wealth. They used bone instead of ivory for cosmetic applications; they employed common pottery, not fine ware; they imported no wines.[66]

Thus, based on the evidence of the houses from first century Sepphoris discovered so far (Tiberias has not been excavated adequately for such an assessment[67]), we would have to say that a small percentage of the inhabitants of Lower Galilee lived in an urban setting, and in plush but not extravagantly lavish houses. Those in the villages ranged from rather comfortable to very simple structures. Probably there were

---

Recent Research," in L. I. Levine, ed., *The Galilee in Late Antiquity*, 322.

64. See E. Netzer and Z. Weiss, *Zippori* (Jerusalem: Israel Exploration Society, 1994) 21–23; Carol L. Meyers and E. M. Meyers, "Sepphoris" in E. M. Meyers, ed., *OEANE* IV, 531–532; J. Reed, *Archaeology and the Galilean Jesus*, 126; and Z. Weiss and E. Netzer, "Hellenistic and Roman Sepphoris: The Archaeological Evidence" in Rebecca Martin Nagy, Carol L. Meyers, E. M. Meyers, Z. Weiss, eds., *Sepphoris in Galilee: Crosscurrents of Culture*, 29–37; K. G. Hoglund and E. M. Meyers, "The Residential Quarter on the Western Summit," in *Sepphoris in Galilee*, 40.

65. See N. Avigad, "How the Wealthy Lived in Herodian Jerusalem," *BAR* 2 (1976) 22–35. E. M. Meyers, "The Problems of Gendered Space in Syro- Palestinian Domestic Architecture," D. L. Balch and Carolyn Osiek, eds., *Early Christian Families in Context* (Grand Rapids: Eerdmans, 2003) Where Meyers indicates that the "Great Mansion" of Jerusalem had a living area of 600 square meters while a large house excavated at Sepphoris (building 84.1) had an area of 300 square meters.

66. Reed, *Archaeology and the Galilean Jesus*, 126.

67. See Y. Hirschfeld, "Tiberias" in E. Stern, ed., *NEAEHL* IV, 1466–1467.

also the very poor residents of villages, and those who dwelled on the outskirts of the cities that lived in mud huts, tents, or caves.

CONCLUSION

If the reader had lived in Lower Galilee in the first century AD, chances are he/she would have lived in a village of less than 2000 inhabitants. The village would have consisted mostly of simply made houses haphazardly planned, unpaved streets, perhaps a public building or two, and a few open areas used on market day or by nomadic persons for pitching their tents. If the reader were fortunate enough to have lived in one of the two cities, he/she would have known wide thoroughfares, impressive architecture, and various forms of entertainment. If the reader had lived in a village, he/she would probably have been engaged in agricultural pursuits, but certain kinds of industry (especially pottery production) would also not have been out of the question.

8

Roof Tiles and How They Relate to the Interpretation of the Synoptic Gospels

Robert W. Smith

"ROOF TILES, MARBLE FLOOR fragments, tesserae, and chunks of mortar are regularly regarded as little more than rubbish at Roman and Byzantine era archaeological sites, but they are worthy of careful consideration." Dr. Reuben Bullard made this assertion to his students at the Abila of the Decapolis Expedition in 1984.[1] He then proceeded to assign each to the task of looking after the processing and registry of one of these classes of materials that may have otherwise been neglected.[2] These heavy architectural elements are often underappreciated. They are dug from the ground, sometimes by the wheelbarrow load. Some are tagged, bagged, carried, cleaned, and counted. A select few are measured, labeled, and drawn.

Nonetheless, such a study can help develop a roof tile typology for the region. A more thorough comprehension of roof tile production and style can also enhance New Testament scholarship. This is especially true with regard to one pericope in the canonical Gospels.[3] The study of

---

1. The Abila of the Decapolis Expedition was directed by W. Harold Mare from 1980–2004.

2. John Wineland was assigned tesserae, the polychrome cubes of cut stone from which mosaics are made. Kraig Stanforth was assigned marble and fragments of the *opus sectile* floors. Steve Ray was assigned mortar, and Robert Smith was assigned roof tiles.

3. This was something that could make the wrestling with roof tiles worthwhile, and still keeps me excited about pursuing the sometimes tedious tasks of archaeology decades later. The interaction with my archaeological mentor, Reuben Bullard, and the Abila expedition, in his favored words, "changed the course of my life."

roof tiles reveals how seemingly insignificant details can illuminate or complicate one's understanding of the Biblical texts.

This chapter proceeds in three steps. First, it offers observations about the history of roof tiles and roofing systems in the ancient Near East. Second, it describes the recovery and reconstruction of roof tiles and roofing systems at the site of Abila in Jordan. Third, it gathers together this knowledge of roof tiles and roofing systems in order to consider the account of the healed paralytic in Capernaum as recorded in the synoptic gospels (Matthew 9; Mark 2; Luke 5). It is hoped that this will encourage archaeologists to be diligent in examining and preserving mundane materials such as roof tiles, as they may hold the potential of helping to address significant questions. Similarly, it is hoped that this study will encourage students of the Bible to use archaeological evidence carefully.

THE HISTORY OF ROOF TILES AND ROOFING SYSTEMS

The history of roofing systems in the Levant begins with the flat packed clay roof. Such constructions were typical of Levantine homes for generations.[4] From the Jewish past, as preserved in the Old Testament books, the flat roof is clearly evidenced. The space on top of a house was used as a working space (Josh 2:6), a refuge from annoyances of life (Ecc 21:9), a place to hold private conversations in the evening (1 Sam 10:25), a place to host guests (1 Sam10:26; 2 Kgs 4:10), a place for nocturnal ambulation (2 Sam 11:2), and as a place to be seen (2 Sam 16:22) and from which to be heard (Isa 15:3). The roof was also the venue for religious observances of the Jews (Jer 32:29, Neh 8:16) and pagans (Jer 19:13; Zeph 1:5). Its use was so common that a parapet around the perimeter was required under the Mosaic Law to remove culpability for persons falling off such a roof (Deut. 22:8). In the first century references are found in the New Testament to Peter praying on a roof (Acts 10:9), and to proclamations of Jesus' message from rooftops (Matt 10:27).[5] The flat roof of houses in the Levant persists to this day with the new materials of concrete and iron reinforcements.

Access to a flat roof was gained by ladders and exterior staircases within courtyards. This type of roof was made using large dimension

4. Aharon Kempinski and Ronnie Reich eds., *Architecture of Ancient Israel* (Jerusalem: Israel Exploration Society, 1992) 26.

5. See Charles Warren, "Roof," in James Hastings ed. *A Dictionary of the Bible Vol 4*, ed. James Hastings (Edinburgh: T. & T. Clark, 1898) 311–313, for summary of Biblical references and Ottoman era customs.

beams laid horizontally at regular intervals to span the space between the closest parallel walls. Reeds, small branches, thatching, or matting were then laid on top of and perpendicular to the large beams spanning the gap between the beams. A thick layer of clay material was placed on the flat supportive structure, usually made of large unfired mud bricks laid closely together and then covered with a finishing coat of clay that was packed into place and allowed to bake in the sun (See Figure 1).

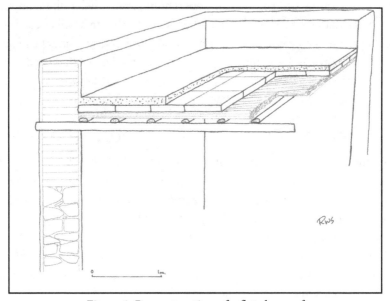

Figure 1: Reconstruction of a flat clay roof

The dried mud bricks provided immediate strength, having the advantage of not being squeezed through the underlying materials, thus being a substantially lighter load on the roof than wet mud.[6] The dried mud bricks also helped to distribute the weight of the construction workers as they installed the roof.[7] This clay roof was effective in arid regions, keeping the occupants cool in the summer and dry in the winter. The roof would last as long as rain water was not permitted to pool, and as long as it was

6. The typical Abila flat rooftile is a finger thick (slightly less than 2 cm). This stands in contrast to the ca. 15 cm thickness of the clay or plaster on the flat roofs. The weight of a square meter of packed clay 15 cm thick not counting the lumber would be over 80 kg/m 2 as compared to 40kg/m 2 for a pantile roof with cover tiles held in place by mortar. Tile roofs do not require thicker walls than a flat roof.

7. The use of mud bricks in making a flat roof was observed by the author in Syria during the summer of 1987 while working at Tel Tunenir.

regularly maintained by packing a new finishing layer of clay with a roller to replace what had eroded away. Well made and maintained flat clay roofs were substantial enough for considerable activity, and could easily support the weight of a family without threat of collapse. Evidence for the use of clay roofs at Abila and other archaeological sites is rarely found since continued occupants often cleared away collapsed materials. The clay from such clay roofs deteriorates together with mud-brick walls into clay rich soil that can be found covering stone remains of foundations and floors.

Roof tiles were made possible with the development of pyro-technology and ceramics. The plastic properties of clay allowed it to be shaped in a variety of forms as it dried and was fired. Clay objects were deliberately fashioned and fired as early as the Neolithic era. In time and place, hand-molded pottery gave way to wheel thrown and mold-made vessels. Some hand molded vessels and objects continued to be used throughout the history of the Ancient Near East. Sun dried bricks were used in wall construction, and by the time of the Bronze Age were being formed in rectangular molds.[8] In conjunction with sun baked bricks, fired bricks were used at sites where durable material was required for the exterior of walls or for steps.[9] Some of the fired bricks of Babylon were molded in raised relief to depict deities, and fired with colored glazing to create the grandeur of the Ishtar Gate. While there was great creativity in the architectural use of fired roof tiles, they were not employed in Palestine until after the conquest of the Greeks and Romans.

The use of roof tiles appears to have developed in the Aegean. The Greeks of the Archaic Era widely employed roof tiles. The idea was carried to their colonies around the Mediterranean. In Magna Graecia and Ionia, roofing technologies were copied by the colonial settlements. Two basic systems rose to prominence.

---

8. The hard labor of the enslaved Hebrews included brick making for Pharonic constructions (Exod 1:11–14; 5:6–18). A sample of a 38 cm long mud brick made with mud and straw and stamped with the cartouche of Ramesses II is held as British Museum, object E 6020.

9. See the ca. 35 cm x 35 cm fired brick stamped with the name of Nebuchadnezzar in the Western Asiatic exhibition of the British Museum (object number WA 90136).

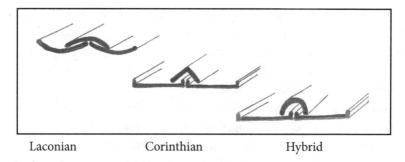

Laconian   Corinthian   Hybrid

Figure 2: Classical systems of rooftile arrangements

The Laconian system (see Figure 2) had quadrangular curved tiles (*kaluptaer*) laid side by side in a row, concave side up, on a supportive sloped wooden framework.[10] The next row of similarly curved quadrilateral tiles was laid partially overlapping the down-slope row. The cracks between the adjacent tiles were then covered by a similarly shaped tile turned upside down. This interlocking grid had the advantage of simplicity and economy. Tiles could serve in either a convex or concave position if they were made the same size. Beyond the Laconian system, a second roofing system is identified as "Corinthian" (see Figure 2). This arrangement employed broad flat rectilinear tiles with raised rims along most of the length of the long sides (*stegastaeres/solanes*). These, too, were laid in horizontal rows. Subsequent rows of flat tiles above overlapped the tiles below to the point where they abutted the projecting rims. The cracks between the adjacent flat tiles were covered by angular cover tiles. The flat tiles (also known as pantiles) were more easily manufactured, and were more stable.

Basic elements of the Laconian and Corinthian rooftile systems were combined into a Hybrid System (see Figure 2) in the colonies of Sicily and Aeolia. Here the flat pantiles of the Corinthian system were joined with the curved cover tiles that looked similar to the Laconian crack-covering system. The decorative elements of antefixes, friezes, and revetments that fascinate students of roof tiles from the sites of Classical Greek and Etruscan monuments were not used frequently by those who adopted this hybridized roofing system.

The Romans who had formerly employed wooden shingles (*scandulae*) adopted roof tiles (*tegulae*) as their roofing system of choice be-

---

10. The slope of Greek, Roman, and Byzantine tile roofs typically had a pitch of 20–30 degrees. Roofs of steeper pitches were more susceptible to sliding.

ginning in the third century BC.[11] The flat pantile (*tegula*),[12] combined with a curved cover tile (*imbrex*), was employed in Roman monumental architecture, and the simpler alternating curved tiles were used more widely in domestic settings. Undecorated utilitarian tiles were the norm.[13] Vitruvius greatly appreciated the durability of ceramic building materials, but unfortunately does not have a section devoted to roof tiles in his magisterial *On Architecture*.

In time, Rome was able to acquire and consolidate its hold on the Levant. With the political domination also came influence on the material culture. Unlike the earlier Seleucids, the Romans did not pursue a confrontational cultural policy. They chose, at first, to rule much of the Levant through local client-kings so as to diminish cultural tensions. Herod the Great, as a client-king under Augustus, however, projected his aspirations for greatness, and curried political favor[14] through a large scale building program which included monumental structures built with Roman engineering and architectural traditions. Many of these structures, like the porticoes in Herod's Palace and the Temple in Jerusalem, had tiled roof systems. The evidence for the utilization of roof tiles in the region of Palestine is limited by the paucity of excavations of domestic structures of the first century. The utilization of tiles appears to have been uncommon in first century Palestine, but this could be the result of the ancient practices of recycling roof tiles. These could be crushed to make binding grog for new ceramic materials.[15]

---

11. Pliny, *Natural History* 16:36.

12. Roman pantiles varied in size from 38–77 cm [15–30 in] in length and from 28–56 cm [11–22 in] in breadth, and came in standard dimensions according to Ing. Carlo Roccatelli, See Carlo Roccatelli and Enrico Verdozzi *Brickwork in Italy: A Brief Review from Ancient to Modern Times,* "Part 1: Brick in Roman Antiquity: Manufacture and Size," The American Face Brick Association (Chicago: The Association, 1925).

13. For the most recent and comprehensive study of Greek rooftiles see Nancy A. Winter, *Greek Architectural Terracottas from the Prehistoric to the End of the Archaic Period* (Oxford: Clarendon Press, 1993).

14. Josephus, *Wars* 1:21.

15. At Abila the practice of recycling tiles is evidenced in the use of floor tiles from the bathhouse to make an Islamic era glass smelting kiln in Area C. There is little evidence of the use of fired brick in construction at Abila since there was plenty of easily workable limestone available. Pantiles that have had their side ridges broken off (*Tegulae fractae*) have not been observed as being used as bricks at Abila, as is commonly seen in Rome.

Builders in the Later Roman and Byzantine periods used roof tiles for monumental structures in the Levant. The most common place where tile roofs were employed was in basilicas. The traditional flat packed clay roof continued in domestic construction. Sloped tile roofs continued to be used in churches and monumental structures of the Islamic period in the Levant.

ROOF TILE MANUFACTURE
AND ROOFING SYSTEMS OF ABILA

Roof tiles were employed in the covering of all five of the Byzantine era church buildings excavated at Abila from 1984–2008. Study of archaeological reports from other church buildings excavated in the local region of Palestina Secunda show that they were the standard roofing material of similar monumental structures throughout the Byzantine and Islamic periods. While these ceramic materials were employed in monumental architecture like churches,[16] there is little evidence for them being used in domestic architecture. Flat packed clay roofs were the norm for domestic architecture in the Levant from the Canaanite through the Ottoman period. The cultural elite and aspirants to such status in the Roman era who had extra resources may have sought to copy the architecture of Athens and Rome in their homes, though this would have been the exception. There is little evidence for the use of roof tiles in the domestic architecture of the populated centers of Palestina Secunda or the earlier sections of the region from the first century. The traditional flat roof provided additional space for a family, and worked well in this region where there was low humidity and precipitation. A sloped tiled roof was lighter and less susceptible to problems than a flat roof, especially when a large space was being spanned. The drawback was that the sloped roof did not provide the useable space afforded by a flat roof. Evidence for the continued utilization and maintenance of flat packed clay roofs is seen in the discovery of cylindrical stone compaction rollers at Abila in the ruins of secondary structures built within the ruins of Basilicae.[17]

16. Mosaic depictions of church structures in the Madaba map and the depictions of cities in the mosaics of Umm ar-Rasas consistently show the hybrid style of tiles being employed.

17. Stone rollers have been found in the Abbasid era domestic structures made of architectural fragments subsequent to a great earthquake in AD 748 on the floors of the churches in Areas A, D, DD, and E.

The sloped tile roofs of the Byzantine era churches were supported by heavy cut stone masonry exterior walls and interior stone columns, arches, or piers. These sturdy stone supports held aloft a wooden framework of trusses and rafters that supported roof tiles, following the hybrid style of flat pantiles and curved cover tiles. None of the wooden frameworks of the roofs have been found, as most of them would have been recycled for construction or used as fuel. The many iron nails found on the church floors testify to the fact that large dimension timber was employed, with the nails being driven through the wood and then bent over to secure them. Shed roofs along the side aisles, and peaked roofs covering the nave above clerestory windows created great open spaces. This type of roof required more high quality lumber than a flat roof, making it more expensive to form and fire, but resulted in a superior, lighter, and lower maintenance roof.

The roof tiles of Abila were manufactured using local materials. Workable clay, sufficient water, fuel for kilns, and labor were readily available. Local production was encouraged by the expense, weight, and breakability of tiles in transport. Clay would have been dug at a local source where it had eroded from the surrounding fields and stored in a depression. It was then carted to a potter's yard, or perhaps prepared *in situ* in the Wadi Qwelbah at a level spot near the perennial stream that was cleared off for the purpose. Highly levigated clay, like that needed for fine wheel thrown pottery, was not essential. The clay merely needed to be free of inclusions larger than sand particles. A good deal of fine organic matter and sand also was included as temper. The temper in Abila tiles includes grog made of crushed pottery, as well as quartz and basalt sand. A few pantile fragments from Abila show the results of a lack of temper in the surface of the tile where slurry of more levigated clay formed the surface. These tiles developed superficial cracks on the surface as they dried, but were fixed in the firing.[18] Collecting clay and combining it with water was easily accomplished at Abila, and required only modest skill. Children may even have been involved in treading chaff into the mix. The clay would have needed to be of a stiff consistency, with air pockets completely driven out of the clay. The inclusion of temper in the clay was important to reduce the effects of shrinkage as the tiles dehydrated. Local potters who could throw thin walled cooking pots had more than enough skill to make tiles.

18. See Abila Rooftiles Registry AE 1982 Area A Locus 3011, #140.

More challenging would be making regularly shaped pantiles that would fit well together. The tiles could be hand-shaped or formed using a flat board, but they would have lacked uniformity. A standardized product was needed if the tiles were to fit snugly together. At Abila, the Byzantine era pantiles are generally about a finger width thick (ca. 2 cm) with ridges that stand another finger width tall and wide. These ridges run the length but give way to a flat flange at one end of the tile. This flange, about a palm's width (ca. 14 cm), enables the tile to be overlapped and "locked down" with another row of tiles (See Figure 3).

ROOFTILE FRAGMENT FROM ABILA

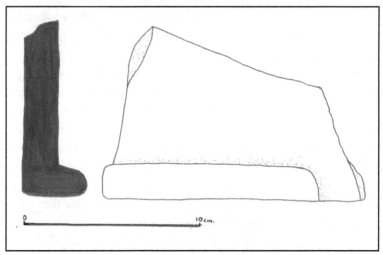

Figure 3: Pantile fragment from Abila. Note the transition
from the side ridge to the flange.
Tile fragment: AE 84, A5, 5001, 4, #8

No intact roof tiles have been found or have been able to be fully re-constructed. However, from fragments it can be seen that some of pantiles were as large as 64 cm long and 40 cm wide.[19]

A pantile-making technique, using a simple wooden molding frame of a rectangular shape, would have been efficient in producing a uniform product (see Figures 4, 5, and 6).

---

19. The dimensions of the pantiles may provide insight as to the measuring system employed in Byzantine Abila and the rest of the region.

How to make a Pan Tile like those found at Abila

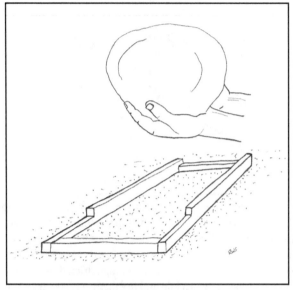

Figure 4: Place wooden pantile molding frame
on a level sanded surface. Put c. 5000 cm3 of prepared clay
into the center of the molding frame

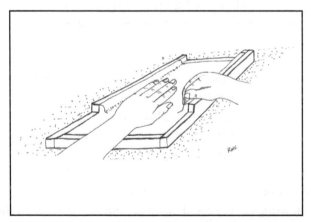

Figure 5: Press the prepared clay into the molding frame squeezing out
any voids. Push extra clay up against the long sides of the frame. Pinch
off the ends of the side ridges. Take wet hands and smooth off the top
of the tile. Draw a wet finger over the top of the side ridges

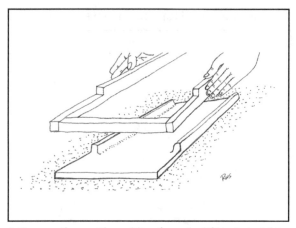

Figure 6: Remove the pantile molding frame by lifting it straight up. Take
wet fingers and run them around the sides of the tile and correct any
deformations made while removing the mold. Allow the tile to sit in the
sun for a week. Then stack the tiles on end in a dry place and allow them
to dry for an extended period. When enough dried tiles are amassed,
stack then carefully in a kiln and fire them at c. 800 degrees C

A slightly increased frame size was needed to accommodate the
slight shrinkage of the product as the wet clay material dried.[20] The
frame was likely laid on level ground that had been scraped flat and
cleared of vegetation, and then sprinkled with sand. This is evidenced
in the coarse sand adhering to the bottom of Abila pantiles. This layer of
sand prevented the tiles from sticking to the ground after they had dried
in the sun, after which the prepared clay mixture was then pressed into
the dampened frame removing any excess clay. The process for removing excess clay may have varied. Most simply, the top of the tile could
have been molded by hand. A second method would be to strike off the
excess material by dragging a straight piece of wood across the top of the
form in both directions, leaving the ridges on the sides. A third method,
suggested by a narrow groove along the base of the ridge on some tiles, is
that a taunt string or wire could have been employed to cut off the excess
clay. Evidence for the method of removing excess clay from the frame
was largely obscured by the tile maker who most likely smoothed the
top surface with wet hands while the frame was still in place, and then

20. In the experimental production of a flat rooftile in Cincinnati after the Abila
1984 expedition, there was about an eight percent shrinkage since the clay was lacking
in temper.

smoothed it again when the frame was lifted away around the edges. The size and shape of ridges on the sides of pantiles show some variation. It was important that the ridges not be substantially thicker than the rest of the tile so that there would be even drying and firing, adding subsequent strength. Thick tiles had thick ridges, and thin tiles had thin ridges. Small irregularities in the side ridges were not greatly important as they would be covered over with curved cover tiles affixed with mortar. In some tiles, wet fingers were pressed across the top of newly formed wet ridges.[21] The resulting depressions served the functional role of improving the bond of the mortar holding the cover tiles in place.

Figure 7: Large drawing in the lower left of figure shows
a pantile fragment with goat hoof prints made while still leather hard,
AE 84, A9, 9001, 5, #109
Small drawing on the upper right shows a pantile fragment
with a possible marking of the tile, AE 82, A4, 4002, 3, #148

Cover tiles, like the pantiles, were not simply shaped as free form objects (See Figure 8). Uniformity in size was important if they were to make a good roof. The prepared clay could have been spread out in a flat even layer on the ground and then cut by a string into the shape of a truncated triangle, though more likely it was made by pressing the clay

---

21. See also the rooftile AE 82, A, WS 19 published in *Near East Archaeological Society Bulletin* 14 (1983) 20.

into an appropriately shaped wooden form that was laid on a piece of cloth instead of on the bed of sand like the pantiles. This wooden form was made in proportions that complimented the pantiles. The cover tiles were approximately the same length as the pantiles, and tapered in width when laid flat from ca. 25 cm to 15 cm. The tile maker sometimes made two parallel depressions on the larger end of the tile by drawing his fingers across the still malleable clay.

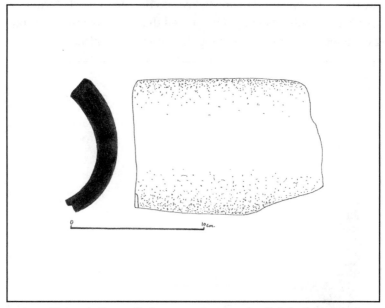

Figure 8: Cover tile fragment showing the slightly thicker finished edge and the stretching of the middle of the tile, AE 84, D12, 12006, 7, #120

These depressions were made to provide greater adhesion to the mortar, thus helping to hold the cover tile in place above, while protecting the crack between pantiles in the row below. After the wooden frame was removed, the cover tile might have been permitted a little time to dry before the still pliable clay form was transferred to a place where it could be draped over a rounded form such as a tree branch, and then bent so that it acquired a semicircular shape along the long axis. The final smoothing of the top of the cover tile then took place by drawing wet hands across the top.

As the newly formed pantiles and cover tiles began to dry, they were sometimes intentionally impressed with writing or architectural modifications like nail holes. Marks that identified the manufacturer or the number of tiles emerged in fifth century Sicily, and became increasingly common.[22] Only one roof tile fragment has been recovered at Abila that may have been marked. It has two "horseshoe" or "C" shaped impressions (See Figure 7).[23]

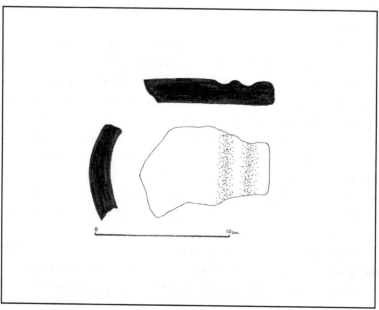

Figure 9: Cover tile fragment showing a finished end that is finished with two grooves to improve mortar adherence, AE 84, A5, 5001, 4, #36

Such marks are not like those made by the Legions that occupied the Levant, and who left their marks on tiles. These marks do not appear to be tally marks, since those were usually hidden on the sides. They could be incidental, i.e. caused by materials that burned away during firing, or by the probing cane of a supervisor who was inspecting the rate at which the tiles were drying. Other such unintended impressions, such as animal tracks, were sometimes made. One example of this was found at Abila in a pantile that bears testimony to a small goat or sheep wandering across drying tiles.[24]

The tiles were allowed to dry thoroughly in the potter's yard before being stacked on edge. Tiles were probably made in the early summer

22. Roger McWhirr, *Roman Brick and Tile*, British Archaeological Reports International Series 68 (Oxford: University Press) 23.

23. AE 82, A4002 #248.

24. AE 84, A9, 9001, 5, #109.

when the climate becomes more arid and the temperatures rise. After sufficient tiles were made ready, they would have been stacked carefully in a kiln so that they would not be warped, and so that the hot gases could circulate evenly. A pottery kiln has been found at Abila on the windy upper slope of the Wadi Qwelbah, making it clear that less sophisticated roof tiles could have been fashioned at this site.[25] Since Abila clays are rich in iron and lime, when combined with sufficient temperatures, the color of the finished tiles was affected. When heated to over 600 degrees centigrade, the tiles would have glowed red hot. The lighter colored tiles suggest that they were fired at hotter temperatures. The air supplied to the kiln during the cooling phase was also important in determining the color of the tiles. In the Roman and Early Byzantine eras, an oxidation atmosphere was maintained by sustaining a supply of air. In Later Byzantine and Early Islamic pottery and tiles, a reduction atmosphere was created in cooling kilns by cutting off the air supply, thus reducing the iron, resulting in tile with a darker color.[26] Excavations at Abila have uncovered a very few of these darker grey tiles. This process was adopted in the Islamic era as a matter of aesthetics.[27] The tiles found at Abila have been made of a highly levigated clay, fired at high temperatures, producing a very thin and hard product with more sharply defined ridges on the sides.

Once the tiles were cooled and transported to the construction site where the timber framework of trusses and purlins was in place, the tiling process would have begun with the bottom row being laid across two purlins. The Abila tiles appear to have been kept in place by their weight

25. On the east side of Abila a pottery kiln containing unfired stacked pottery was found at the site of H36 in 1992. A report on this kiln can be seen in R.W. Smith. "Abila Tomb Excavations: 1992," *Near East Archaeological Society Bulletin* 37 (1992) 40–60, 56.

26. For a brief explanation of the colors of Levantine pottery see D. Homes-Fredericq and H. J. Franken, *Pottery and Potters-Past and Present: 7000 Years of Ceramic Art in Jordan. Ausstellungskatalogue Der Universitat Tubingen Nr 20* (Tubingen: Attempto Verlag, 1986) 15–18.

27. At nearby Jerash, pantiles have been found stacked in anticipation of making repairs to the roof, and several intact cover tiles have been found in an Umayyad era church. These pantiles evidence the inclusion of ridges along three sides in some tiles that have a slightly keystone shape. Other rectangular tiles with ridges running the length of the tile, leaving no flange, have also been found. These tiles all have been made in the reduction kilns of the time. See Vincent A. Clark, "The Church of Bishop Isaiah at Jerash" in *Jerash Archaeological Project 1981–1983. Vol 1.*, ed. Fawzi Zayadine (Amman: The Department of Antiquities of Jordan, 1986) 303–22, 332–37.

and by the low angle of the roof. Each subsequent row of pantiles rested at the bottom on the flange of the tile below, and at the top on a purlin. The overlapping of the sloped tiles helped to create a tight roof. The pantiles of Abila do not suggest the use of mortar to hold them in place. Between the ridges on the sides of adjacent pantiles, lime mortar helped to secure the cover tiles over the crack. The lower row of cover tiles were butted against the pantiles above, and were subsequently overlapped by the next row of cover tiles. This process was continued up to the peak of the roof where mortar and curved tiles would have sealed the top of the roof. It is possible that the flat roof tiles could have been laid on a bed of clay spread over reeds and small branches that spanned the purlins,[28] though evidence of this technique at Abila has generally been washed away from the tiles. Some tiles have been found with some mortar on the bottom side. This technique would have bonded the tiles to the roof, making the tiles less likely to be dislodged.

ROOF TILES AND ROOFING
IN NEW TESTAMENT CAPERNAUM

Roofing systems are of interest to architectural historians and social scientists interested in the interaction of people and the exchange of ideas and culture. Students of the life of Jesus and early Christianity also have an interest in the cultural setting of the first century in which Jesus lived. At the current time there is considerable discussion regarding the extent of Hellenization in Galilee, with some scholars reconstructing great cultural tension between changing urban centers and a resistant countryside.[29] Others find less tension.[30] The presence or absence of roof tiles may be a small indicator of Hellenization in this debate. An awareness of that distant time and place with its different lifestyles helps in the

28. Shader N. Rababeh, *How Petra Was Built: An Analysis of the Construction Technique of the Nabataean Freestanding Buildings and Rock-Cut Monuments in Petra, Jordan*. British Archaeological Reports International Series 1460 (Oxford: Archaeopress, 2006) 54.

29. John Dominic Crossan and Jonathan L. Reed, *Excavating Jesus: Beneath the Stones, Behind the Texts*, Revised ed (New York: HarperSanFrancisco, 2007) 118–135. Crossan and Reed describe Capernaum as a traditional Jewish town in the first century that would have been culturally resistant to Hellenization.

30. Morten H. Jensen, *Herod Antipas in Galilee: Literary and Archaeological Sources on the Reign of Herod Antipas and Its Socio-economic Impact on Galilee, Wissenschaftliche Untersuchungen Zum Neuen Testament 2. Reihe, 215* (Tubingen: Mohr Siebeck, 2006).

understanding and interpretation of the Gospel accounts of the message and person of Jesus. The indicators of context provided by the Gospel provide one measure by which these sources may be tested as they are compared to extra-biblical sources or to preserved artifacts. Hence, roofing systems come to be of interest, as there is a reference to roofing in the New Testament.

An account of the healing of a paralytic in Capernaum is found in the Synoptic Gospels (Matt 9:1–8; Mark 2:1–12; Luke 5:18–26). Matthew places the event in "his [Jesus'] own city," Capernaum (Matt 4:13).[31] This brief account includes details such as the paralytic being carried by men to Jesus, and includes the statements such as "Your sins are forgiven," and "Rise, take up your bed, and go home" (Matt 9:2–6). Matthew's account of the healing says nothing about the event taking place indoors, or how access was gained to Jesus. Mark records the same story in greater detail. Here the event takes place at Capernaum where Jesus "had come home" (v. 1) a crowd gathered at the building where Jesus was found. "So many gathered that there was no room left, not even outside the door" (v. 2). Since the four men carrying the paralytic could not get their friend to Jesus through the unyielding crowd, "they made an opening in the roof above Jesus and, after digging through it, lowered the mat the paralyzed man was lying on" (v. 4). With respect to this discourse, Mark's account is similar to Matthew's, with the slight variation in the description of what the man had laid upon: "Rise, take up your pallet and go home" (v. 11).

The harmonization of these two accounts raises no great issues. If Jesus was speaking Aramaic, as was common amongst Galilean Jews, then "bed" and "pallet" would be synonyms that identified the object to be carried when Jesus' words were translated into Greek. Luke's account is as extensive as that in Mark. It does not clearly indicate that the episode took place at Capernaum, but like Mark's account, affirms that it took place indoors. The New International Version asserts the men tried to take the paralytic "into the house" (v. 18), but the word for "house" is not in the Greek text, and the New American Standard translation "to bring him in" is more precise. The assumption that Jesus was in a domestic structure must be recognized for what it is, namely a hypothesis. The texts of the Synoptics do leave open the possibility that the

---

31. The New American Standard Version is employed throughout this paper unless otherwise indicated.

structure could have been a "house" such as that of Simon Peter (Matt 8:14; Mark 1:29; and Luke 4:38), or even a public building or synagogue (Mark 1:21; Luke 4:38) where there was seating (Mark 2:6). The supposition that Jesus was in Peter's house is not indicated in the Gospels. Luke's account affirms the obstruction of the crowd, and that the men carrying the paralytic found a way to get past the people when "they went up on the roof and let him down through the tiles (*dia ton keramon*) with his stretcher, right in the center, in front of Jesus" (v. 19). Note the specific mention of "tiles" (*keramon*). Subsequently, Jesus is reported as saying "your sins are forgiven . . . take up your stretcher and go home" (vv 20–24). Once again, there is a different Greek word for the item that the paralyzed man had been lying on and subsequently ordered to take back home. The terms "stretcher" (Luke 5:19, 24), "pallet" (Mark 2:4, 9, 11), or "bed" (Matt 9:2, 6) are equivalent translations of Jesus' direct discourse. It is the description of how the paralytic's friends opened the hole in the roof through which the man was lowered that has come to be a subject of discussion, and a point upon which the reliability of the Gospel of Luke is challenged.

In Capernaum the Hellenzing influence of the prevailing Roman culture must have been felt by the Jewish population. This influence is evidenced by coins, but not by fired roof tiles.[32] Extensive work in Capernaum by the Italian excavator, Virgilio Corbo, has exposed the Late Roman era white limestone synagogue, an adjacent black basalt Byzantine era basilica, and beneath them a first century synagogue and an *insula* that reportedly is built around the home of Simon Peter. The more clearly Romanized remains of Capernaum at Tel Hum appear to have been located east of the Franciscan property where Vasillios Tzaferis has exposed an Early Roman era bathhouse and other structures.[33] The second century bath house that has been excavated is situated on the remains of a similar earlier structure. Unfortunately, it has been covered by remains from a later period that are considered worthy of preservation.[34]

32. John Dominic Crossan, *Excavating Jesus: Beneath the Stones, Behind the Texts* (New York: HarperSanFrancisco, 2001) 85.

33. Vasillios Tzaferis, et al, *Excavations at Capernaum*, Vol 1:1978–82 (Winona Lake, IN: Eisenbrauns, 1989) 198–204.

34. John C. H. McLaughlin, "Capernaum from Jesus' Time and After," *Biblical Archaeology Review* 19.5 (September 1993) 57.

The presumption that Peter's first century house has been found in Capernaum beneath the foundations of a Byzantine octagonal pilgrimage church,[35] has led some to look at that *insula* as a possible venue for this story. The layout of this first century house, a central stone paved room six by six and a half meters with an adjacent courtyard, would have accommodated the crowd pressing to see Jesus. The excavators found inscriptions that indicate that it had long been venerated, and subsequently resurfaced over the years with three layers of plaster. While the archaeologists did not find any roof tiles in the first century strata beneath the plastered layers of the floor, they did find that in this *insula*, and the one adjacent, that the ca. 60 cm wide walls were constructed of basalt fieldstones interstitially dry-packed with cobbles and pebbles. The general lack of mortar in the walls of the houses thus far excavated in Capernaum has led to the conclusion that "walls so constructed could not have held a second story. Nor could the original roof have been masonry; no doubt it (the roof of "Peter's House") was made from beams and branches of trees covered with straw and earth."[36] This type of wall could have supported a sloped tile roof or a flat roof that was made with clay and other components, as there was less weight to support than a masonry one supported by corbelling. The problem is that the roof of this structure has not been preserved. The archaeological reports of the Capernaum excavations make no mention of the discovery of roof tiles in first century strata. This negative evidence has been interpreted as excluding the use of roof tiles, thus settling the question as to the type of roof through which the paralytic was lowered. The possibility still remains, however, that tiles could have been used in some first century houses in Galilee. According to Morten Jensen, some tiles have been found in first century strata at Cana, but have not been found in first century strata of the Galilean urban centers of Tiberius and Sepphoris.[37] This same observation is true in the nearby Decapolis cities of Hippus, Gadara, and Abila. The problem is that first century remains are generally disturbed by the large population of the region in the Late Roman and Byzantine eras.

35. Virgilio Corbo, *Cafarnao I: Gli edifice della citta*, (Jerusalem: Franciscan Printing House, 1975) 25–111.

36. James F. Strange and Herschel Shanks, "Has the House Where Jesus Stayed in Capernaum Been Found?" *Biblical Archaeology Review* 8 (1982) 34.

37. Jensen, Chapter 5.

There are at least three opinions regarding the interpretation of the roofing system in the story of the healing of the paralytic.[38] First, there is the opinion that gives priority to the Gospel of Mark and its presentation of a flat, packed, clay roof. Second there is the opinion that gives priority to the Gospel of Luke and its sloped, ceramic tiled roof. Third, there is the opinion that seeks to harmonize these two, seemingly different, reports.

The creation of a hole in a flat clay roof, sizable enough to pass a man through it, would have been a difficult task. It would have required some digging tools to break into the hard clay and break the reeds spanning the space between the rafters. This activity would have dropped a shower of debris and dust upon those below. Effective repair of such a hole would have been difficult. The roof would have subsequently been compromised. The damage, however, would not have been an insurmountable obstacle. Clearly, as communicated by the text, this was a desperate act committed by desperate men.

The creation of a hole in a sloped tiled roof, sufficient to pass a man through it, would have been a relatively simple task. The lower end of a cover tile would have been easily lifted, breaking the bond of mortar affixing it to the tiles below. Once a series of cover tiles were removed, the row of pantiles below would have been easily removed as well, exposing a narrow gap through which a person in a flexible pallet could be lowered. This process would have only taken minutes, and could have been conducted with little disruption below. If two rows of tiles were removed, then a piece of supporting woodwork between the rafters would have also had to be removed. However, for the men carrying the paralytic across such a sloped roof, the task would have been perilous. The men would have needed to walk carefully on the supported parts of the tiles so that they would not break through the roof themselves or slide off to the ground below.

In 1939, C. C. McCown rejected reconstructions of Roman houses with the tile roofs and tiled canopies of Syrian houses. He affirmed the flat mud roof theory based on the claim that Luke translated Semitic

---

38. See H. Keith Beebe, "Domestic Architecture in the New Testament," *Biblical Archaeologist* 38.4 (1975) 102. Beebe suggests that a stone arch and slab technique would explain how a hole was made in the ceiling. This reconstruction is rejected here, as this would not have used clay or tiles. Furthermore, this technique, though present in Byzantine era Galilee, was not employed in the first century.

customs to his Hellenistic audience.[39] Following this reasoning, Craig S. Keener asserts that "Luke changes this Palestinian roof structure to the tiles more familiar to his own readers, as preachers today change details when retelling biblical stories to make them relevant to their hearers."[40] The description of lowering the paralytic "down through the tiles" thus, really meant "through the roofing," with no specific reference to the construction materials that constituted the roof.

Interestingly, the verbs used in Mark's account can be harmonized with Luke's description "through the tiles"(5:19). The first verbal action in Mark is literally "an unroofing" (*apostegazo*) (2:4). This provides no indication of the materials from which the roof was made. The second verb, appearing in the same verse (*exorusso*), has a range of meanings that circle around the making of an opening by the removal of material.[41] The first century roofs of the temples of Petra made by Herod the Great's rival, Aretas IV, are reconstructed by archaeologists as having roof tiles laid on a clay substrate.[42] This technique combined the new durable ceramic surface with a familiar substrate that was now inclined. In such a roof, both the tiles and the clay substrate would have to be removed in order to make a hole in the roof (See Figure 10).

39. C. C. McCown, "Luke's Translation of Semitic into Hellenistic Custom," *Journal of Biblical Literature* 58.3 (September 1939) 213–220.

40. Craig S. Keener, *The IVP Bible Background Commentary: New Testament* (Downers Grove, IL: InterVarsity Press, 1993) 202.

41. The NIV here uses the words "dug through," which is seen to support the action required to work through packed clay, though the originals text can also be translated as "tear out," which would fit the removal of clay-based roofing materials like rolled clay and mold-made sun-baked mud bricks.

42. Shaber M. Rababeh, *How Petra Was Built: An Analysis of the Construction Technique of the Nabataean Freestanding Buildings and Rock-Cut Monuments in Petra, Jordan.* British Archaeological Reports International Series 1460 (Oxford: Archaeopress, 2006) 54.

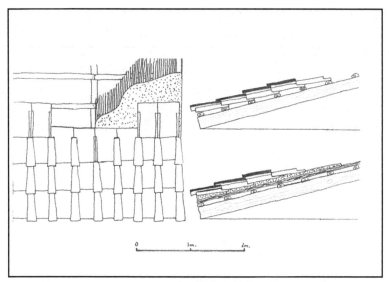

Figure 10: Reconstruction of a tiled roof showing substructures

The word *keramos*, employed in Luke 5:19, typically refers to fired clay products, but in some contexts can mean "clay" like that used by a potter.[43] If the word was used in the singular, then Mark and Luke could both have been speaking of a flat packed sun-dried clay roof. Since Luke uses the plural *ton keramon*, it is more likely that he was referring to distinct pieces of clay-based material. Hand molded sun-dried square clay bricks are only differentiated from tiles by their thickness. Such brick/tiles would not appear in the archaeological remains other than as mud brick detritus, and would be consistent with the absence of roof tiles in Capernaum.

CONCLUSION

Archaeological research of domestic architecture in first century Palestine has not been extensive, but it is apparent that fired roof tiles were not widely employed in the Galilee of Jesus' day. However, this does not remove the possibility that Jesus could have been confronted by a paralytic lowered through a tiled structure, either a house or a public building that has yet to be unearthed or one that has not been preserved.

---

43. *BDAG* 540. Note a reference to potter's earth in the Flinders Petrie Papyri in J.P. Mahaffy & J.G. Smyly, *Cunningham Memoirs*, no. 11 (Royal Irish Academy: Dublin 1905) 327.

The description in Mark could describe the opening of a hole in a sloped tile roof. The digging would have been extensive if the sloping tiles were set on a clay bed that was supported by reeds. It remains possible, but less likely, that the roof being described in both Mark and Luke was a flat roof, and that Luke described the mud bricks or packed clay removed from the roof as *keramoi*. In either reconstruction, Mark and Luke can be seen as giving harmonious accounts that fit the cultural milieu of the first century.

9

Digital Publication of Pottery

John Mark Wade

BROKEN PIECES OF POTTERY, commonly referred to as "potsherds" or "sherds," litter the landscape of almost every ancient site in the Middle East. This is due to the short life span of vessels, especially those used on a daily basis. The sherds come both from accidental breakage and from cooking pots shattering when subjected to repeated heating and cooling. These sherds are scattered around the site, pushed into corners, reused for various purposes, cast into cisterns, or thrown into the refuse heap of the site. When a complete vessel is found, it is usually the result of being crushed in-situ on the final living surface of a site under the collapsed remains of mud brick and stone walls (See Figure 1).

Figure 1: Excavation of a broken storage jar in-situ

One goal of the archaeologist is to develop a greater understanding of what is known about the culture being investigated through the collection of pottery.[1] To do this, the archaeological team collects, counts, and studies a sample of the sherds recovered during the excavation. The retrieval and processing of pottery sherds is a mammoth undertaking for even a small excavation site. With such an investment of time in this process, the archaeologist must find ways to maximize the retrieval of data from each sherd.

The most common statistic collected about pottery during the field work is the total number of sherds and generic forms of vessels recovered. These raw data give a gross estimation of the types of activities that occurred within a structure or site. Changes observed in the form of vessels are noted, as these can be used as the basis for suggesting the passage of time when coupled with stratigraphic change within a site. Archaeologists use these subtle changes in form and composition to suggest contemporaneity between regional sites when more accurate dating material is lacking.

After the archaeologist collects the pottery, it must be published in a way so that others can benefit from what has been discovered. The traditional way of publication is drawing each sherd by hand using pencil and paper and then publishing it within a paper-based publication. In contrast to this traditional method are more contemporary, computer-based approaches. This study presents the author's own efforts to discover a more efficient way to digitally draw sherds for publication. It is based upon experiences gained by working with the ceramic corpus recovered by the Karak Resources Project in Jordan.[2] It should also be noted that while this study gives focus to the "how" of pottery drawing, it does not fully address the question of "why" pottery is drawn or how it is best presented within the practice of archaeological reporting. These are questions ripe for discussion.

1. For excellent pottery references see Ruth Amiran, *Ancient Pottery of the Holy Land: From Its Beginning in the Neolithic Period to the End of the Iron Age.* New Brunswick: Rutgers University Press, 1970; Ralph E. Hendrix, Philip R. Drey, and J. Bjornar Storfjell, *Ancient Pottery of Transjordan.* Berrien Springs: Institute of Archaeology/ Horn Archaeological Museum Andrews University, 1996; Larry G. Herr, and Warren C. Trenchard. *Published Pottery of Palestine.* Atlanta: American Schools of Oriental Research, 1996.

2. For more information about the Karak Resources Project see the Virtual Karak Resources Project Website. http://www.vkrp.org/.

REASONS FOR NEW METHOD

The process of electronically drawing pottery was developed out of the frustration of trying to learn how to "draw pottery" using the traditional method. It became obvious that a better and faster way to draw pottery must exist. The traditional method was too labor intensive. Further, the traditional method was prone to errors as seen in the sherd traced in the picture where the pencil can slip away from the sherd's edge, or when bulges appear in the thickness of the line due to overlapping pencil strokes (See Figure 2).

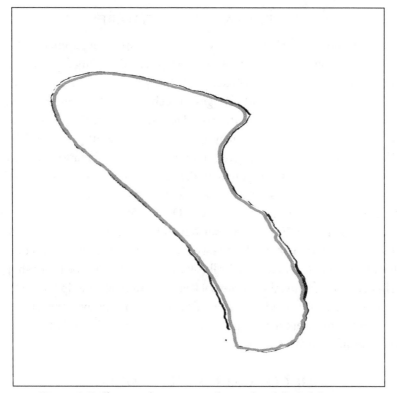

Figure 2: Differences between mechanical and digital drawing

The digital method was developed to harness the power of technology to do the drawings. Others have developed digital methods that required investing large sums of money to scan pottery using laser technology. However, most archaeological excavations have very modest budgets, making the use of such technology completely out of the question. Therefore, a low cost alternative method of digitizing pottery sherds and drawing the pottery from the image needed to be developed.

There are at least three benefits of digitizing and drawing sherds. First, the drawing based on a digital image is very precise. Second, the resulting data from the scan and drawing can be published through a digital medium more quickly at a lower cost to the excavation. Even if the results will ultimately be published in a paper format, digital images can be quickly formatted to make them "camera ready" for final publication. Third, the digitized sherd is a color image. The color image of the sherd has the potential of giving the archaeologist more information about the clay matrix and the technical skill level in the firing process.

EQUIPMENT AND SOFTWARE

Scanning pottery requires some very basic computer equipment. First, a "fast" computer with a "large" amount of RAM, a "large" hard drive and a "large" monitor are needed. Both of the terms "fast" and "large" are relative given the rapid changes in technology. The computer that this process was developed on was a Dell 8100 Dimension Pentium 4, 1.3 megahertz with 128 megabytes of RAM and a 40 gigabyte drive. The monitor was a 19-inch Dell Trinitron. This combination was one of the first Pentium 4 computers on the market. The scanner was an HP Scanjet 5740c flatbed scanner. Over the period of six years since originally purchased, two external drives (80 and 250 gig.), a 128 megabyte video card, and a DVD-RW burner were added for more storage, speed, and backup. For printing the results, two color printers were added, an Epson Stylus 82C inkjet and a Dell color laser printer. Adobe Photoshop, a high end professional software package, was used for manipulating the scanned images, providing a great deal more control over the images. Becoming proficient using this software takes a large time commitment, but it ultimately saves time.

PROCESS OF DIGITIZING POTTERY

The first step in the process of digitizing pottery is to select sherds for analysis from all the sherds collected during the excavation. This part of the process begins while the excavation is still working in the field. The pottery is washed on the same day that it is excavated to remove the excess soil. After the pottery dries then it is "read" by the archaeologist to determine, in general terms, the chronological period when the pottery may have originated, and the number of vessel types (bowls, jars, and jugs) that were found. The archaeologist uses diagnostic pieces of pottery (rims, handles, bases, and decorated pieces) to determine the number and type of vessels. From the initial pottery readings, representative pieces are selected for possible publication.

Next, the pottery that is selected for publication is registered. Registration means that each sherd selected is assigned a unique identification number. An example of an identification number is: M01.D.E4.28.1. The complete identification number contains all the information about where the sherd was found. Without this information, the sherd is of little value because there would be no control over the source of the excavated piece. The unique identification number is broken down in the following chart to show what each segment means.

M	Mudaybi', the site on the Karak Plateau in Jordan being excavated by the KRP Team
01	2001 is the year the sherd was excavated
D	Field D is in the northwest corner of the site
E4	Square E4 is the identification of the square in the site grid where the sherd was found
28	Locus 28 is the unit of soil where the sherd was found that is clearly defined in three dimensions of width, length, and depth within the square
1	the first registration number in the sequence of sherds found in locus 28

An important step in the registration process is to determine the diameter of the rim opening of the vessel based on the sherd. The pottery registrar uses a chart called a "diameter gauge" that contains arched lines spaced 2.5 mm apart that equals 5 mm (or half cm) increases in the diameter of the sherd rim opening. The measurements from the chart usually are rounded to the closest centimeter. Rarely are rim openings perfectly round, so there always must be some minor flexibility in every measurement. The measurement is made on the inside of the rim. The larger the sherd, the easier it is to determine the rim diameter.

The next step is cutting the sherds to give a clean, flat view of the profiled shape and interior of the sherd. The cutting process is done in the lab using a standard wet-cut saw normally used for cutting ceramic tiles in home construction. The cut is done at a 90-degree angle to the top of the rim to expose a cross section of the sherd. Scanning of the sherd begins by first determining the "stance" of the sherd. The stance is the angle that the sherd needs to be rotated for the rim of the sherd to be in the correct vertical angle if the vessel was placed on a flat surface. The sherd is rocked forward and backward on its edge until a point is found where the most contact between the flat surface and the rim's edge is found. This point is probably the most likely stance for the vessel.

Once the stance is determined, then the sherd is placed on the scanner as closely as possible to the angle. There is always some subjectivity in this process that can be corrected later during the final checking. The important thing about a scanned sherd is that the angle can be rotated easily in the software in fractions of degrees. This is an important difference between drawing the sherd by hand and drawing it digitally. Once the angle of the stance on a sherd is drawn by hand it is much more difficult to change.

When scanning a sherd, a clear plastic sheet like an overhead transparency for large sherds or a clear hard CD case (it seems to work best) is placed on the glass of the scanner to protect it from being scratched by the sherd. This is an inexpensive way to protect the glass on the scanner bed. The transparency introduces a small, but acceptable amount of distortion into the scan. When the transparency or CD case becomes too scratched, it can be replaced.

After the cut sherd is placed on the scanner, it is covered with some type of box since the lid of the scanner is not designed for three-dimensional objects. The box limits the amount of extraneous background light that is included in the scan. A lid of a photocopier paper box works very well for a cover. The interior of the lid can be left brown or covered with paper. White paper seems to define the edges of the sherd a little better than brown or black paper.

I tried various PPI (pixels per inch) settings for the scanning process. PPI is the correct terminology for scanner and monitor display resolutions. It is roughly the same as DPI (dots per inch) that is used when talking about printer resolution. 1200 PPI works the best. The higher the resolution, the greater the enlargements can be made on the screen and in prints without pixilation occurring. There is little visible difference on the computer monitor between 1200, 2400, and 4800 PPI because of the limitation of computer screen technology. Printed results, on the other hand, are noticeably different when comparing 1200 PPI to a 4800 PPI resolution file. However, the size differential between the two files is 16 times larger for the 4800 PPI. If the goal is for printed results, then higher resolution is desirable. The original goal for this method was digital publication, so I limited the size to match current screen resolution.

With higher resolution comes a larger file. The difference in size between a 1200 PPI and a 2400 PPI scan of the same object is about 1:4 ratio. For example, the scan of a small sherd at 1200 PPI will produce an image of four megabytes. The same sherd scan at 2400 becomes almost 16 megabytes. The same sherd at 4800 PPI is about 64 megabytes. Some of the larger sherds scanned while developing this method at 1200 PPI exceeded 100 megabytes. The magnitude of the problem can easily be seen. When the scanned files become too large, they become unwieldy, bogging down even the fastest current computer. Thus, the 1200 PPI resolution is a compromise between the limitation of the hardware and publication on the one hand, and the needs of the researcher on the other hand.

Photoshop imports the scan directly from the HP scanner. The image is cropped to the smallest area possible to reduce the size of the file. Initially it was thought a centimeter scale on the scanner bed with each sherd would be needed, however, the scale proved to be unnecessary since the scanner process is virtually a 1:1 ratio. Thus, a centimeter on the scanner equals a centimeter on the computer screen in the software.

The original scan is saved as a TIFF (Tag Image File Format), and the file is named according to the number assigned to the sherd by the pottery registrar. This number includes the site, year, field, square, locus, and the individual sherd registry number. This number is unique. Each time the scan is modified, a designation of "cp" for color plate, "bp" for black and white (b/w) plate, or "d" for complete drawing are added to the file name. Sometimes the interior and exterior of the sherd are scanned when there are surface treatments that may have significance. A designation of "icp" for inside color plate, and "ocp" for outside color plate is added. Therefore, the numbering scheme would appear like the chart below.

M01.D.E4.28.1	Original profile scan before modification
M01.D.E4.28.1bp	B/W profile drawing of the sherd with scale
M01.D.E4.28.1cp	Color profile of sherd with scale
M01.D.E4.28.1d	B/W reconstructed drawing of the complete vessel rim with scale
M01.D.E4.28.1icp	Color scan of the inside face of the sherd
M01.D.E4.28.1ocp	Color scan of the outside face of the sherd

The files are always saved as an uncompressed TIFF because formats such as JPG compresses the file each time it is saved, leading to the loss of pixel data.

After the original scan file is saved, the next step is to clean up the scan by replacing the background with black on the color scan. Various drawing tips in Photoshop were tried. The easiest to use was the airbrush at 19-pixel spray point size set at 100% hardness, 1% spacing, 100% roundness, and 100% pressure. When tracing the sherd, it is enlarged on the computer monitor to 200%, making a centimeter of the scanned sherd fill the width of the 19" monitor. The outside of the sherd is traced with black. The advantage of the digital drawing is that the edge of the sherd that is printed in the electronic drawing is in truth the edge of the sherd and not the outer edge of the black pencil line, as shown in the current method of drawing. The inner line in the photo is the outline of the sherd drawn digitally to show the difference in accuracy between pencil and digital drawings. As can be seen from this comparison the digital drawing is cleaner and more accurate than the pencil drawing (See Figure 2).

Once the tracing of the perimeter of the sherd is complete, then the eraser tool is used to widen the traced line. The block eraser seems to work best for this process. After the line around the sherd is widened enough, then the Marquee tool is used to highlight an area and replace it with black. This is the fastest method for replacing the remaining background with black, as seen in this sequence of photos. The background is replaced for two reasons. The first reason is to clearly define the edge of the sherd in the scan, while the second reason is to give the image uniformity of appearance for presentation and publication (See Figures 3–5).

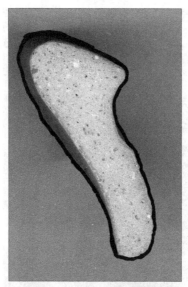

Figure 3: Scanned sherd outlined in black
(original image is in color)

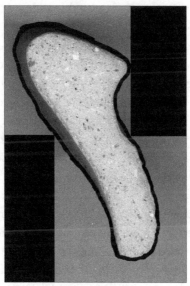

Figure 4: Marquee Tool used to replace large blocks of background
(original image is in color)

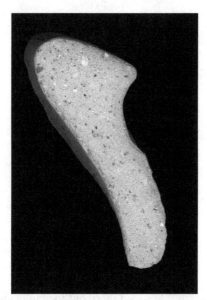

Figure 5: Final plate (original image is in color)

The next step is to copy and paste the color scan from the working scan to the black background color template, using the copy tool. The template was developed to standardize the look of the sherds when they appear in slide shows or publications. It contains a 5 cm scale at the top, and the registration number is always included on the final picture of each version of the sherd. The template was developed by trial and error to find a size that matched the dimensions of most sherds. Since this template is in "true color, 16.7 million colors," its size is 35 megabytes. In contrast, the b/w template is 11 megabytes because all the color data have been removed and replaced with grayscale.

The template and the original must have the same resolution of 1200 PPI, or the size will be skewed. Since the file name is modified each time by adding a letter combination to the end of the file name, all the file versions can be saved into the same directory. The original scan is always retained until all the processing is complete, and then it is removed from the hard drive by saving it to a CD or DVD.

The process is a little more cumbersome when used to create the black and white drawing because the sherd must be traced with white on the outside of the sherd. The next step is to change the outlined scan to grayscale. Then the sherd itself must be outlined in black on the inside, as seen in Figures 6–7.

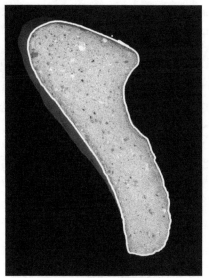

Figure 6: Pottery section
originally being reworked to make b/w image

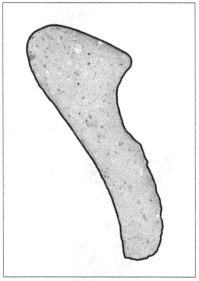

Figure 7: Color and background removed from image.

The Magic Wand tool was first tried to highlight the interior of the sherd to make the entire sherd black. This method did not work because the sherd is not a solid color, and it left jagged edges and many pixels that had to be erased manually. The quickest method seemed to be the Eraser block and Marquee delete method. Once the sherd is completely black and the background is completely white, the sherd is copied and pasted onto the b/w template. The file is saved according to the sherd naming conventions noted earlier.

After all the above steps are complete, there will be two profiles of the sherd, one in color, and one in black and white. The sherd appearance is always standardized so the interior of the vessel faces the left side of the color scan and black and white drawing. This standardization means that sometimes the sherd must be flipped horizontally. This a very simple change to make using Photoshop (See Figures 8–10).

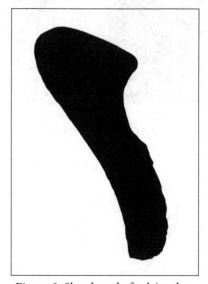

Figure 8: Sherd ready for b/w plate

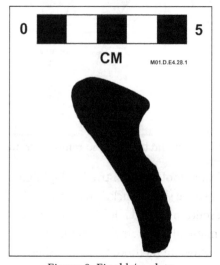

Figure 9: Final b/w plate

The final step is to extrapolate the rim of the sherd into a complete vessel from the black and white sherd drawing. The extrapolation is based on the probable size of the interior diameter of the opening of the rim determined during sherd registration. The probable size is determined using the diameter gauge chart noted earlier.

This final step is begun by copying the black and white image onto a new template that is large enough to accommodate the full width of the vessel. This template is expanded as needed to match the size of the vessel. The black and white drawing is copied on the right side of the template and then flipped horizontally to make the left side identical; then the black image is erased, leaving only the outline. The centimeter scale that is built into Photoshop is used to determine the spacing of each side of the central axis of the rim. Then it is a simple process of connecting the two sides with the appropriate number of horizontal lines and one vertical line in the center (See Figure 10).

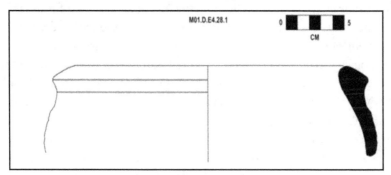

Figure 10: Final drawing of upper part of vessel based on rim sherd

The final black and white drawing is almost 70 megabytes in size at the 1200 PPI resolution. The combined total for the three scans/drawings of this one small sherd is about 115 megabytes. At this rate only 6 sherds can be saved on a 700 megabyte CD-ROM. Lately, I have saved our final files to DVD. Once the scans and drawings are in this format they can be manipulated into various electronic and paper publication formats.

FUTURE PLANS

A goal of this research is to find a way to publish pottery profiles and scans in a timely manner for use by the scholarly community and other interested individuals. The Internet is the obvious choice. Sharing data in an organized format is necessary, though the large size of the files at this time makes sharing impossible on the current Internet. With the next generation of Internet, file size will be less of a problem, though this solution is many years away for most educational institutions. CD-ROMs and DVDs may be the most practical way of sharing large volumes of data in the short term.

Standardization of descriptive terminology is critical for a database to be of any value. All sherds must be described using a controlled vocabulary. This vocabulary would standardize how a pottery vessel is described. This description must be very precise, plus there must be agreement by those who input the data on what to name each part of a pottery vessel. This may be the most difficult part of this project because Middle Eastern archaeologists tend to work independently and often are slow to cooperate.

Color descriptions all use the same standard guide, the Munsell Soil Color chart, which has become the "de facto" standard for describing the color of sherds. This chart was originally designed for describing the color of soils in the United States, but it seems to work for the color readings on most pottery sherds. There is also a way to standardize the color settings on a computer screen through software associated with the Munsell chart. With standardization the data can be saved into a searchable database for use in the scholarly community for comparative analysis that will enhance the study of pottery in the Middle East.

The level of technological achievement during a given period may be studied through an analysis of the clay matrix of the sherd seen in the color scan. The study of the technological level includes the consistency of the preparation of the clay, the temper inclusions added to the fabric, and the firing temperature used. From each of these the archaeologist learns something about the culture and environment in which the pottery was made.

The provenience of the manufacturing of the pottery, whether local, regional, or from some distance from the site may come to light through the study of the clay matrix of the sherd. This information can tell the archaeologist something about the intra site trade and longer distance trade in which the inhabitants of the site may have participated. The future of ceramic analysis is very promising, as new technologies are innovatively applied to help answer the current archaeological and historical questions.

Dr. Reuben G. Bullard was an innovator in his time as he applied geology principles to the archaeological fieldwork at Tell Gezer and other sites in the Middle East. He taught his students to look at the world inquisitively. It is the author's hope this small contribution to the field of archaeological honors Dr. Bullard's memory as a great scholar, teacher, mentor, and friend.

10

Antiquarian Power in Ancient Mesopotamia

Sara Fudge

MODERN PEOPLE ARE INTERESTED in the past for many reasons: curiosity, beauty, identity. Ancient people were drawn to the past as well, but for reasons that moderns may find surprising. Curiosity or esthetics may have played a part, but in addition to these interests, some ancients believed that by paying homage to the past they could safeguard their own present and future. This is because the past was viewed with special respect; it possessed antiquarian power.

This survey will focus on how the ancient inhabitants of Mesopotamia endeavored to tap into the power of the past through the possession of, or association with, significant ancient artifacts (ancient, even to them). Specifically, this survey will glance in three directions. The first is toward ancient documents. A variety of supernatural texts were pursued and preserved as amulets to safeguard their owners. Second, this survey will glance in the direction of foundation deposits. These deposits were often placed at the base of a temple or palace when a structure was built or restored. Third and finally, the present survey will glance in the direction of relics, and in particular, statues. These objects were perceived as projections of glory and power and were maintained in collections that resemble modern museums.

Motivations for remembering one's past are varied. Richard Ellis offers four motivations for the practice of depositing tablets at temple foundations. These motivations are of interest to this study as we look at how and why ancient people remembered their past, not only for the sake of foundation deposits alone, but for other areas as well. One motivation is to sanctify and dedicate an object or building to the gods.

The second motivation is for protection against evil spirits and divine offense. The third is for commemoration, or "to preserve a record of one's pious or grandiose efforts."[1] The fourth incentive is for elaboration or beauty, and thus is intended to impress the gods. These four motivations reflect the need that the ancients had to appease the gods and thus bring good fortune to their lives. The use of antiquarian power considers these four concerns.

POWER IN TEXTS

Texts may contain spells, potions, or other special wording. Ancient people believed that when quoted or performed, these would bring about good or bad results. However, the texts themselves may also carry this power.

Around the third quarter of the second millennium BC, a process began among the scribal schools of Mesopotamia that "froze" (or standardized) much of the traditional corpus of literary texts. Oppenheim refers to this body of texts as the "stream of tradition." The stream of tradition is "what can loosely be termed the corpus of literary texts maintained, controlled, and carefully kept alive by a tradition served by successive generations of learned and well-trained scribes."[1] Student assignments included the copying of texts, creating libraries of significant literary works that were passed down through the generations.[2] The culmination of this process can be seen in Ashurbanipal's library discovered in Nineveh. This process likely began much earlier. Shulgi (2093-2046 BC), ruler of the Ur III Dynasty, commissioned the scribal schools to make copies of his hymns. "In other words, it was his ingenious idea to charge the scribal schools not only with the composition of his hymns, but also with the dissemination and transmission of them for future generations. Thus, it is due to Shulgi that royal hymnology,

---

1. A. Leo Oppenheim, *Ancient Mesopotamia: Portrait of a Dead Civilization* (London: The University of Chicago Press, 1977) 13.

2. Pedersén notes the difference between a library and an archive. An archive usually consists of one copy of the text and includes writings such as letters, and legal, economic and administrative documents. Libraries may contain several copies of one text and include writings such as literary, historical, religious, and scientific tests. Olof Pedersén. *Archives and Libraries in the Ancient Near East 1500-300 B.C.* (Bethesda, Maryland: CDL Press, 1998) 3.

including of course the hymns of his father, became an integral part of scribal curriculum and tradition."[3]

The idea of a canonized group of documents from Mesopotamia has been a greatly discussed issue among modern scholars. One definition of "canon" determines whether the texts in this "stream of tradition" can be considered canonized. The words that scholars assess as being essential for a group of texts to be canonized include "accepted," "genuine," "inspired," "sacred," "authoritative," "authentic," and "sanctioned."[4] The biblical canon was closed as certain texts were decisively included in the canon while other works were declared uncanonical. The corpus of material was fixed, not to be altered by later generations. In contrast, the Akkadian canon continued to grow. This can be seen by the continued work in astronomical omina as late as the first century BC. Mesopotamian civilizations fell before a fully completed canon could be established. "Assyriologists have been striving for a century to finish this unfinished task, to produce such a final cuneiform canon."[5] Ancient scribes did not seem to be concerned with a finalized canon. This idea of the "stream of tradition," and the process of standardizing certain texts, is significant to this study for it shows the importance of maintaining and preserving ancient works. This was done as texts were protected the texts, and used for the sake of good fortune.

One of the greatest collections of texts in the ancient world was Ashurbanibal's library. Ashurbanipal (669–627 BC), the Assyrian king who ruled at the height of the Neo-Assyrian Empire, obviously had a draw to antiquities as evidenced by his exceptional text collection found in Nineveh. It is a reflection not only of his scholarly interests, but also his desire to connect with the past. Excited to build his library, Ashurbanipal wrote the following to his aide, "Seek these [tablets] out

3. Jacob Klein, "From Gudea to Shulgi: Continuity and Change in Sumerian Literary Tradition," in *DUMU-E2-DUB-BA-A: Studies in Honor of Åke W. Sjöberg*, eds. Hermann Behrens, Darlene Loding, Martha T. Roth, Occasional Publications of the Samuel Noah Kramer Fund, 11: VAS 24, no. 43 (Philadelphia, 1989) 301.

4. For a discussion on the understanding of the term "canon," see William Hallo, "Canonicity in Cuneiform and Biblical Literature," in the *Biblical Canon in Comparative Perspective: Scripture in Context IV*, eds. K. Lawson Younger, Jr., William W. Hallo and Bernard F. Batto, *Ancient Near Eastern Texts and Studies* 11 (Lewiston: The Edwin Mellen Press, 1991) 1–20.

5. Hallo, "Canonicity," 10; See also, William Hallo, "Assyriology and the Canon," in *The American Scholar* 59, no. 1 (Winter 1990) 105–8.

and send them to me . . . No one is to withhold any tablet from you. And if there is any tablet or ritual which I have not mentioned to you and you get knowledge of it and it is good for my palace, search it out, confiscate it, and send it to me."[6]

A closer look at some of these documents will help one to better understand what was important to the people, and their motives for collecting them. A letter found in the library, possibly from Ashurbanipal himself, reads as follows:

> Royal command to Kudurranu . . . As soon as you see my tablet, take charge of [three named men] and the scribal experts known to you in Borsippa, and collect all the tablets that are in their houses, and all the tablets deposited in the temple Ezida, (in particular): Tablets (with texts) for *amulets* for the king:. . . four stone amulets for the head of the royal bed and its foot[7]

This text goes on to list several tablets and their ritual significance.

Another part of Ashurbanipal's collection was amulets. An amulet is an ornament that is worn or kept as a charm against evil. Ashurbanipal was anxious to secure some of these texts for their protective value. These were not gathered merely to add to his collection, or to be able to boast of the largest library in Mesopotamia. These texts held a certain power that the king desired. They held the secrets to the future, protection, and success. Saggs writes that, "In ancient belief the person who occupied the throne was particularly vulnerable to the slings and arrows of outrageous fortune, and what Ashurbanipal wanted was supernatural protection for himself and his palace."[8]

Ashurbanipal wanted four of these tablets for his bed to protect him against any evil that might threaten him or his kingdom. He believed they held the power to do this. There is something magical about a spoken or written word. Once a word is vocalized or etched out, it seems to come alive. Ashurbanipal recorded the following:

> I wrote on the tablets the wisdom of Nabu . . . and I checked and collated them.

6. *Kouyunjik Catalogue*, xxii.

7. Cuneiform Text from Babylonian Tablets in the British Museum XXII (London, 1906), pl. 1, no. 1, translations by H. W. F. Saggs, *Babylonians: Peoples of the Past* (Norman: University of Oklahoma Press, 1995) 146–47.

8. Saggs, *Babylonians: Peoples of the Past*, 147.

> I placed them for *futurity* in the library of the temple of my lord Nabu . . . in Nineveh, for my *life*, for the *guarding of my soul*, that I might *not have illness*, and for *making firm the foundation* of my royal throne [italic mine].[9]

Notice the power that these texts have.

1. "[F]or futurity": This may have two different connotations. Ashurbanipal may have been thinking of his own future. By owning and caring for these influential texts, he was hoping to secure a bright and prosperous future for himself. They acted as a safeguard against the attacks of evil spirits, as an amulet would do for him. The second thought may be for the future of his nation, for those who follow him. Not only is he safeguarded, but so are his descendants and any who follow him.

2. "[F]or my life": Like most people, Ashurbanipal was hoping for a long life. He was looking for a way to guarantee that he would not be assassinated, killed in battle, or experience any other unnatural or untimely death.

3. "[F]or the guarding of my soul": The soul may exist in a tormented state in the next world if proper protocol is not adhered to in the present life. This could be a fate worse than death. An improper burial or a neglected grave could result in a troubled spirit that experienced no rest or peace. Ashurbanipal sought protection against such a fate in the next world.

4. "[T]hat I might not have illness": While he is here on the throne living the long life he hopes for, he is petitioning the gods for a healthy life. These texts, which serve as amulets, are to protect him from disease and any form of malady.

5. "[F]or making firm the foundation of my throne": Now, what good is a long healthy life if there is turmoil in the kingdom? Ashurbanipal wants his throne protected from attacks from his enemies, whether they are foreign nations pressing in on him, or incursions from within the palace that may threaten the stability of his rule.

---

9. Streck Asb 2, 354–75, translation by Saggs, *Babylonians: Peoples of the Past*, 144. Italics added to note key points.

Ashurbanipal's motivation for collecting and revering the ancient texts was not merely for their beauty in scholarship or for his personal interest in history; rather, they held hope for the future. They were a means by which the present and future could be secured. It may also be inferred (as we will see with foundation deposits and statues) that as Ashurbanipal collected texts from neighboring nations his motivation may have been to obtain some of the power and good fortune of his neighbors. To steal that good fortune from them made him more powerful than his neighbors.

Israel had a reverence for their sacred writings. This is expressed most vividly in their handling of the texts. Scribes were trained to copy every word and letter exactly. Scriptures were handled with sacred reverence. When a text was retired from active use it was deposited in a special location called a *genizah,* Scripture was not to be destroyed. Power, though, was not to be sought in the scroll itself. The Scripture was to reflect the power of God, not to be that power.

POWER IN FOUNDATION DEPOSITS

Ancient people looked in many places for power beyond themselves. Another area that captured their attention and drew promise for favor and success was in connecting objects with temple foundations.

Foundation deposits date back as early as the Protoliterate period, possibly as early as the Ubaid period (5000-3750 BC), and continued through the time of the Parthians (ca. 238 BC to AD 224). While some of these were dedicatory inscriptions designed to be displayed where all could see, others were designed for the distinct purpose of being buried or hidden. These inscriptions, called *temennu,* may be found on clay prisms, clay nails, bricks, barrel cylinders, small statues, cups and bowls, beads, and stone slabs. They may be made of gold, silver, or other precious metals. They may be deposited in the temple, or at its foundation. The deposits placed at the foundation of the temple were obviously not intended to be read by the public. Their message was for the gods and for future kings who meticulously restored the temple.[10]

It has been said that Nabonidus, king of Babylon, was the first archaeologist.[11] This is based on his excavations of ancient temples look-

10. Oppenheim, *Ancient Mesopotamia*, 148.

11. See Campbell-Thompson, "Decay and Fall of Babylonia under Nabonidus," in *The*

ing for buried artifacts. This was proposed by Campbell-Thompson who
gave a description of Nabonidus that has characterized him for many
years. He wrote, "He [Nabonidus] was a scholar with a most conservative respect for old records and customs, and was never happier than
when he could excavate some ancient foundation-stone."[12] Dougherty
describes the popular view of Nabonidus as follows:

> According to the former estimate of Nabonidus, an impulse aris-
> ing from antiquarian tastes was the leading factor in his life. He
> was pictured as a king who exhibited no concern for the political
> and military welfare of his empire. Digging down to old foun-
> dations and reading the inscriptions of his predecessors were
> regarded as his principal occupations.[13]

The noted scholar Oppenheim writes of Nabonidus, "The last ruler
of Babylonia, Nabonidus (555-539 BC), provided a somewhat queer
'finis' to the independence of Babylonia."[14] Was Nabonidus a lunatic
randomly excavating old foundations at the expense of his empire, or is
there some other explanation for his behavior? Some have suggested that
Nabonidus had more concern for his kingdom than previously thought.
Dougherty admits it is difficult to determine what motivated Nabonidus'
decision to move his residence to Tema, which has baffled scholars and
caused them to question his leadership.[15] David Weisberg suggests that
Nabonidus was interested in "staying power." In order to strengthen his
kingdom, he had to focus on "military defense, farming and husbandry,
trade and market, and maintenance of tradition."[16]

This "maintenance of tradition" is where Nabonidus has been mis-
understood. A study of temple buildings reveals a very strong tradition
of maintaining a sacred site for the temple. It was acceptable to build
new temples on newly sanctified sites, but it was preferred to restore

New Babylonian Empire, The Cambridge Ancient History III (Cambridge, 1954) 218.

12. Ibid., 218.

13. R. P. Dougherty, *Nabonidus and Belshazzar. A Study of the Closing Events of the Neo-Babylonian Empire,* Yale Oriental Series Researches XV (New Haven: Yale University Press, 1929) 158.

14. Oppenheim, *Ancient Mesopotamia,* 163.

15. Dougherty, *Nabonidus and Belshazzar,* 158–59.

16. David Weisberg, "The Antiquarian Interests of the Neo-Babylonian Kings," in *Capital Cities: Urban Planning and Spiritual Dimensions,* ed. Joan Goodnick Westenholz (Jerusalem: Bible Lands Museum Jerusalem, proceedings of the symposium held on May 27–29, 1996).

previously sanctified sites on the foundations of earlier built temples. A *temennu*, or foundation deposit, was placed at the foundation of the temple by the ruler. Nabonidus took pride in excavating these ancient sites to expose the foundations of previous temples and their foundation deposits. He then added his own foundation deposit to the one found of the earlier ruler who built the first temple. In doing so, he hoped, by association with the honored ruler of the past who built the temple, to gain the favor of the gods. As the earlier ruler, such as Hammurabi, was blessed and favored by the gods, so may he experience by association the same blessings, glory and success as this ancient ruler had experienced.

The following are examples of Nabonidus' foundation stones.

> I deposited with my (own) inscription an inscription of Hammurapi, an ancient king, (written) on an alabaster tablet which I found inside it (a ruined temple); I placed (them) forever.[17]

> I rebuilt Ebabbara, their temple in Sippar, on the foundation of Naram-Sin, an ancient king . . . I deposited my inscription inside, together with the inscription of Naram-Sin, the earlier king.[18]

Nebuchadnezzar, Nabonius' predecessor, reflects this same concern and desire for power obtained through his *temennu* in association with that of Naram-Sin.

> I praised Lugal-Marada, my lord, and I searched carefully for the ancient foundation of Eigikalama, temple in Marad, whose old foundation no earlier king had seen since the old days; . . . I found the foundation of Naram-Sin, king of Babylon, my distant ancestor. I did not alter his inscription, but deposited my inscription together with his. I laid its (the temple's) foundations on the foundation of Naram-Sin, king of Babylon.[19]

This practice of searching for the *temennu* was not limited to the Neo-Babylonian period. There is clear evidence for this in the Old Babylonian Period as well. Shamshi-Adad I, who lived twelve hundred years before Nebuchadnezzar, and ruled early Assyria, was concerned about the same issues. He placed his foundation deposit with the great

---

17. Nabonidus VAB, 4, 420.

18. Nabonidus BAV, 4, 320–32.

19. YOS, 1, no. 44:I 24–27.

ruler Manishtushu.[20] He actually anticipated future interest in his foundation deposit. He wrote,

> ... let (a future ruler) anoint my foundation inscriptions with oil, let him offer a sacrifice and return them to their place, (but) he who does not anoint my foundation inscriptions, does not offer a sacrifice, does not return them to their place, or(?) removes my foundation documents, deletes my name, and writes his own name there (may the gods punish).[21]

Scripture does not mention whether Solomon placed a *temennu* at the foundation of his temple during its construction. Continued activity in Jerusalem today does not allow for the archaeological work needed to discover such a find. But Scripture does record God's blessing for this temple. This would be the coveted favor every ruler seeks for his kingdom.

> And the LORD said to him, "I have heard your prayer and your supplication, which you have made before Me; I have consecrated this house which you have built by putting My name there forever, and My eyes and My heart will be there perpetually. And as for you, if you will walk before Me as your father David walked, in integrity of heart and uprightness, doing according to all that I have commanded you *and* will keep My statutes and My ordinances, then I will establish the throne of your kingdom over Israel forever, just as I promised to your father David, saying, 'You shall not lack a man on the throne of Israel.'"[22]

Note the mention of David. Here is the association with the successful predecessor. This association with David, the great ruler and warrior, will have a very familiar ring through the years to come. David is noted as one whom the Lord loves, and as one whose reign was the epitome of success, is the one of whom scribes will refer to as the model for future kings. This echoes back to Babylonian rulers name-dropping with Naram-Sin, Manishtusu, and Hammurabi, all great rulers of the past. "And he [Josiah] did right in the sight of the LORD and walkedin all the ways of his father David, nor did he turn aside to the right or to the left."[23] Israel had been warned to keep the superstitious nature

20. Ellis, *Foundation Deposits*, 173.

21. AOB, 1 24 v 3ff, Translation from *The Assyrian Dictionary* N part 1 vol. 2., 367.

22. 1 Kgs 9:3–5; The Lord's words continue with a warning to those who fail to observe his commands and degrees, 1 Kgs 9:6–9.

23. 2 Kgs 22:2.

out of their association with the past as their neighbors had done. The power did not come from their ancestor, David, rather, it comes from the Lord.

POWER IN RELICS

In Ancient Mesopotamia several cities have been excavated that appear to have had a museum of sorts located near or in the palace or temple (same as the libraries). Historians have labeled these as museums since they appear to be collections of antiquarian objects found in a single location and collected for a specific purpose. As noted with libraries and other antiquarian interests, here too it will be evident that these collections held a more meaningful purpose than curiosity alone. Many of the artifacts found in these museums were there for their beauty, antiquity, and intrinsic value, but there were also many objects found in the collections which very likely held a sense of authority and even power that was valued and sought after. These collections included items such as cult statues, votive items, royal statues, and ancient stelae commemorating an earlier king's victory. To procure an object that commemorated a ruler's victory was in essence to attain the victory itself. This included one's own national rulers, or rulers of notoriety, or legends of other nations. This would make the motive for collecting such priceless artifacts a search for prosperity, success, and good fortune.[24]

Cult statues and votiveware are known to carry with them supernatural significance, and therefore, are considered prized pieces in any museum. It may not be as evident that a royal statue or victory stele could also carry this special significance. This was addressed with the power that comes as one ruler adds his *temennu* (foundation deposit) to that of a successful ruler from an earlier period. The greatness of one ruler may conceivably and hopefully rub off on another by association. Thus, cultic items, as well as statues, laws, or stelae of great rulers were sought out by ambitious leaders.[25] These ancestral rulers need not be

24. Significant "museum" collections have been excavated at Susa, Ur, Nippur, Babylon, and Sippar. These are all located within Mesopotamia (except Susa), and all contain objects from outlying areas. The museum at Susa contained some of the most significant objects from Babylon, including the Code of Hammurabi. See P. Calmeyer, "Museum," in *Reallexikon Der Assyriologie*, 8 Band, Begründet von E. Ebling und B. Meissner, (Berlin: Walter de Gruyter, 1993).

25. See William Hallo, "Cult Statue and Divine Image," in *Scripture in Context II: More Essays on the Comparative Method*, ed. W. Hallo, J. Moyer, L. Perdue (Winona

deified in their life to carry such influence, though some were. Egypt was known to have deified their pharaohs. Mesopotamia had deified a few of its Sargonic kings, though this was not a regular practice of Mesopotamian rulers. Nonetheless, kings such as Hammurabi (not deified) were regarded as powerful in their day, as well as posthumously. This may also be applied to non-royal ancestors. Ancestral worship was widely practiced throughout the ancient world. The same rationale that motivated rulers to seek power from their predecessors, motivated the layman to ancestral worship: good health, success, and protection.

While excavating the tell of Susa in Persia (earlier Elamite territory), Jacques de Morgan hoped to find Persian treasures, and bring to light an array of Persian culture and tales of Persian history. He accomplished this, and unexpectedly found a wealth of Babylonian objects. He had uncovered an Elamite "museum" that held an array of Babylonian objects: a diorite victory stele of Sargon of Akkad (2340–2284 BC), a statue of Manishtushu (2275–2260 BC), a victory stele of Naram-Sin (2260–2223 BC), and the famous Code of Hammurabi (1792–1750 BC). Elam had a great reverence for Babylonian culture, and had at times invaded Mesopotamia, carrying away among her spoils of war not only monetary wealth of gold, prisoners, and other valuables, but they had also carried away victory stelae, law codes of the famous Hammurabi, and statues of very powerful Babylonian rulers. This collection is a good example of one nation capturing from their enemy, not only their wealth and workers, but also their power. Nations would "kidnap" the statues of the rulers and gods of their enemies as a sign of conquest. When a city lost its emblems of power, it lost its approbation that was associated with them. The same transfer of power and authority followed the statues as with the texts. They carried significance, bringing the owners and those who revered them good fortune. These relics were not merely for exhibit and the fascination of on-lookers. Hallo writes of the cult-statue, "The loss of the cult-statue was no small matter. It involved the inexorable disruption of the cult and implied the withdrawal of divine favors."[26] The restoration of the statue was a sign that the divinity once again dwelt in the city/temple. The royal statue, as well, carried with it "favors" and "divinity."

Lake, IN: Eisenbrauns, 1983)..

26. Hallo, "Cult Statue and Divine Image," 13.

This practice of associating power with an image of a powerful leader extended centuries beyond the Babylonian period. Alexander the Great beat all the odds against him in his eastern campaigns; he was obviously one whom the gods favored. Statues of him were treasured by those who hoped to gain that same favor.[27]

This fascination with images of past rulers is an extension of ancient humanity's superstition regarding foundation deposits and texts. These items carry with them, or one could say, possess in and of themselves, a desired power. The ancient world was a very superstitious one. Consumed with the fears over, and consequently, the attempt to control the gods, demons, and the souls of ancestors was critical. Much effort was invested into reading, understanding, and manipulating these forces to one's advantage through extispicy, necromancy, oracles, auspices, omens, incubation, and other means. In this context power is "contagious;" it may be obtained through association with antiquarian objects such as foundation deposits, texts, and statues of those who had found favor in the eyes of the gods. Even today we hear the phrase, "I hope some of your good luck rubs off on me."

As ancient people looked to their own ancient past they were seeing something quite different than we would expect. Modern people approach their history in search of knowledge and heritage. Ancient people searched for the approval and control or power over their own circumstances and destiny.

27. J. J. Pollitt, *Art in the Hellenistic Age* (Cambridge: University Press, 1993) 3; See Plutarch, *Plutarch's Lives* with an English translation by Bernadotte Perrin, Vol. 7, The Loeb Classical Library (Cambridge, Mass.: Harvard University Press 1990).

11

Aspects of Warfare in the Bible: Insights from Egypt

Kevin Morrow

IN THE INTRODUCTION TO his classic work on ancient warfare Yigael Yadin states, "A study of human history cannot therefore be complete without a study of the military events of the past."[1] Over the past two centuries archaeology has produced a collection of discoveries that form a grand gallery of illustrations of life in the ancient Near East. Within the reliefs and inscriptions is a narrative dominated with militaristic accents. This ancient drama is best captured in the observation: "Then it happened in the spring, at the time when kings go out to battle" (2 Sam 11:1).[2] The landscape of the Fertile Crescent is a veritable battleground whereon geo-politics was most clearly represented in the application of armed might, witnessed in the destruction debris of dead cities with their toppled walls, gates, and towers.

Outside of Egypt, however, many key biblical passages thirst for proper context. Egypt is too often ignored as a rich resource for biblical studies, leaving the discipline poorer and some scholarly works barren of meaning. Attention needs to be paid to Egypt! Emphasis on Egypt in this study is motivated by the conviction that the legacy of Egypt has much in common with certain biblical material such as warfare, yielding rich insights into key Old Testament texts. Sa-Moon Kang points out that the focus of many scholars has been limited to Assyrian sources and the Assyrian concept of divine war in the first millennium.[3] On the

1. Yigael Yadin, *The Art of Warfare in Biblical Lands in Light of Archaeological Study*, 2 Vols (Jerusalem: International Publishing Company, 1963) 1.

2. All Scriptural citations are from the New American Standard Bible, unless otherwise indicated.

3. Kang, 5.

issue of Egyptian historiographical influence, K. L. Younger, Jr. stresses, "There can be little doubt that the Egyptians' influence on the historical literature of ancient Israel was much more than is usually considered."[4] James Hoffmeier expresses surprise over the marginalization of Egypt in biblical studies, considering that Egypt and Canaan were next-door neighbors and Mesopotamia was not;[5] a fact pointed out by Kenneth Kitchen in the Forward to John Currid's book, *Ancient Egypt and the Old Testament*.[6] Says Hoffmeier, "There is still much light Egyptian royal inscriptions of the New Kingdom can shed on Hebrew military writing."[7] Another reason for emphasizing Egypt in this study is the 400 years of contact between Egypt and Israel, and the magnitude of God's warring activity in Egypt, comprising the first fourteen chapters of Exodus and prompting the earliest explicit statement of God as warrior in the Old Testament (Exod 15:3). This historical epic took place sometime during Egypt's New Kingdom period, a golden age marking the beginning of Egypt as a militaristic state, and the army becoming a regularized institution. This was a time of warrior-god kings and the age of the blue war-crown, which came into being during the Eighteenth Dynasty.[8] Egypt was at its zenith when God "came down" (Exod 3:8) to deliver His people as the Divine warrior-savior.[9]

THE DIVINE WARRIOR AND SALVATION

It is therefore not surprising that warfare pervades the biblical record. Much of the militaristic emphasis in Scripture should be understood against this broader milieu. In Exodus, God "comes down" as a warrior-savior to liberate His people. Numbers documents the draft and military divisions of the tribes, preliminaries for the invasion of Canaan. Joshua

---

4. K.L. Younger, Jr. *Ancient Conquest Accounts: A Study in Ancient Near Eastern and Biblical History Writing* (JSOTSup 98; Sheffeild: JSOT Press, 1990) 165.

5. J. Hoffmeier, "Understanding Hebrew and Egyptian Military Texts: A Contextual Approach" in *Context of Scripture, Vol 3: Archival Documents from the Biblical World*, ed. William Hallo and K. Lawson Younger, Jr. (Lieden: Brill, 2002) xxi.

6. John Currid, *Ancient Egypt and Old Testament* (Grand Rapids: Baker Books, 1997) 9.

7. Hoffmeier, xxii.

8. Pierre Montet, *Eternal Egypt* (London: Phoenix Press, 1964) 40.

9. Even though Egypt developed a military machine, they were not bloodthirsty warmongers, but were conservative, and traditionally peaceful. See Kang, 88.

and Judges narrates the wars of Canaan, the acquisition of the land, and territorial divisions (Josh 21:43–45). The books of Samuel, Kings, and Chronicles are full of conflict, both domestic and foreign. "Day of the Lord" language, war-judgment oracles, and apocalyptic imagery embellish the Major and Minor Prophets. Even the New Testament is laced with war elements, especially Divine warrior ideology, which finds expression in numerous passages such as Jesus' casting out demons, calming storms,[10] marching into Jerusalem as the conquering hero,[11] and the epochal moment of Christ's death on the cross (Heb 2:14). Finally, Revelation boldly portrays the glorified Messiah as the divine warrior-judge with eyes ablaze, seated on a white horse, and distributing God's wrath upon His enemies (Rev 19:11ff).[12]

A difficult challenge facing biblical theologians has been agreeing on the central locus of Old Testament theology, around which the whole of Scripture is said to be fashioned and unified. Various proposals have been made, including *land, covenant,* and *messianic* or *promised line.* Thomas Olbricht offered the best proposal when he said, "God is at the center of OT theology."[13] God manifested Himself in various ways, by numerous names and epithets such as Creator, Husband, Groom, Shepherd, Judge, and Savior to name a few. But one of the popular recurring images in the Bible is that of Divine warrior, as represented in Isaiah: "The Lord will go forth like a warrior, He will arouse His zeal like a man of war. He will utter a shout, yes, He will raise a war cry" (Isa 42:13). Patrick Miller observes that the "dominant and controlling images that Israel carried of its God were *warrior, judge,* and *king.*"[14] He

10. See Bruce A. Stevens, "Jesus as Divine Warrior," in *The Expository Times* 94, no. 11 (Aug 1983) 328.

11. See Paul B. Duff, "The March of the Divine Warrior and the Advent of the Greco-Roman King: Mark's Account of Jesus' Triumphal Entry into Jerusalem," in *Journal of Biblical Literature* 111, no. 1 (1992) 55–71.

12. The reader must understand that the image of warfare in the N.T. takes on a figurative flavor. Jesus' warrior-like character is manifested in healings, raising the dead, love and sacrifice.

13. Thomas H. Olbricht, "The Theology of the Old Testament," *The World and Literature of the Old Testament,* ed. John T. Willis (Austin: Sweet Publishing Company, 1979) 298.

14. Patrick Miller, *The Religion of Ancient Israel* (Louisville: Westminster John Knox Press, 2000) 7.

further states that, "The image of Yahweh as divine warrior . . . continued to play a major role throughout the history of Israel's religion."[15]

This popular epithet (i.e. warrior) stands at the very heart of salvation history-theology, beginning with the *proto-evangelium* ("first gospel") of Gen 3:15, and climaxing in Jesus' death, burial, resurrection, and final battle in John's Apocalypse. This perspective is espoused by John Goldingay, who notes, "There is no development toward more emphasis on peace in the First Testament, as there is not in the New Testament, which ends with a book that much emphasizes God's activity as warrior."[16] Salvation and war were understood as two inter-locking concepts in ancient times. In Egyptian sources, such as the Carnarvon Tablet I, Amun commissioned kings to engage Egypt's enemies in warfare because Amun's desire was to "save" Egypt.[17] Jeremiah illustrates this by equating God's militaristic character and salvation in a negative question, "Why are you like a man dismayed, like a mighty man who cannot save" (Jer 14:9). The term "mighty man" is synonymous with "warrior" as translated in the *NIV*. In the so-called "war oracle" of Exod 14:13–14, Moses told Israel, "Do not fear! Stand by and see the *salvation* [italics mine] of the Lord which He will accomplish for you today; for the Egyptians whom you have seen today, you will never see them again forever. The Lord will *fight* (italics mine) for you." Here God's fighting is equated with salvation. The overthrow of the Egyptian army (Exod 14:27) is the salvific event that Israel would visibly witness (Deut 7:19; Josh 24:7), as commanded by Moses. Thus in Exod 15:3 God is appropriately called "warrior." Marc Brettler associates the Divine warrior metaphor with salvation language in the Book of Psalms,[18] which is appropriate since psalms of praise often have their origin in salvation realia, e.g. Song of the Sea (Exod 15), and Song of Deborah (Judges 5). Richard Nysse adds strength to the argument when he contends that if the "Yahweh-is-a-Warrior" theme were jettisoned from the Bible there would be immense confusion in understanding certain key issues like

15. Miller, 8.

16. John Goldingay, *Old Testament Theology, Vol 2: Israel's Faith* (Downers Grove, IL: InterVarsity Press, 2006) 151. See also Charles Scobie, *The Ways of Our God*, pp. 858, 861.

17. Sa-Moon Kang, *Divine War in the Old Testament and in the Ancient Near East* (Berlin: Walter de Gruyter, 1989) 88.

18. Marc Brettler, "Images of YHWH the Warrior in Psalms," *Semeia* no. 61 (1993) 137.

salvation.[19] Says Nysse, "Themes of liberation, creation, and hope would either be weakened or need to be drastically recast."[20]

DOCUMENTING WARFARE

Why document wars, especially in the Bible? According to Jeffrey Niehaus, "History-writing itself was established on the theological foundations of divine election and covenant."[21] Wars were often recorded to pay tribute to patron deities (Amun in particular), based on the belief that the gods had ordained the battle, and empowered the king to overcome the enemy. At the beginning of Thutmosis III's campaign texts, recorded on the walls of the Karnak temple, it states: "His majesty commanded that the [victories which his father Amun gave him to be recorded as] an inscription in the temple which his majesty had made for [his father Amun in order to record] each campaign along with the booty."[22] In the Bible, such memorials, or testimonials, often appear as celebratory poems, or tributes to the Savior-King. They also function as stern reminders of God's character and role, sensitizing His people to their covenant obligations, and encouraging future generations concerning His ability to protect and deliver. The much-debated "Book of the Wars of the Lord" in Num 21:14 might have been an anthology of praise hymns compiled for such a purpose. This passage serves as the basis for labeling many of Israel's wars as "Yahweh Wars," as opposed to "Holy Wars," a non-biblical term coined by F. Schwally.[23] Many of the monuments of Egypt bear toponyms, or names, of conquered cities, groups of bound captives, lists of spoils, and travel itineraries. We find similar data in the books of Deuteronomy and Joshua. Charles Krahmalkov compares the topographical lists of Ramesses II and Ramesses III with Joshua 15, showing that they all describe the Hebron district with the same topographical details.[24]

19. Richard Nysse, "Yahweh Is a Warrior," *Word and World* 7, no. 2 (Spr 1987) 193.

20. Ibid., 194.

21. Jeffrey J. Niehaus, "The Warrior and His God: The Covenant Foundation of History and Historiography," in *Faith, Tradition, and History Old Testament Historiography in Its Near Eastern Context* (Winona Lake, IN: Eisenbrauns, 1994) 302.

22. COS, "The Annals of Thutmose III (2.2A)," trans. J. Hoffmeier, 8.

23. Gerhard von Rad, *Holy War in Ancient Israel*, trans. Marva J. Dawn (Grand Rapids: Wm. B. Eerdmans, 1991) 6.

24. Charles R. Krahmalkov, "Exodus Itinerary Confirmed by Egyptian Evidence,"

Wars were also written down to glorify kings. As Spalinger notes, "Egyptian scribes gloried in writing military stories depicting their ruler as a victorious hero waging war against the vile enemy."[25] At the conclusion of Khamose's war report of the campaign against the Hyksos, it says, "Have everything which my majesty has done by strength put upon a stela which occupies its place in Karnak in the Theban Nome forever and ever."[26] Both in Egyptian and biblical texts, the detailing of wars was often a daunting challenge, based on the amount of data to be documented and possibly the time constraints placed upon scribes for publication. Scribes accompanied Egyptian armies on military expeditions, keeping daily records of the events: "Everything which his majesty did to this city, to that feeble enemy and his feeble army, was recorded daily."[27] Egyptian scribes employed a variety of literary methods for publishing their war reports, one of which was *iw.tw* form, or short summary, similar to the epistolary style of Middle Kingdom reporting.[28] Thutmose III's Armant Stela is called a "summary" of the acts of his bravery.[29] A similar style of reporting appears in the Book of Joshua. A good example is Josh 10:29–43, which recounts the southern campaign of Canaan. Here we find a summary-style formula employed to condense the account into a manageable text. Only the scantiest details are provided for each city in the war itinerary, which generally moves from north to south. It is especially important to recognize that in each section credit is given to Yahweh for success, e.g. "The Lord gave Lachish into the hands of Israel" (Josh 10:32).

STRIKE AND SMITE

One of the key militaristic terms found in the Old Testament, especially Exodus, is the word "strike," or "smite," which finds artistic representation in Egyptian royal iconography where pharaohs are shown striking their enemies. On the fringes of the eastern Delta at Tell el-Retaba, once

---

BAR 20, no. 5 (Sept/Oct 1994) 6–7.

25. Spalinger, 121.

26. "The War Against the Hyksos," in James B. Pritchard, *Ancient Near Eastern Texts Relating to the Old Testament*, (New Jersey: Princeton University Press, 1955) 93. Hereafter, Pritchard's first volume will be called ANET.

27. COS, "Annals of Thutmose III," 12.

28. Spalinger, 2.

29. COS, "Gebel Barkal Stela of Thutmose III (2.2B)," trans. J. Hoffmeier, 18.

a Ramesside military post, the temple of Atum still exhibits a scene of Ramesses II in the act of slaying a Semite before Atum. This standard war gesture in the art of Egypt (and other cultures) is at least as old as the ceremonial Narmer Palette, which shows Narmar grasping the hair-knot of an enemy with his left hand while wielding a mace in his right, preparing to strike the enemy. The royal titulary (a title consisting of five names) for some of the pharaohs consisted of such epithets as "Great in Strength," and "Smiter of the Asiatics." In the Gebel Barkal stela Thutmosis III boasts: "It was my mace which overthrew the Asiatics, my club which smote the Nine Bows."[30] The word "strike" (*naka*) is often used to define the warlike nature of God and introduces many of the plagues, e.g. "I will strike the water that is in the Nile" (Exod 7:17); "I will smite your whole territory with frogs" (Exod 8:2); "Strike the dust of the earth, that it may become gnats" (Exod 8:16); "strike down all the first-born" (Exod 12:12); and "I will strike the land of Egypt" (Exod 12:13). While the act of striking or smiting denoted retribution, it is clearly to be understood as a militaristic action term, possibly functioning as a polemic against Egyptian royal ideology.

GOD'S ROLE IN WARFARE

During the New Kingdom warfare was understood as the will of the gods. According to Kang, in Egyptian texts the word for "military" (*wdyt*) corresponds with the word for "command" (*wd*).[31] War was never arbitrary. To engage in warfare was to carry out the will of the gods. In Deut 7:16 God tells Israel, "You shall consume all the peoples whom the Lord your God will deliver to you." In the victory hymn of Thutmosis III, Egypt's enemies are said to be Amun's enemies. Amun, or the "victorious father," even ordains the extent of territory Thutmosis would conquer.[32] This is similar to the Beth-Shean Stela of Ramesses II, where Amun-Re establishes the boundaries of Egypt, and gives Ramesses "a sword against all foreign countries."[33] God told Israel He would fix their boundaries from the Red Sea to the Euphrates (Exod 23:31). In Egypt the decision of the king was absolute, but on momentous occasions such as military expe-

30. COS 16.
31. Kang, 90.
32. COS, "The Annals of Thutmose III (2.2A)," 9.
33. Kang, 95.

ditions into Nubia, Lybia, Canaan, Retenu,[34] or Naharin,[35] the oracular pronouncement of Amun gave concrete legitimacy to the event. In one of Seti I's inscriptions it states multiple times that Amun decreed the king's valor: "It is the might of Father Amun who has decreed for you valor and victory over every foreign country."[36]

In numerous passages of the Bible God's will is sought first before entering the field of battle. King Jehoshaphat desired an oracle from God before entering into battle at Ramoth-Gilead (1 Kgs 22:5). In Judges 1 the tribes inquire of God, "Who shall go up first for us against the Canaanites, to fight against them?" David prayed before attacking the Philistines (1 Sam 23:1). The wars of Canaan were divinely ordained (Gen 15:16), and preparations began in the wilderness with the formation of a standing army and war camp, with the Ark of the Covenant (and Tabernacle) as the centerpiece around which the tribal divisions were placed, each with their own standard (Num 1–3). The arrangement of the Hebrew camp has parallels in Egypt, such as the description of Ramesses II's camp at Kadesh or Thutmosis III's camp at Megiddo.[37] Wall scenes of the Kadesh campaign portray an open camp arranged in a square with the tent of the deity and king in the center, similar to the camp arrangement in Numbers. The Ark played a pivotal role in Israel's wars, the singular icon of Yahweh's presence in the midst of His people. In Joshua 3 the Ark leads Israel into Canaan. When Ramesses II marched into battle the god Amun said, "Behold, I am in front of you."[38] In Exodus 23 God decreed that His angel would go before Israel into Canaan. The notion of divine guidance preceding the army was a popular concept in ancient times.

Then there is the issue or promise of terror. God promised Israel that He would send His "terror" ahead of them, and throw the enemy into "confusion" (Exod 23:27).[39] Amun-Re is credited with using a comet,

---

34. Retenu is a term that includes the Lebanons and Syria.

35. Similar to the Hebrew "Aram-Naharayim" (Gen 24:10). The Egyptians employed the term Naharin to describe the area around the great bend of the Euphrates and the Habur Triangle, the biblical Padan-Aram.

36. COS, "Karnak, Campaign From Sile to Pa-Canaan, Year 1 (2.4)," trans. K. Kitchen, 24.

37. Yadin, *Aspects of the Conquest*, 9.

38. Kang, 101.

39. Deut 7:23; Josh 10:10.

which created fear in the enemy, causing them to "fall headlong."[40] Also, Amun-Re put the "dread" and "fear" of Thutmosis into his enemies. In the Gebel Barkal stela, Thutmosis III says of Amun, "Among the foreigners he placed the fear of me so that they might flee far from me."[41] God put the "dread and fear" of Israel before their enemies (Deut 2:25).

The gods also often promised to subdue enemies. In the Libyan campaign Ramesses III tells that Amun-Re made the enemy prostrate under his feet.[42] Thutmosis III brags that Amun placed "everyone on whom the sun shines" under his sandals.[43] While this is symbolic language of triumph, it represents a common idea in the ancient world. It can be found in Joshua's act of having his officers place their feet on the necks of Israel's enemies (Josh 10:24), an image also reminiscent of Christ's ultimate victory over sin and death (Gen 3:15).[44]

The arm/hand idiom in Egyptian and biblical texts clearly reflects strength and power to deliver or conquer, both being symbols of triumph. The formulaic phrase "outstretched arm" occurs nearly twenty times in the Old Testament, and it is always in reference to the power of God. Reflecting on the liberation from Egypt, the author of Deuteronomy said, "The Lord brought us out of Egypt with a mighty hand and an outstretched arm and with great terror and with signs and wonders" (Deut 26:8). This anthropomorphism is related to God's creative abilities in Jeremiah 32:17. Karen Martens treats the phrase "with a strong hand and an outstretched arm" within the military setting, and suggests that it might be "the fundamental metaphor" of Exodus.[45] In Exodus 6:6 God states that He will redeem Israel with "an outstretched arm and with great judgments." A similar phrase is found in Exodus 7:4: "I will lay My hand on Egypt and bring out My hosts, My people the sons of Israel, from the land of Egypt by great judgments." Martens believes the expression, "with a strong hand," is a stock phrase that was later embellished with additional formula, such as "outstretched arm."[46] The phrase

40. COS, "The Gebel Barkal Stela of Thutmose III (2.2B)," trans. J. Hoffmeier, 17.

41. COS, "The Gebel Barkal Stela," 17.

42. Kang, 98–99.

43. COS, 17.

44. 1 Cor 15:25–27; Eph 1:22; Heb 2:8.

45. Karen Martens, "With A Strong Hand And An Outstretched Arm: The Meaning of the Expression," *Journal for the Study of the Old Testament* 15 No 1 (2001) 123.

46. Martens, 129.

certainly embraces salvation through judgment, and includes any and all actions of God in Egypt. It should be understood as a militaristic term within the context of salvation.

This expression is ubiquitous in Egyptian campaign texts, taking on different forms: "strong arm," "powerful arm," "great of arm," and "potent with his arm." Its frequency in the biblical narrative of Exodus leads Hoffmeier to consider polemical connections. Hoffmeier notes, "What better way for the exodus traditions to describe God's victory over Pharaoh than to use Hebrew derivations or counterparts to Egyptian expressions that symbolized Egyptian royal power."[47] Amun "strengthened the powerful arm of my majesty."[48] In the Gebel Barkal account, Thutmosis III is said to have a "powerful arm, smiting foreigners," and is "a warrior who extends his arm on the battlefield."[49] The Memphis and Karnak Stelae mention, "Possessor of a Powerful Arm," which appears as one of Amenhotep II's many names.[50] Likewise, Seti I is called "Mighty of Arm," and "potent with his arm."[51] The Egyptians also portray their enemies as "weak of arms,"[52] or exhausted of arms because Pharaoh's uraeus overpowered them.[53]

BE COURAGEOUS FORMULA

Roland De Vaux points out that due to the nature of holy war, faith was indispensable. Thus God's people were to have no fear. Those who did were to be sent away (Deut 20:8).[54] In the Kadesh inscription, Amun asserts, "I am the Lord of Victory, who loves bravery."[55] Paul-Eugene Dion makes a good case that "fear not" should not be regarded as an exclusive

47. James K. Hoffmeier, "The Arm of God Versus the Arm of Pharaoh in the Exodus Narratives," *Biblica* 67 (1986) 387.

48. COS, "Annals of Thutmose III," 10.

49. COS, "The Gebel Barkal Stela," 14.

50. COS, "The Memphis and Karnak Stelae of Amenhotep II (2.3)," trans. J. Hoffmeier, 20.

51. James Pritchard, "A Campaign of Seti I in Northern Palestine," in *The Ancient Near East, Vol. 2: A New Anthology of Texts and Pictures* (New Jersey: Princeton University Press, 1975) 182. Hereafter Pritchard's second volume will be cited as ANET 2.

52. ANET, "The War Against the Hyksos," 90.

53. COS, "Annals of Thutmose III," 11.

54. Roland De Vaux, *Ancient Israel Its Life and Institutions* (Grand Rapids: Wm. B. Eerdmans Publishing Co., 1961) 259.

55. COS, "Battle of Qadesh," 35.

element in holy war ideology, as opposed to the more prominent phrase, "God X has given Y into your hand."[56] The purpose here is not to argue solely from a holy war perspective, but to simply show that such an encouragement formula is attested in both Egyptian and biblical war texts, regardless of frequency. Kang notes that prior to battle kings often voiced a final encouragement to their troops.[57] In preparation for the assault at Megiddo, Thutmosis III commanded, "Be courageous, be courageous, keep awake, keep awake."[58] This is similar to the command given three times to Joshua by God: "Only be strong and very courageous" (Josh 1:6–9), and once by Israel's officers (Josh 1:18).[59] This will be reciprocated by Joshua to his officers in Josh 10:25, along with a promise of God-given victory. Hezekiah encouraged the military officers in preparation for Assyria with the same formula: "Be strong and courageous, do not fear" (2 Chron 32:7). The legitimacy of his statement is based on the presence of God, who will "help us and fight our battles" (2 Chron 32:8). According to Kang, Ramesses II told his troops and a shield-bearer to "steady" their hearts.[60] In Exod 14:13–14 Moses told Israel: "Do not fear! Stand by and see the salvation of the Lord which He will accomplish for you today; for the Egyptians whom you have seen today, you will never see them again forever. The Lord will fight for you while you keep silent." Both Egyptian and biblical texts demonstrate the usage of an encouragement formula common to the western Crescent.

FIRE AND THE URAEUS CROWN

M. Weinfeld lists eight common elements of divine war which have parallels throughout the ancient Near Eastern world. Among these elements he mentions "pillar of fire and cloud," as well as "god's fire consuming the enemy."[61] Fire is a popular expression of divine activity in war and judgment (Ps 50:3; 2 Sam 22:9). In the Exodus narrative, God manifested Himself in a pillar of cloud by day and a pillar of fire by night (Exod

56. Paul-Eugene Dion, "The 'Fear Not' Formula and Holy War," *Catholic Biblical Quarterly* 32 (1970) 565–70.

57. Kang, 102.

58. COS, "Annals of Thutmose III," 11, 12. This command appears to be directed toward the sentries in the second case.

59. Deut 31:6, 7; 2 Sam 10:12.

60. Kang, 102–3.

61. Kang, 6.

13:21), leading and protecting Israel. Fire describes the theophany of the burning bush, as well as the grand spectacle at Sinai/Horeb, where God's glory is likened unto a "consuming fire" (Exod 24:17; Heb 12:29). Elsewhere, the fire of God devoured the cities of Sodom and Gomorrah (Gen 19), consumed Nadab and Abihu (Lev 10:2), 250 Israelite rebels (Num 16:35), and three groups of 50 men sent to Elijah by Ahaziah (2 Kgs 1). God encouraged Israel that He would be Israel's vanguard into Canaan, leading them "like a devouring fire," destroying and subduing Israel's enemies (Deut 9:3).

In ancient Egypt, pharaohs often wore a serpent-crested diadem as a part of their royal regalia, known as the uraeus crown. This up-reared cobra was a potent charm infused with supernatural power, and symbolized pharaonic strength. Perhaps the most popular image of this is found on the brow of Tutankhamun's burial mask, which displays the serpent goddess Wadjet, goddess of Lower Egypt, aside the vulture deity Nekhbet, goddess of Upper Egypt. In battle the uraeus was thought to strike fear in the hearts of Egypt's enemies, and fight against them through the manifestation of fire, protecting the king while creating fear and weakness in Egypt's enemies, and even in Egyptians.[62] Numerous battle texts contain this motif.

The Gebel Barkal Stela portrays Thutmosis III entering into the enemy lines while "a blast of his flame is against them with fire, turning into nothing those who lie prostrate in their blood. It is his uraeus that overthrows them for him, his flaming serpent that subdues his enemies."[63] John Currid points out that the Egyptians believed the cobra crown was imbued with great magic.[64] Uraeus is called "Great of Magic" in Ramesses III's Medinet Habu account of the war against the Sea People.[65] It also states that "the flame was prepared before them" and "the full flame was in front of them."[66] Similarly, Khamose boasts that the Hyksos "saw my fiery blaze."[67] In Thutmosis III's Megiddo campaign his uraeus "overpowered" the Asiatics, and weakened their arms.

---

62. COS, "The Victory Stela of King Piye (Piankhy) (2.7)," trans. Miriam Lichtheim, 50.

63. COS, "Gebel Barkal Stela," 14.

64. Currid, 91.

65. ANET, "War Against the Peoples of the Sea," 263.

66. Ibid. 262–63.

67. "The War Against the Hyksos," ANET 2, 92.

[68] In the Bible fire is often described as issuing forth from God, or going before Him. It is said of God, "A flame goes forth from his mouth" (Job 41:21; Ps 18:8). In Psalm 50:3: "fire devours before Him," while in Psalm 97:3 God's "fire goes before Him and burns up His adversaries." Currid treats the issue of biblical polemics, revealing the purposeful criticism of Egyptian cultural and religious concepts in certain biblical texts.[69] It is especially intriguing to see how Currid connects the uraeus cult with the serpent contest found in Exodus 7:8–13. Although Currid makes no mention of a polemical parallel between the uraeus cult and the pillar of fire in Exodus 13, it is very tempting to see such a connection based upon the abundant usage of such imagery in Egyptian war texts. Exodus 13:19–20, which bears war imagery, describes how the pillar theophany moved to Israel's rear flank and stood as a bastion between the "camp of Egypt and the camp of Israel." In verse 24, God "looked down on the army of the Egyptians through the pillar of fire and cloud and brought the army of the Egyptians into confusion." The Egyptians replied, "Let us flee from Israel, for the Lord is fighting for them against the Egyptians" (13:25). What the up-reared uraeus was said to do against the enemies of Egypt, Yahweh did for Israel. The victory hymn of Exodus 15 gives no attention to the pillar element, but neither does it mention any of the plagues. It celebrates the culmination of God's actions against Egypt, the climax being the drowning of the Egyptian army in the Red Sea. Thomas Dozeman observes that the "annihilation of the enemy by Yahweh marks the moment of salvation for Israel and prompts the victory hymn."[70]

INTELLIGENCE AGENCIES

Yadin describes the efficiency of the information services (spying) during the period of the Conquest, basing his information on Egyptian texts.[71] One of those texts is the "Bulletin" Text of the Battle of Kadesh, where one of Ramesses II's professional scouts captures two spies of the "Fallen One of Hatti" (Hittites).[72] Of course, one of the popular biblical

68. COS, "Annals of Thutmose III," 11.

69. Currid, 83ff.

70. Thomas Dozeman, *God at War: Power in the Exodus Tradition* (New York: Oxford University Press, 1996) 3.

71. Y. Yadin, "Military and Archaeological Aspects of the Conquest of Canaan in the Book of Joshua," in *Jewish Biblical Quarterly* 32 No 1 (2004), 9.

72. COS, "The Battle of Qadesh—The "Bulletin" Text (2.5B)," trans. K. A. Kitchen, 39.

stories relates to the reconnaissance mission of the 12 spies sent from Kadesh-barnea (Num 13:1). The Megiddo report of Thutmosis III describes the "reporting" of the enemy, as Egyptian scouts were constantly monitoring the actions of the enemies to the north of the Carmel range. After consulting with his officers about the Aruna Pass, "intelligence reports" were brought to Thutmosis III concerning the "feeble enemy."[73] In Numbers 21:32, Moses sent spies to Jazer. Joshua 2:1 records the sending of two spies into Canaan to gather intelligence, especially on Jericho (Josh 7:2; 14:7; Judg 18:14). It is almost certain that most of the people in southern Canaan and the Transjordan kept a watchful eye on Israel's movements through Sinai. Even though Hyksos' rule did not include a strong surveillance of their subject territories, the Hyksos king, Apophis, dispatched a secret courier to his Nubian ally in the south, a strategy that was thwarted by the Egyptian scouts of Khamose of Thebes.[74]

DOXOLOGY OF WAR

Worship was the appropriate response to military success. Praise and worship appear in the Bible as both pre and post-war celebratory acts. Julius Wellhausen believed that war was worship for Israel.[75] Robert Lowery calculated that out of 404 verses comprising the Book of Revelation, 155 of them resemble content from the Book of Exodus. According to Lowery, two of the key interlocking themes from both books are "worship" and "warfare." Lowery also concludes that "Worship is warfare."[76] The religious or spiritual nature of warfare in the Bible is reflected in the prescriptions to keep the war camp holy (Deut 23:14) in the preparations of Israel prior to crossing the Jordan (Josh 3–5), and in the pre-war sacrifice offered by Saul (1 Sam 13). The most popular mode of war doxology was the praise hymn, believed to reflect the "victory song" motif popular in ancient Near Eastern texts. Examples of these abound in Psalms. Kitchen points out that Exodus 15, one of earliest praise hymns, is a

73. COS, "Annals of Thutmosis III," 9.

74. Anthony Spalinger, *War In Ancient Egypt: The New Kingdom* (Malden, MA: Blackwell Publishers, 2005) 3–4.

75. Longman, 20.

76. Robert Lowery, "The Dwelling." Sermon. Ozark Christian College Chapel (Fall 2006). This sermon may be obtained online at http://occ.edu/Chapel/OCC.Chapel .Archives.L.aspx.

"triumph hymn" having much in common with royal triumph hymns etched on the monuments and stelae of Egypt's pharaohs.[77]

According to Thutmosis III's annals, once the enemy at Megiddo had been conquered and the spoils of war collected, the whole army shouted and gave praise to Amun for the victory.[78] Younger says that hymns of praise often followed the announcement of the defeat of Egypt's enemy.[79] Hymns celebrating Khamose's victory over the Hyksos can be found at the conclusion of his victory monument.[80] Longman proposes that the victory song motif is the same as the "new song" found in Isaiah (Isa 42:10),[81] and that it has a close connection with the salvation brought about by God's warring activity.[82] As a part of this doxological response to warfare, the temple, or sacred precinct, often played a vital role. Egyptian kings would bring back the best of the spoils of war and place them in the temple as tribute to Amun. In Joshua 6:19 and 24, the spoils of Jericho were to be placed in the treasury of the Lord. The city of Jericho, which was placed "under the ban" (ḥerem), was considered as whole burnt offering to Yahweh, a tribute to Him as the first-fruits of battle. Ramesses II comments on building a "Memorial Temple" for Amun, filling it with captives.[83] One victory account reads thus: "Giving adoration to [Amun] for the victories [which he] had given to his son… Giving offerings to [Amun]-Re-Harakhty consisting of oxen, fowl, short-horned cattle."[84] The Gebel Barkal inscription mentions that Thutmosis III offered much of his kingdom's tribute, including goods from Punt to Amun, placing them into Amun's temple for compensation for his protection on the battlefield.[85] The doxology of war in both Egypt and the Bible is representative of the general perception of the relationship between man and the divine. The divine ultimately is the authority over

77. K. Kitchen, *On the Reliability of the Old Testament* (Grand Rapids: William B. Eerdmans, 2003) 252.

78. COS, "Annals of Thutmose III," 13.

79. Younger, 170.

80. Anthony J. Spalinger, *Aspects of the Military Documents of the Ancient Egyptians* (New Haven: Yale University Press, 1982) 48.

81. Psalm 40:3; 96:1; 144:9

82. Tremper Longman III and Daniel G. Reid, *God is a Warrior* (Grand Rapids: Zondervan, 1995) 44–45.

83. COS, "Battle of Qadesh," 34.

84. COS, "Annals," 13.

85. COS, "Gebel Barkal Stela," 17.

history, and is the sole source of victory, and therefore, the guarantor of salvation.

CONCLUSION

Cyrus Gordon underscored the "contextual approach" to biblical studies when he said, "No one interested in the nation that produced the Bible can afford to be unfamiliar with the whole of the 'ancient Near East.'"[86] When the Bible is viewed against its proper historical, literary, and cultural background, it is plain to see that it shares much in common with the world of the ancient Crescent, especially Egypt. As previously stated, attention must be paid to Egypt. Egyptian Royal Inscriptions provide rich comparisons for biblical aspects of warfare, supporting the claim that the Bible reflects a second millennium milieu, and illuminating numerous passages that might otherwise be deprived of their proper context and historicity.[87]

---

86. Cyrus Gordon and Gary Rendsburg, *The Bible and the Ancient Near East* (New York: W. W. Norton & Company, 1997) 32.

87. The writer would like to express his deep appreciation to the Ozark Christian College Reference Librarians, John Hunter and Barbara Gardner (former Reference Librarian), for their Second-Mile service in tracking down resources, and for John's aiding in the editorial process. Thanks also to Mark Scott, Academic Dean, and Tom Lawson, Faculty, for their insights and suggestions with the overall presentation.

12

Dark Ages and Little Ice Ages: Millennial Scale Climate Change and Human History[1]

Nigel Brush

O NE OF THE THINGS that scientists love most is the discovery of patterning in their data. This is especially true of multidisciplinary
scientists who are trying to link together data from several different
fields. First of all, patterning reduces the infinite complexity of individual instances to finite collections of similar instances. Secondly, the
existence of patterning suggests common origins, or common development through similar processes, or stimuli. Finally, patterning opens
up the possibility of predictability; scientists can begin to build models
that attempt to explain how patterns arose in the past, or describe what
patterns may reoccur in the future. Although social scientists (such as
archaeologists and historians) have adopted the same scientific methodology as natural scientists (such as geologists), the highly flexible and
adaptive nature of human thought and culture has largely thwarted their
efforts to develop predictive laws or models concerning human behavior.
Nevertheless, one significant pattern that archaeologists and historians

1. Dr. Reuben Bullard was one of those rare teachers who could inspire as well as
instruct his students. He was so successful at imparting his love of geology, archaeology,
and ancient history to his students that some of us have only been able to find intel-
lectual fulfillment in multidisciplinary studies where we could simultaneously pursue
all three of these passions. One of the areas where the multidisciplinary approach has
been particularly productive is in the realm of climate change. Within the past decade,
geologists have begun to unveil a new vision of recent earth history that has significant
implications for both archaeologists and historians. Dr. Bullard would not have been
surprised by this development since he always believed that geology could serve as a
bridge between the natural sciences and the social sciences.

have discovered in their study of human history is a reoccurring cycle of cultural expansion and contraction. The periods of expansion are often remembered as "golden ages," while the periods of contraction are frequently described as "dark ages."

DARK AGES

The idea of an age of darkness (Lat. *tenebrae*) was first developed by the Italian humanist Francesco Petrarch (AD 1304–1374) in order to contrast the time in which he lived (a dark age), with the previous glories of the ancient Roman Empire. He believed that this dark age began when Christianity became the religion of the empire, and when "barbarian" (non-Roman) emperors assumed the rule of Italy. It was Petrarch's fervent dream that the Roman Empire would someday return to its former position of dominance in the world, if only the citizens of Rome could be educated about their glorious past.[2] At the end of his epic poem *Africa*, he expressed this longing for a new, brighter age:

> My life is destined to be spent 'midst storms and turmoil. But if you, as is my wish and ardent hope, shall live on after me, a more propitious age will come again: this Lethean stupor surely can't endure forever. Our posterity, perchance, when the dark clouds are lifted, may enjoy once more the radiance the ancients knew.[3]

By the fifteenth century, many humanists, such as Leonardo Bruni, had convinced themselves that Petrarch's dream had been achieved through the Italian Renaissance, and thus began to refer to the period between the collapse of the Roman Empire in the 4th Century (the Classical world) and the Renaissance in the 15th Century (the Modern world) as the "Middle Ages."[4] This thousand-year-period would subsequently be subdivided into the Early, High, and Late Middle Ages. A growing knowledge of these sub-periods led to the recognition that significant cultural achievements had been made during the High Middle Ages; thus, the use of the term Dark Ages was frequently restricted to only the Early Middle Ages. (Later, some scholars would argue that the

---

2. Theodore E. Mommsen, "Petrarch's Conception of the 'Dark Ages'," *Speculum* 17 (1942) 233–37.

3. Francesco Petrarch, *Petrarch's Africa*, trans. Thomas G. Bergin and Alice S. Wilson (New Haven: Yale University Press, 1977) 239.

4. Mommsen, 241–42.

Early Middle Ages were "dark," only in the sense that modern people had little information about this distant time period.) By the seventeenth and eighteenth centuries, the Age of Enlightenment gave scholars another reason to view the Middle Ages as a backward time, a time dominated not by reason, but by faith. In the eighteenth and nineteenth centuries, reaction against the growing atheism, humanism, and secularism of the modern age led to the Romantic Movement and its various incarnations, such as the Gothic Revival and the Pre-Raphaelites, which glorified the Middle Ages (particularly the High Middle Ages) as an Age of Faith rather than an Age of Darkness. Therefore, Petrarch's original concept of a dark age has seen many revisions and reformulations over the centuries.

In the twentieth century the idea of Dark Ages was revised once again, this time by archaeologists attempting to describe catastrophic episodes in the past when large numbers of cultures and civilizations seem to have collapsed simultaneously. In his book *What Happened in History* (1942), Gordon Childe used the term "dark age" to refer to the time of chaos at end of the Early Bronze Age,[5] as well as at the end of the Late Bronze Age:

> So the Bronze Age in the Near East ended round about 1200 B.C. in a dark age, blacker and more extensive than those that opened our last chapter. Not in a single State alone, but over a large part of the civilized world history itself seems to be interrupted; the written sources dry up, the archaeological documents are poor and hard to date.[6]

While excavating at Ras Shamra (Ugarit) in Syria, the French archaeologist, Claude Schaeffer, identified four major destruction layers, three of which corresponded with the dates for the end of the Early, Middle, and Late Bronze Ages. Later (1948), in a book entitled *Stratigraphie comparée et chronologie de l'Asie Occidentale (IIIe et IIe millénaire) Syrie, Palestine, Asie Mineure, Chypre, Perse et Caucase*,[7] Schaeffer examined the evidence for similar destruction layers at some forty sites throughout the Mediterranean world. He believed that the widespread destructions

---

5. Gordon Childe, *What Happened in History* (Baltimore: Penguin Books, 1942) 159.

6. Ibid., 194.

7. Claude F.A. Schaeffer, *Stratigraphie comparée et chronologie de l'Asie Occidentale (IIIe et IIe millénaire) Syrie, Palestine, Asie Mineure, Chypre, Perse et Caucase.* (London: G. Cumberledge, 1948).

of cities across the Near East were the result of some natural agent (such as earthquakes).

Unfortunately, the work of Childe and Schaeffer on dark ages was largely ignored by archaeologists during the next thirty years, due to the prevailing bias in the scientific community against any hint of environmental determinism[8] or catastrophism. It was not until the 1970s and 1980s that several archaeologists began to use dark age models to explain major periods of cultural disruption in individual countries such as Egypt,[9] Greece,[10] and England.[11] In the 1980s, with the growing concern over the environmental impacts of global warming, acid rain, and the ozone crisis, as well as the discovery of an asteroid-induced, world-wide catastrophe at the end of the Cretaceous Period,[12] scientists began to re-access their attitudes toward catastrophism and environmental determinism. Archaeologists and historians began to assemble evidence for individual dark ages that had settled over many nations at the same time such as at the end of Early Bronze Age,[13] at the end of Late Bronze Age,[14] and at the end of the Classical Age.[15] However, it was not until the end of the twentieth century and the beginning of the twenty-first century that Childe and Schaeffer's vision of multiple dark ages was fully revived in the work of individuals such as Baillie,[16] Burroughs,[17] or Chew.[18]

8. Eugene Linden, *The Winds of Change: Climate, Weather, and the Destruction of Civilizations* (New York: Simon & Schuster, 2006) 91–92.

9. Barbara Bell, "The Dark Ages in Ancient History I: The First Dark Age in Egypt," *American Journal of Archaeology* 75 (1971).

10. A. M. Snodgrass, *The Dark Age of Greece* (Edinburgh: Edinburgh University Press, 1971); V. R. Desborough, *The Greek Dark Ages* (London: Ernest Benn, 1972).

11. C. Burgess, "Population, Climate and Upland Settlement," *British Archaeological Reports* (British Series) 143 (1985).

12. Walter Alvarez, *T. rex and the Crater of Doom* (Princeton: Princeton University Press, 1997).

13. H. Weiss et al., "The Genesis and Collapse of Third Millennium North Mesopotamian Civilization," *Science* 261 (1993).

14. Robert Drews, *The End of the Bronze Age: Changes in Warfare and the Catastrophe ca. 1200 B.C.* (Princeton: Princeton University Press, 1993).

15. David Keys, *Catastrophe: An Investigation into the Origins of the Modern World* (New York: Ballantine Books, 1999).

16. M. G. L. Baillie, *A Slice Through Time: Dendrochronology and Precision Dating* (London: Routledge, 1995); Mike Baillie, *Exodus to Arthur: Catastrophic Encounters with Comets* (London: B.T. Batsford, 1999).

17. William James Burroughs, *Climate Change in Prehistory: The End of the Reign of Chaos* (Cambridge: Cambridge University Press, 2005).

18. Sing C. Chew, *The Recurring Dark Ages: Ecological Stress, Climate Changes, and*

As research into these periods of widespread cultural decline and collapse continued, Petrarch's original dark age was retained. However, archaeologists and historians subsequently identified at least four additional dark ages that have occurred during the past 6000 years. Each of these dark ages lasted for at least 500 years.[19] Although Petrarch believed that he was living in the dark age that had descended upon Europe following the collapse of the Roman Empire, it can now be argued that he was actually born just after the close of a golden age, the High Middle Ages (AD 1000–1300). The world in which Petrarch lived was actually descending into a new dark age that would last until (at least) AD 1700.

Based on archaeological and historical records, as well as pollen profiles that record reoccurring periods of deforestation, Chew[20] has identified 5 dark ages: Phase 1 (3800/3400–2400 BC), Phase 2 (2200–1700 BC), Phase 2a (1200–700 BC), Phase 3 (AD 300/400–900), and Phase 4 (AD 1300–1700). However, since we are presently uncertain as to how many (even older) dark ages may eventually be identified, it would probably be better to start numbering these dark ages from the most recent event (See Table 1).

Table 1: Dark Ages	
Dark Age I	AD 1300–1700
Dark Age II	AD 300/400–900
Dark Age III	1200–700 BC
Dark Age IV	2200–1700 BC
Dark Age V	3800/3400–2400 BC

Dark Age I corresponds to the period of the Late Middle Ages in Europe. Dark Age II begins around the time of the collapse of the Roman Empire, and ends with the start of the High Middle Ages. David Keys has focused on Dark Age II in his book *Catastrophe: An Investigation into the Origins of the Modern World*, and Joel Gunn has also examined this period in *The Years Without Summer: Tracing A.D. 536 and its Aftermath*.[21] Dark Age III begins with the end of the Late Bronze Age Period in the

---

System Transformation (New York: AltaMira Press, 2007).

19. Ibid., 13.

20. Ibid., 41–54.

21. Keys; Joel Gunn, ed., *The Years Without Summer: Tracing A.D. 536 and its Aftermath* (Oxford: Archaeopress, 2000).

eastern Mediterranean, and is the focus of several books, including: *The Crisis Years: The 12th Century B.C.*, and *The End of the Bronze Age: Changes in Warfare and the Catastrophe ca. 1200 B.C.*[22] Dark Age IV starts with the end of the Early Bronze Age Period, and is discussed in such works as: "The Genesis and Collapse of Third Millennium North Mesopotamian Civilization," and *Third Millennium B.C. Climate Change and Old World Collapse.*[23] Dark Age V, presently being the oldest, is the least understood (as can be seen in the 1400 year span assigned to this episode). Chew identified this dark age solely on the basis of a major period of deforestation from 3854 to 2400 BC; he notes that archaeologists and historians have not yet identified a dark age for this period.[24]

When one examines the historical, archaeological, and geological evidence for these dark ages, a series of reoccurring patterns emerge in the cultures and societies that were in existence during these chaotic times. The first four dark ages (Dark Ages I–IV) all share most (if not all) of the following traits (See Table 2):

Table 2: Characteristics of Dark Ages	
Culture	*Society*
decrease in literacy	decrease in social stratification
decrease in subsistence	decrease in communal tombs
decrease in technology	decrease in centralized authority
decrease in arts	decrease in territory
decrease in architecture	decrease in urbanization
decrease in trade	decrease in population
Human Environment	*Natural Environment*
increase in famines	increase in cold wet/periods
increase in plagues	increase in droughts
increase in social anarchy	increase in storms
increase in warfare	increase in floods
increase in migrations	increase in deforestation
increase in religious activity	increase in soil erosion and debris flows

22. William A. Ward and Martha Joukowsky, eds., *The Crisis Years: The 12th Century B.C.* (Dubuque: Kendall/Hunt, 1992); Drews.

23. Weiss et al.; H. Nüzhet Dalfes et al. eds., *Third Millennium BC Climate Change and Old World Collapse.* (Berlin: Springer, 1997).

24. Chew, 48.

Many different theories have been advanced to explain these reoccurring dark ages, including: (1) migrations,[25] (2) raiders,[26] (3) ironworking,[27] (4) earthquakes,[28] (5) drought,[29] (6) internal factors,[30] (7) plagues,[31] (8) over specialization in the agricultural system,[32] (9) systems collapse,[33] (10) change in trade networks and patterns of production,[34] (11) new style of warfare,[35] (12) volcanic eruptions,[36] (13) asteroid impacts,[37] and (14) climate change.[38] Such debates often seem irresolvable since at least some scientific evidence can be assembled to support each of the competing hypotheses. For many years geologists faced a similar impasse as they sorted through a plethora of theories that had been advanced to explain the widespread destruction of terrestrial and marine communities (such as dinosaurs and ammonites) at the end of the Cretaceous Period. They were finally able to resolve this problem by identifying a single causal agent (an asteroid) that had produced multiple effects upon earth's ecosystems. In the past decade, geologists have

25. Gaston Maspero, *The Struggle of the Nations*, ed. A.H. Sayce, trans. M.L. McClure (New York: Appleton, 1896).

26. Henry A. Ormerod, *Piracy in the Ancient World: An Essay in Mediterranean History* (1924; reprint, Chicago: Argonaut, 1967).

27. Childe.

28. Schaeffer.

29. Rhys Carpenter, *Discontinuity in Greek Civilization* (New York: Norton, 1968).

30. T. P. Culbert, *The Classic Maya Collapse* (Albuquerque: University of New Mexico Press, 1973); Mario Liverani, "The Collapse of the Near Eastern Regional System at the End of the Bronze Age: The Case of Syria," in *Centre and Periphery in the Ancient World*, ed. M. Rowlands, M. Larsen, and K. Kristiansen (Cambridge: Cambridge University Press, 1987).

31. William H. McNeill, *Plagues and People* (Garden City: Anchor Press, 1976).

32. Philip Betancourt, "The End of the Greek Bronze Age," *Antiquity* 50 (1976).

33. Nancy Sandars, *The Sea Peoples: Warriors of the Ancient Mediterranean 1250–1150 B.C.* (London: Thames and Hudson, 1978).

34. Carlo Zaccagnini, "The Transition from Bronze to Iron in the Near East and in the Levant: Marginal Notes," *JAOS* 110 (1990).

35. Drews.

36. Keys; Baillie, *Slice Through Time*; Baillie, *Exodus to Arthur*; C. Burgess, "Volcanoes, Catastrophe, and Global Crisis of the Late 2nd Millennium B.C.," *Current Anthropology* 10 (1989).

37. Patrick McCafferty and Mike Baillie, *The Celtic Gods: Comets in Irish Mythology* (Stoud: Tempus, 2005).

38. Burroughs.

discovered another causal agent capable of producing multiple effects in both natural and cultural systems: little ice ages. This agent appears to hold the key to explaining the pattern of reoccurring dark ages.

LITTLE ICE AGES

The term "Little Ice Age" was initially coined by François Matthes in 1939 to describe the cooler conditions that have prevailed since the Climatic Optimum ended some 5,000 years ago.[39] However, as scientific scrutiny of climatic records intensified during the second half of the twentieth century, it was discovered that the climate of the Holocene Epoch (10,000-years-ago to present) was not as stable and benign as had long been imagined. Instead of a gradual rise in temperature from the end of the Ice Age to the Climatic Optimum, and then a gradual fall in temperatures from the Climatic Optimum to the present, scientists began to uncover evidence for much more dramatic climatic excursions during this time period. The twentieth century, rather than being the coolest century since the Climatic Optimum, was actually the warmest and most stable period in the past 600 years. Prior to the 1850s, the world's climate had been much cooler and more unsettled than at present. Geologists and climatologists have subsequently taken Matthes' term, "Little Ice Age," and restricted its use to designate the period of cooler, wetter climate between AD 1300 and 1850. During this time, glaciers experienced a period of growth and expansion in a number of mountain ranges around the world.

As scientists developed more sophisticated techniques for studying climate change, they found that the Little Ice Age had been preceded by a warm, stable period, similar to the one in which we presently live; this period (AD 900–1300) was designated as the Medieval Warm Period, and corresponded with the time of the High Middle Ages. This warm period was bracketed by the Little Ice Age at its end, and another cool wet period at its beginning. By carbon-dating pieces of wood in glacial moraines, geologists began to realize that glacial advances during the Holocene were not confined to the Little Ice Age. In 1967 Porter and Denton, working in western North America, identified moraines deposited during the Little Ice Age event, as well as during two earlier glacial advances at 2600 BC and AD 600–800.[40] Six years later, Denton

39. F. E. Matthes, "Report of Committee on Glaciers, April 1939," *Transactions of the American Geophysical Union* 20 (1939).

40. S. C. Porter and G. H. Denton, "Chronology of Neo-glaciation in the North

and Karlén confirmed these three advances by studying moraines in Alaska, Canada, and Sweden; they also found three additional advances at 1350–450 cal. BC, 3800–2900 BC, and 6000 BC They pointed out that each of these periods of glacial advance lasted between 600–900 years.[41] Working in the Alps, Heuberger (1974) subsequently identified seven glacial advances during the past 9000 years,[42] and Patzelt (1974) added an eighth.[43] During the last quarter of the twentieth century, the work of these early pioneers in Holocene glacial geology would subsequently be confirmed, corrected, refined, or expanded by other geologists using a variety of new climatic proxies, including ice cores, sediment cores, tree rings, coral reefs, and speleothems. In the 1990s, Gerard Bond and his colleagues, using mineral grains that had been dropped onto the seafloor of the North Atlantic by icebergs during cool periods, were able to identify nine little ice age events in the past 12,000 years.[44] These little ice age events seem to have a periodicity of 1650 + 500 years. Based on cosmogenic isotopes such as beryllium-10 (recovered from ice cores) and carbon-14 (recovered from tree rings), these cold phases were shown to occur during periods of decreased solar irradiance.[45] Thus, like the reoccurring pattern of dark ages discovered by archaeologists and historians, geologists have identified a reoccurring pattern of little ice ages.

Jean M. Grove, in her book *Little Ice Ages Ancient and Modern*, noted that the Little Ice Age was a global phenomenon that was characterized by "measurable meteorological, geomorphological and vegetational changes."[46] Among the physical changes she identified (See Table 3) were drops in temperature, shifts in climate zones, and increases in severe weather.[47]

American Cordillera," *American Journal of Science* 265 (1967).

41. G. H. Denton and W. Karlén, "Holocene Climatic Variations-Their Pattern and Possible Causes," *Quaternary Research* 3 (1973).

42. H. Heuberger, "Alpine Quaternary Glaciation," in *Arctic and Alpine Environments*, ed. J. D. Ives and R. G. Barry, (London: Methuen, 1974).

43. G. Patzelt, "Holocene Variations of Glaciers in the Alps," in *Les méthods quantitative d'étude des variations du climate au cours du Pléistocene* (Paris: Colloques Internationaux du Centre National de la Recherche Scientifique, no. 219, 1974).

44. Gerard Bond, et al., "Persistent Solar Influence on North Atlantic Climate during the Holocene," *Science* 294 (2001).

45. Ibid.

46. Jean M. Grove, *Little Ice Ages: Ancient and Modern*, 2 vol., 2nd ed. (London: Routledge, 2004) 1:4.

47. Ibid., 2:591–604.

Table 3: Characteristics of Little Ice Ages
drops in temperature of 2 degrees C or less around the world
drops in temperature of up to 4 degrees C in more limited areas
advances of mountain glaciers and the Greenland ice sheet to more forward positions
shifts of snowlines from higher to lower elevations
shifts of climate zones from higher to lower latitudes
increases in climate instability with sometimes rapid, decadal-length shifts
increases of flooding and debris flows in some areas
increases of drought, falling water tables and lake levels in some areas
increase of windiness, dustiness, and dune formation in some areas

These meteorological, geomorphological, and vegetational changes not only characterized the Little Ice Ages, but also other (earlier) little ice ages. Moreover, as Grove pointed out, these climatic changes had significant impacts, not just on plant and animal communities, but also upon human populations.[48] Indeed, many of the same climatic disruptions that are characteristic of these little ice ages were also recorded by individuals living during Dark Ages I-IV, or by archaeologists and historians studying these periods of cultural collapse. Therefore, is it possible that the agent causing the dark ages that have been identified by archaeologists and historians is the little ice ages that have been identified by geologists and climatologists?

SYNTHESIS

If we compare the time ranges for the little ice ages documented by Bond and his colleagues[49] with the five dark ages identified by Chew,[50] as well as two additional dark ages (#6 and #10) identified by Weiss and Bradley,[51] we find that the date ranges for these two phenomena correspond very closely with each other. Moreover, Baillie has identified seven brief periods during the last 7200 years during which tree ring growth in various parts of the world was at a minimum. If climatic conditions were so severe during these periods that even trees experienced little growth, it is likely that human agriculture was also under great stress. Five of

48. Ibid., 2:604–38.

49. Bond et al., 2131.

50. Chew, 41–54.

51. Harvey Weiss and Raymond S. Bradley, "What Drives Societal Collapse?" *Science* 291 (2001) 609.

Baillie's seven "narrowest-ring events"[52] fall within these dark age/little ice age periods (See Table 4):

Table 4: Chronology of Little Ice Ages, Dark Ages, and Narrowest Ring Events (NRE)				
Little Ice Ages		Dark Ages		NRE
Little Ice Age #1	AD 1400–1900	Dark Age #1	AD 1300–1700	
Little Ice Age #2	AD 400–800	Dark Age #2	AD 300/400–900	AD 540
Little Ice Age #3	1400–800 BC	Dark Age #3	1200–700 BC	1159 BC
Little Ice Age #4	2600–2000 BC	Dark Age #4	2200–1700 BC	2345 BC
Little Ice Age #5	3800–3200 BC	Dark Age #5	3800/3400–2400 BC	3195 BC
Little Ice Age #6	6600–5400 BC	Dark Age #6	6400 BC	
Little Ice Age #7	7400 BC			
Little Ice Age #8	8400 BC			
Little Ice Age #9	9400–9200 BC			
Little Ice Age #10	10,900–9600 BC	Dark Age #10	10,000 BC	

Therefore, it is highly likely that instead of there being multiple causal agents responsible for the pattern of reoccurring dark ages during the past 12,000 years, there was but one, reoccurring, causal agent. This agent was little ice ages that had multiple impacts upon both the human and natural environments. In other words, the reoccurring pattern of cultural expansion and contraction (golden ages and dark ages) that archaeologists and historians have identified in their study of human history, was the direct result of the waxing and waning of global climate (warm periods and little ice ages). These shifts in climate were being driven by a millennial-scale periodicity in solar irradiance.

Little ice ages had multiple impacts on cultures across broad regions of the earth. These climatic impacts were highly variable, with some areas becoming colder and wetter, while other areas became warmer and drier as climate bands shifted from higher to lower latitudes. Although these shifts may have been ultimately advantageous to some areas (i.e. hot areas that became cooler, or dry areas that became wetter), abrupt climate shifts most likely would have been initially disruptive to most cultures because all cultures typically developed complex, long-term adaptations to the prevailing climatic regimes. These adaptations could have been easily or rapidly modified. Consequently, little ice ages put many cultures under stress as people attempted to readjust to new environmental conditions.

52. Baillie, *Slice Through Time*, 77.

The most important impact that climate change would have initially had on cultures across the world would have been upon their subsistence systems. Many of the plant and animal communities that peoples previously relied on for food or other purposes would have been severely affected by the change in climate. Some plants and animals may not have been able to survive these climatic shifts, while others might have experienced significant reductions in their numbers, or were forced to drastically alter their ranges. Under these circumstances there would have been growing scarcities of food and other raw materials. Competition for these resources would have intensified, both inside and outside of cultures, thus resulting in rising levels of tension and hostility. Therefore, it is not surprising that societal collapse and warfare often became endemic during these cold pulses. Moreover, in areas that were already marginal in terms of available resources (such as those at higher elevations or higher latitudes), the climate changes may have been so disadvantageous that many of the peoples occupying these regions could have been forced to abandon their homes and migrate to less rigorous environments. Such large-scale mobilizations of people would most likely have put additional stress on cultures in less marginal environments who were already attempting to adapt to the new environmental conditions. With crop failures and famines resulting from the climatic disruptions, ensuing warfare, and mobilization of large numbers of people, it is not surprising that disease and plague outbreaks often accompanied these cold pulses. These agents ultimately would decimate urban centers, and cause steep declines in population levels, all resulting in the contraction of territories, and the collapse of empires. During such unsettled periods, any additional environmental disruptions (such as major volcanic eruptions or earthquakes) would have only exacerbated these cultural and societal problems.

In the face of great stress and calamity, all cultures and societies probably had fall-back positions to which they may have reverted. Earlier modes of resource procurement or societal organization are often simpler and more reliable than later adaptations. In other words, a culture's collective knowledge of past adaptive strategies could have served as an insurance policy against unforeseen change. At the outset of a dark age many peoples may have been forced to revert to older technologies and societal frameworks to survive the rigors of a little ice age. Consequently, at the beginning of a dark age, cultures and societies might often have seemed to be taking a step backward in time to earlier life-ways. However, during the course of the dark age/little ice age, the challenges of survival often stimulated the development of completely new technologies and societal configurations. When the dark age/little ice age ended, survivors, instead of just picking up where their pre-dark age ancestors left off, may have actually possessed new tools and skills that allowed them to reach much higher levels of cultural development during the next phase of warmer, more settled climatic conditions. These warm ages would have then appeared as "golden ages" when compared with what came before (a dark age) or after (another dark age).

In light of the preceding factors, it is not surprising that some of the "ages" that archaeologists and historians had previously created in order to divide up human history and prehistory into manageable units (i.e. Early/Middle/Late Bronze Age or Early/High/Late Middle Ages), can readily be superimposed over the chronology of little ice ages that geologists have developed from various climatic proxies. Little ice ages/warm periods have strongly influenced the pace of human societal and cultural development. The transitions from cool to warm periods are often marked by the rapid and widespread adoption of technological and societal innovations whose development was stimulated by the rigors of the natural and cultural environment during the preceding little ice age/dark age. When catastrophism was reintroduced into geology in the last quarter of the twentieth century, geologists found a similar correspondence between major catastrophes and the "periods" and "eras" that they had previously created in order to divide up geological time into manageable units. Instead of technological and societal innovations, geologists had used the appearance and disappearance of various organisms in the fossil record to designate the beginning and ending of various eras (Paleozoic, Mesozoic, and Cenozoic) and periods (i.e. Permian, Triassic, Jurassic, Cretaceous). The abrupt disappearance of a number of species from the fossil record at the end of a period or era (such as the dinosaurs at the end of the Cretaceous Period/Mesozoic Era) was the direct result of a major mass extinction that had been generated by a catastrophe (an asteroid impact). Adaptive radiations of new species into many (now empty) ecological niches marked the beginning of a new period or era (such as the appearance and spread of new mammals in the Tertiary Period/Cenozoic Era). Therefore, even as Dark Age I and II correspond with the end of the High Middle Ages and the Classical Roman Period, and Dark Ages III and IV correspond with the end of the Late and Early Bronze Ages, archaeologists and historians may find evidence for Dark Age V and VII through IX in the stages or sub-stages of already established chronologies.

In conclusion, archaeologists and historians have identified a cyclical pattern of expansion and contraction in cultures and civilizations that spans the past 12,000 years of human history/prehistory. The periods of expansion are often remembered as golden ages, while the periods of contraction are frequently described as dark ages. Using a variety of climatic proxies, geologists have identified a cyclical pattern of warm and cool periods that span the last 12,000 years of earth history. The cold periods in this cycle are called little ice ages. Both of these cycles operate on a millennial time scale. Moreover, when the cycle of warm and cold periods is superimposed over the cycle of cultural expansions and contractions, there is a strong correlation between their time ranges. The periods of cultural expansion (golden ages) occur during the warm periods, and the periods of cultural contraction (dark ages) occur during the cold periods. In other words, human cultures and civilizations seem to be highly sensitive to slight changes in the earth's climate. The earth's climate, in turn, is highly sensitive to slight changes in solar irradiation. Thus, the linkage between human history and natural history is far more dynamic than we had previously imagined.

Dr. Bullard's work anticipated such deep connections between climate and human history. Indeed, he spent his life looking for such patterns. As a pioneer in archaeological geology, he specialized in the use of geology to help reconstruct the environmental setting of archaeological sites and ancient cultures. He believed that there was a strong correlation between a site, a city, or a culture and its surrounding environment. I think he would have been pleased to learn that geologists, archaeologists, and historians have now forged an even deeper link between the natural environment and human history, a link that not only spans countries and continents but also centuries and millennia.[53]

53. The God whom Dr. Bullard served was Lord of both space and time. As Dr. Bullard often pointed out in class, this God was quite capable of ordering events in the natural world to accomplish His purposes in human history. Although the gradual reemergence of environmental determinism and catastrophism in the latter part of the twentieth century facilitated scientific consideration of Child and Schaeffer's dark ages, the cyclical pattern of warm period/golden age and cold period/dark age could just as readily be understood in terms of divine prerogative. As many theologians have pointed out, death not only serves as a punishment for sin, but as a necessary check on the propagation of evil. The injustice and cruelty inflicted upon humanity by men such as Nebuchadnezzar, Nero, or Hitler, is limited by the mortality of these perpetrators. In a similar manner, God may have placed temporal restraints upon the cultures and civilizations of the world. During their expansive stage, powerful nations may appear invincible and everlasting; yet, they too will meet their end "at the appointed time" (Dan 11:27) perhaps, during a little ice age.

13

Mosaics at Abila[1]

Timothy Snow

Since the Edict of Toleration by the Emperor Constantine in AD 312/3, Christians were free to openly express their beliefs. One way that this manifested itself was through the medium of mosaics. The more ornate mosaics were executed on the walls and domes of the various basilicas. Since floor mosaics served an additional purpose of being walked upon, these usually were less ornate. Whether on the walls or on the floors, mosaics communicated the thinking and sentiments of earlier Christians. Dunbabin remarked:

> However, from the fourth century A.D. onwards mosaics were used very extensively to decorate the sacred buildings of both Jews and Christians. On both banks of the Jordan, but especially in the east, the tradition continued without a break until a late date; the latest known here belong to the eighth century, long after the Arab conquests of the 630's. Their use not only continued in Christian churches, but was also adopted by the Moslem conquerors.[2]

This was no different at the site of Abila. As a Decapolis city whose heyday was in the Roman and Byzantine periods, Abila had no fewer than six basilicas. Each was highly or lowly decorated, depending on

1. I have been with the excavations at Abila during the 1986–2004 and 2008 seasons, mainly under the encouragement of Reuben Bullard and Willard W. Winter to whom I am eternally grateful. In the 1986 and 1988 seasons I worked under the supervision of Dr. Winter, where my interests in basilicas and mosaics were developed. From the 1990 season forward, I served as chief photographer for the excavation while maintaining the prior interests.

2. Katherine M. D. Dunbabin, *Mosaics of the Greek and Roman World*, (Cambridge: Cambridge University Press, 1999) 187.

patrons and/or funds available. Besides the basilicas at Tell Abil, the primary focus of this chapter will center upon the basilicas at Khirbet Umm el 'Amad.

First of all, mosaics can be divided into three main groups: *opus tessellatum*, *opus sectile*, and *opus vermiculatum*. The first two groups have to do with floor mosaics, the latter was commonly used on wall mosaics. There were no intact wall mosaics preserved at Abila. *Opus tessellatum* was the technique "in which pieces of stone or marble were cut to approximately cubic shape and fitted closely together in a bed of mortar, invented in the course of the 3rd century BC though the exact date is controversial."[3] On Tell Abil and Khirbet Umm el 'Amad, *opus tessellatum* mosaics were found outside of the churches proper in areas of the narthex and ancillary rooms. *Opus Sectile* (cut work) was a technique used to lay the flooring in the naves and side aisles of the basilicas. Ling defined this technique as being "a surface decoration obtained by cutting pieces of stone to special geometric or other shapes."[4] The floor patterns at Abila range from basic checkerboard designs to more intricate geometrical patterns. *Opus vermiculatum* is a mosaic technique found on walls. Literally "worm-like," it is "commonly used to describe the technique of pictorial mosaics made with minute tesserae."[5] At Abila, no wall mosaics have been preserved since there are almost no walls left standing. However, minute glass and gold tesserae have been found.

THE MANUFACTURING PROCESS

During the 1986 season a "tesserae workshop" was discovered in the eastern part of the Khirbet Umm el 'Amad basilica in what is known as Area D. John Wineland drew on Winter's supervisor's report on the 1986 season as he described what was found in regard to this.

> The excavation crew nicknamed square D-14 the "tesserae workshop." The staff found a large pile of limestone chips in D-14 during the excavation. Many of these limestone pieces were of long rectangular shape, and were probably used as tesserae blanks. Mosaicists could have broken tesserae off of the end of the blank

---

3. Katherine M. D. Dunbabin, "Mosaic," in *The Oxford Classical Dictionary*, 3rd ed., eds. Simon Hornblower and Antony Spawforth, (Oxford: Oxford University Press, 1996) 996.

4. Roger Ling, *Ancient Mosaics*, (Princeton, NJ: Princeton University Press, 1998) 139.

5. Ibid.

as they constructed the mosaic. These tesserae blanks measure about ten centimeters in length. Each blank was from various shades of limestone. Excavators found in all four different colors of blanks: red, pink, white, and black.[6]

We are given a window on this practice by a fragmentary grave stele at Ostia, probably from the beginning of the fourth century AD. Dunbabin describes this as being "Two men in long sleeved tunics [who] are sitting hammering at small objects which they hold on an anvil-like block. In the foreground an upturned basket spills out a mass of stones marked into squares by a series of straight lines, perhaps stones to be broken up."[7]

Vitruvius, who wrote during the 1st century BC, recorded this process as one of laying mosaic flooring.[8] Three layers were recommended to prepare for the final pavement. The first layer, the *statumen*, would have been composed of stones "not smaller than can fill the hand." On top of this was a well-compacted layer known as the *rudus*. This was composed of broken stone and lime, and spread to a depth of approximately nine inches. The nucleus, a mixture of pounded tile and lime forming a layer not less than six inches thick was laid on top of the rudus. The mosaic pavement was then pressed into a fine surface layer.[9] Given these were ideal standards, they may not necessarily have been the rule in every instance.

Vitruvius did not indicate how the tesserae themselves were made, but it can be surmised that first the stone was quarried, then it was cut into "fingers." From these "fingers," each individual tessera cube could be broken off as needed. Eventually, mosaics came to be mass-produced in the empire,[10] with mosaic workshops flourishing in the Near East, especially in the first half of the fifth century.[11] As with *opus sectile*, each piece would be cut to a special pattern to conform to a specific design.

6. John D. Wineland, *Ancient Abila: An Archaeological History*, BAR International Series 989 (Oxford: Archaeopress, 2001) 31. See also Willard W. Winter, "Abila of the Decapolis–1986: Area D," *Near Eastern Archaeological Society Bulletin* 28 (1987) 52–76.

7. Dunbabin, *Mosaics of the Greek and Roman World*, 281.

8. Vitruvius Pollio, *The Ten Books on Architecture*, trans. Morris Hicky Morgan, (Cambridge: Harvard University Press, 1914) 202–204. In the original work, this was book 7, chapter 1.

9. Ling, 11.

10. Dunbabin, "Mosaic," 996.

11. Christine Kondoleon and Lucille A. Roussin, "Mosaics," in *The Oxford Encyclopedia of Archaeology in the Near East*, ed. Eric M. Meyers, (New York: Oxford University Press, 1997) 4:53.

At places like Abila, a family workshop of mosaicists was probably in operation, with each generation teaching the craft to the next.

The tessera blanks found in the "tesserae workshop" at Abila were made of various shades of limestone: red, pink, white, and black. This is in line with the fact that Byzantine mosaicists worked with a more limited color palette, using no more than ten to twelve colors, as opposed to the Romans who typically used a palette of about thirty colors.[12] We do not know specifically from where these materials were quarried, even though evidence of quarrying was found throughout the site. Dunbabin replied concerning this question that "The mosaicists (also known as *musivarii*, practitioners in wall mosaics, and *tessellarii*, practitioners in floor mosaics) undoubtedly derived their materials from any convenient source they could, and no great effort was required for the basic white and black; but a more complex process would have been required to identify sources of colored stones not otherwise needed for building."[13] At least in the case of the materials found in the "tesserae workshop," it is likely that the source of mosaic materials at Abila are local, or at least from the general area.

Not only did the mosaicist concern himself with the mechanics of laying the pavement, he also planned out the aesthetics of the finished work. Patterns ranged from simpler geometric patterns to intricate pictorial mosaics. As might be assumed, complicated mosaics required more detailed planning on the part of the artist:

> . . . anything more than the simplest of patterns required careful calculations to adapt the pattern to the size and shape of the room. Normally an area known as an edging-band around the circumference of the room was filled with plain tesserae, a task which could have been left to an apprentice or assistant. Within this the area for the design is usually rectangular, occasionally circular or of some more complicated shape; it could be further subdivided in innumerable different ways. The width of the borders had to be determined, ranging from a simple fillet of two or three rows of tesserae to a succession of complex ornamental bands; and the design to cover the main field or fields had to be planned. Even a simple schema, such as a grid pattern, had to

12. S. Thomas Parker, "The Byzantine Period: An Empire's New Holy Land," *Near Eastern Archaeology*, 62, no. 3 (1999) 158.

13. Dunbabin, *Mosaics of the Greek and Roman World*, 280. The terms in parentheses are found on pages 275–76 of the same work.

be carefully calculated to fit the space, with account taken of the width of dividing bands. Many ornamental schemata involved very complex structures of meanders or interlacing bands, or one scheme superimposed upon another, which would be disastrous if not planned in advance.[14]

At the end of the laying process, the final challenge for the mosaicist was to obtain a smooth surface. The preparatory layers had to be sufficiently level, and the tesserae had to be laid in an even manner.[15] Vitruvius wrote concerning this:

> After it is laid and set at the proper inclination, let it be rubbed down so that, if it consists of cut slips, the lozenges, or triangles, or squares, or hexagons may not stick up at different levels, but be joined together on the same plane with one another; if it is laid in cubes, so that all the edges may be level; for the rubbing down will not be properly finished unless all the edges are on the same level plane.[16]

In regards to the churches of Tell Abil (Area A) and Khirbet Umm el ʿAmad (Area D), the mosaics of the interior of the churches ranged from simple geometric patterns to more elaborate *opus sectile* paving. *Opus tessellatum* was found in the narthex and ancillary rooms of the churches. Pictorial *opus tessellatum* was found in the ancillary rooms outside of the basilica at Area D. It has been thought that these rooms may have been the residence of the bishop.

A SURVEY OF MOSAICS ON TELL ABIL

Floor pavers (*opus sectile*) were first discovered at Tell Abil during the 1984 season. The state of preservation of these floors ranged from being partially preserved to being almost completely destroyed. The best preserved section was found on the south side of the church. Michael Fuller, Chief Archaeologist at Abila during the 1984 and 1986 seasons, posited the hypothesis that the nave was paved with marble which was later robbed for reuse, or probably slaked for agricultural lime.[17] The

14. Ibid., 282.

15. Ibid., 288.

16. Vitruvius, 203.

17. Michael Fuller, "Abila of the Decapolis: A Roman-Byzantine City in the Transjordan (Ph.D. diss. Washington University, 1987) 159. See also Horace D. Hummel, "Abila Area A, 1–16," *NEASB* 29, (1987) 65–68.

Area A crew uncovered in the nave of the basilica a checkerboard pattern with white marble and red limestone pavers; the same pattern was also found, in the nave of the Area D basilica. In many instances, except when protected by large fallen architectural fragments, the marble pavers were stolen, leaving only the limestone pavers. Discovery of more *opus sectile* pavers took place during the 1988 season.[18] During the 1990 season excavators found a more ornate section of flooring (See Figure 1). Area Supervisor John Wineland described this saying, "One section of the floor in square A-32 had an ornate section of the floor with curved pieces of limestone pavers of red and black with circular marble pieces.

Figure 1: Ornate *opus sectile* floor from A-32, Area A Church, Abila

This section of floor may have demarcated certain sections of the church. What remains of the floor demonstrates the care and expense put forth to decorate this building."[19] To the west of the intricate curved limestone pieces and marble discs was a floor of rectangular red limestone pavers, small black limestone squares, and regular sized marble *opus sectile* pavers (See Figure 2).

18. See John Wineland, "1988 Abila of the Decapolis Excavation: Area A–Preliminary Report," *NEASB* 32 and 33 (1989) 49–64.

19. Wineland, *Ancient Abila: An Archaeological History*, p. 27. See also John D. Wineland, "The Area A 1990 Excavations at Abila: Area Supervisor's Preliminary Report," *NEASB* 35 (1990) 20–32.

Figure 2: *Opus sectile* floor with red and black limestone pavers,
Area A Church, Abila

During the 1990 season, *opus tessellatum* flooring was found in, what Wineland described as the portico of the basilica. Against a background of white tesserae, intersecting lines of black and red tesserae formed diamond-shaped geometric patterns with a cross at the center of each diamond pattern.[20] More of this floor was uncovered during the 1992 season (See Figure 3).

Figure 3: *Opus tessellatum* floor with diamond pattern
in the portico area, Area A Church, Abila

20. Wineland, 27.

A SURVEY OF MOSAICS
ON KHIRBET UMM EL 'AMAD: AREA D

Excavation began on Umm el 'Amad during the 1984 season, but significant floor pavers were not found until the 1986 season. During that summer, Willard W. Winter supervised excavations there.[21] The first sign of
a floor was discovered in the extreme northwest corner of D-16, which
was in the north aisle of the basilica. The excavation activity unearthed
limestone pavers in a salmon-colored (hematitic limestone) and dark
gray (bituminous limestone) checkerboard pattern. However, the floor
in the center of the square (in the nave) was found with the salmon-
colored limestone pavers intact, while the white marble pavers had been
robbed out. The existence of marble pavers was confirmed when some
were found under nearby column drums which had fallen due to seismic
activity.[22] The red and white checkerboard pattern in the nave and the
red and black checkerboard pattern in the aisles are like those found at
the church at Tell Abil.

The most interesting discovery came near the end of the 1986 season. Square D-3 was extended to the west so that what was a 1-by-4
meter trench would become a full 4-by-4 meter square; near the southwest corner of this square an intricate *opus sectile* pattern located near
the center of the basilica was discovered. This pattern was composed
of eight-sided concave-shaped hematitic limestone pavers, blue-veined
marble disks, and black bituminous limestone lozenges.[23] Unfortunately,
this excavation pattern continued to square D-23, the square adjacent
to D-3 to the west. There was not enough time in the 1986 season to
remove the balk in order to reveal the entire floor pattern. At the beginning of the 1988 season, the balk between D-3 and D-23 was removed to
reveal the extent of the intricate *opus sectile* floor. The extant contiguous
in situ floor pavers measured 1.25 m wide by 2.75 m long.[24] As evidenced
by the impressions in the plaster matrix, the intricate *opus sectile* floor
measured closer to 3 m square (See Figure 4).

---

21. See Willard W. Winter, "Abila of the Decapolis–1986: Area D," *NEASB* 28 (1987)
52–76.

22. Winter, "Abila of the Decapolis–1986: Area D," 66.

23. The composition of materials was ascertained by personal communication with
Reuben Bullard.

24. Willard W. Winter, "Abila of the Decapolis–1988: Area D," *NEASB* 31 (1988) 58.

Figure 4: Elaborate *opus sectile* floor in area D, Square 3, Abila

Continuing throughout the 1988 season, the team that excavated Area D at Umm el 'Amad unearthed *opus tessellatum* flooring outside the basilica proper, first in the southern portions of squares D-27 and D-36X. This flooring was comprised of large tesserae with intersecting blue and red lines against a white background forming diamond patterns with a cross in the middle of each diamond. This is another similarity with the church at Tell Abil.

In the 1990 season more of the above *opus tessellatum* floor was discovered. The floor was pocked by falling architectural fragments which probably fell during seismic activity that occurred in AD 747/8. In one of the ancillary rooms, an extensive well-preserved mosaic was uncovered. In its border, tesserae were arranged into alternating squared and curved designs. The body of the mosaic contained intersecting double lines which formed repeated diamond-shaped panels. In each panel was a circular pattern with a cross superimposed upon it. Within the double lines are single-flower designs which were repeated throughout (See Figure 5).

Figure 5: *Opus tessellatum* floor from Area D Church,
note the impact damage from the earthaquake of 747/748

In another of the ancillary rooms to the south of the west end of the basilica, excavators found a more intricate pictorial *opus tessellatum* floor. The images contained therein included baskets, flowers, interlocking loops, and heart-shaped designs.[25] In D-25, located at the north apse of the basilica, tiny tesserae composed of glass, gold leaf, and foil were found. More likely this was used for pictorial *opus vermiculatum* mosaics on the dome and walls of the apse. These tesserae were light-reflective, and when combined with the angle by which they were set, produced an impressive mosaic.

Winter's team also opened squares D-54 through D-59 along the north aisle of the basilica. With the balks removed, a contiguous *opus sectile* surface which measured 15 m long and 4.5 m wide was exposed.[26]

Work continued on the basilica during the 1992 season. Further work was done in the southwest part of the basilica. Immediately outside the basilica, excavators found a continuation of the pictorial *opus tessellatum* pavement, first discovered during the previous season.

25. Willard W. Winter, "The Area D 1990 Excavation at Abila: Area Supervisor's Preliminary Report," *NEASB* 34 (1990) 32.

26. Willard W. Winter, "The Area D 1992 Excavations at Abila: Area Supervisor's Preliminary Report," *NEASB* 37 (1992) 26.

Figure 6: Pictorial *opus tessellatum* floor from Area D Church, Abila

Winter described the uncovered designs as follows:

> The patterns were of exquisite designs depicting birds, flowers, loaves of bread, pomegranate trees with fruit, baskets filled with grain and berries, an amphora, a symbol of eternal life, and a bowl of stacked figs. For the first time at Abila we have now found a mosaic depicting animal life–two birds, one badly mutilated but evidently eating a pomegranate still hanging from the branch of a tree, and the other largely intact.[27]

Further commenting on this, Wineland pointed out (See Figure 6).

> Many of these designs convey the idea of the abundance of the harvest and the afterlife. Amphorae stored both liquid and dry foodstuffs such as grain, wine, and fruits. Baskets stuffed with the bounty of the harvest also adorned the floor. It is possible that Church officials commissioned the floor as a thanksgiving for an abundant harvest.[28]

THE AREA DD CHURCH AT UMM EL ʿAMAD

The excavation team also opened squares across a hard-packed dirt road to the west of the basilica in hopes of finding a staircase leading to the entrance to the church. Instead, excavators found another tri-apsidal church, perhaps older than the one being excavated. Winter recom-

27. Ibid., 32.

28. Wineland, *Ancient Abila: An Archaeological History*, 34.

mended that this church receive its own area designation. Director W. Harold Mare followed this recommendation. Therefore beginning with the 1994 season, this church was excavated under the supervision of David Vila, and was designated Area DD.

This church was first discovered during the 1992 by the Area D team in their search for a grand staircase leading to the basilica. Instead, they found another three-apsed basilica. When it became plain that this was what they had, Winter decided to cease excavation on these squares and focus instead on the basilica they had been excavating. While they excavated in the apses, the excavators came down on *opus tessellatum* mosaics.

Figure 7: The red, white, and black *opus tessellatum* floor
in square D-76, Abila

The pavement, which abutted the apse in D-77, extended some 75 cm, and was composed of black, white, and red tesserae.[29] The *opus tessellatum* mosaic floor found in D-76, which extended to about one-third of the square, was composed of red, white, and black tesserae. Black and white tesserae formed a row of diamonds, composing the border which extended 25 cm. The body of the mosaic had a repeating pattern of small flowers composed of red, white, and black tesserae (See Figure 7).[30]

In the 1994 season, under David Vila's direction, other patches of opus tessellatum in the floral motif were found in other areas of the

29. Wineland, *Ancient Abila: An Archaeological History*, 33.
30. Wineland, *Ancient Abila: An Archaeological History*, 34.

church. However, in the area between the central apse and the iconostasis, was opus sectile flooring in an alternating limestone and marble checkerboard design oriented in diamond shapes. In the midst of this was a large marble paver with a large cross inscribed therein. In the succeeding off season, this feature was robbed out (See Figure 8).

Figure 8: *Opus sectile* floor with large marble paver with an inscribed cross, area D Church, Abila

CONCLUSION

The church in Area DD was probably older than the one excavated in Area D. Some pieces from the former church were probably used in the construction of the latter. The reuse of items probably included column drums and other materials due to the dearth of such items. However, there are some important differences between this church and the Area D church, and its counterpart on Tell Abil. The most important of these differences is the placement of *opus tessellatum* mosaic inside the basilica proper of the former. The other difference is the placement of the paver installation with the inscribed cross.

The Area A (Tell Abil Church) and the Area D church on Khirbet Umm el 'Amad both had an earlier phase of use. In the case of the one on Tell Abil, it was built on top of the foundation of a previous church, as was found during the 1994 season. That it was a church was indicated by a cross that was etched on the west part of the foundation. We know nothing of the floors of this basilica. In the case of the one on Khirbet Umm el 'Amad, the Area D church was only meters away from the earlier basilica on Area DD. Since Umm el 'Amad is not a tell, there was only one occupational level on this location. Judging by the floors laid in the two churches, these can be regarded as sibling churches. The one on Tell Abil was probably the older of the two.

Worshipers during late Byzantine and early Umayyad times entered each of these churches by crossing a portico covered with opus tessellatum of a diamond-shaped geometrical design of intersecting lines with crosses formed in the center of each diamond. As they entered into either basilica, they would have seen identical red and white checkerboard *opus sectile* in the nave of the church. Each church differed in the design of the *opus sectile* pavement at the center of the nave. The center of the earlier basilica at Tell Abil was covered with a section of rectangular red limestone pavers, small black limestone squares, and regular sized marble opus sectile pavers. Immediately to the east was a section of flooring with curved red and black limestone pavers and marble discs. At the Area D basilica at Umm el 'Amad, worshipers saw a section of octagonal red limestone scallops interspersed with blue-veined marble circles and black limestone lozenges. Floors in the side aisles in each basilica were paved with red and black limestone pavers. The pavement in the apses of both churches is unknown.

Covering the ancillary rooms to the south of the Area D church at Khirbet Umm el 'Amad was an intricate pictorial mosaic containing pictures of interlocking ovals, birds, flowers, loaves of bread, pomegranate trees with fruit, baskets of grain and berries, an amphora, bowls of figs, and birds. In another room, a carpet-like expanse of *opus tessellatum* mosaics covered the floor. Its borders were arranged in alternating squared and curved designs. Its body was decorated with intersecting double lines which formed diamond-shaped panels. Each panel contained repeated designs of circles with superimposed crosses. Inside these double lines were depictions of flowers.

Manifest in these buildings is evidence of the devotion of the Christians of Abila. After periods where Christianity was illegal in the empire, expressions of adoration for their Lord abounded in the reminder of the Roman Empire. These manifestations expressed themselves in the expense of the materials, the time and expense of the workmanship of the craftsmen, and their artistic imagination and ability. This was especially notable not only in *opus tessellatum* mosaics, but in the intricate *opus sectile* flooring found at the center of the basilicas of Tell Abil and Khirbet Umm el 'Amad.[31]

---

31. All photos in this chapter were taken by taken by the author with the exception of Figure 4, which was taken by Rick Bullard, the chief photographer of the 1988 season.

CPSIA information can be obtained
at www.ICGtesting.com
Printed in the USA
BVHW041916130620
581356BV00003B/11